# CHRISTIAN
# APOLOGETICS

ALAN RICHARDSON, D.D.

*Canon of Durham, Examining Chaplain
to the Bishops of Durham and Sheffield*

*Intellectus enim merces est fidei. Ergo noli quaerere
intelligere ut credas, sed crede ut intelligas; quoniam
nisi credideritis, non intelligetis.*

St. Augustine, IN JOAN. EVANG., XXIX, 6.

S.C.M. PRESS LTD
56 BLOOMSBURY STREET, LONDON, W.C.1

First published December 1947
Second impression February 1948
Third impression May 1948
Fourth impression March 1950

Printed in Great Britain by
The Camelot Press Ltd., London and Southampton

# CONTENTS

# PREFACE

THIS PREFACE is not intended for the reader who requires a beginner's introduction to the study of Christian apologetics. He is advised to omit these pages and to start at Chapter One, which is designed to form an adequate introduction to the subject as a whole and to its presentation in this book. After he has read the succeeding chapters, he will then, it is hoped, be able to turn back and read these observations with understanding and profit. The aim of this Preface is to indicate the standpoint and argument of this work by setting it within the wider context of present-day thought upon the problem of the nature of our knowledge, more particularly of our scientific knowledge. Christian apologetics deals with the question of the nature and validity of our knowledge of God, and thus compels us to examine the methods and conclusions of theological enquiry in the light of our general knowledge of the world around us and of ourselves in relation to that world.

In our modern age the consideration of Christian apologetics must inevitably raise the question of the methodology of theological science in relation to that of the sciences in general. Since we live in an age which has been taught to submit every claim to knowledge to the test of the scientific method, no approach on the part of Christian apologists to the modern mind is likely to be effective which does not demonstrate the ability of our theological knowledge successfully to undergo that test and so to justify itself at the bar of rational scientific enquiry. There are doubtless larger philosophical questions concerning the nature of our knowledge, whether of the external world, or of ourselves, or of other people, or of God, and with these questions an essay upon the philosophy of religion would be expected to be concerned; but in this book we are not called upon to deal with them directly, since in the present confused state of epistemological thought it is hardly incumbent upon the Christian apologist to attempt to solve problems towards which no generally agreed philosophical attitude is forthcoming amongst metaphysicians. In the following chapters we shall be dealing not with the philosophy of religion but with Christian apologetics; and the principal question with which the Christian apologist to-day must come to grips, if he is to make vital contact with the mind of his age, lies in the sphere of scientific methodology rather than in that of metaphysics and epistemology as such, although, of course, we are well aware that it is impossible to discuss scientific method at all without implying consequences for philosophy. We shall be compelled to consider the relationship between the sciences (including theological science) and philosophy.

The study of Christian apologetics thus confronts us with the question of the methodology of theological science in relation to that of the sciences in general, for in it we are concerned with the problem of the validity of theological knowledge. We are therefore committed to a critical examination of the method of theological science in the light of a consideration of scientific method as such. This task has rarely been attempted by students of Christian apologetics since the adoption of the modern scientific theological method in the nineteenth century. There are several reasons why the study of Christian apologetics has been neglected in the twentieth century. One of them is that workers within a particular scientific field are wont to ignore the more general question of scientific methodology as such, and even to take for granted the methods of their own particular science, because their whole attention is absorbed in their own special research; they wish to get on with their allotted task as scientists, and are not seriously interested in the methodological and philosophical questions which underlie it. Theologians have been wont to pursue their own studies without pausing to reflect upon the method of their science in relation to scientific method in general; indeed, like many workers in other scientific fields, they are frequently hardly aware that such questions exist or are important. That is why, as we sometimes hear it complained, we are so rarely offered any kind of definition or explanation of what theology is; we are told only what it concerns, or what its subject-matter is. Theological science, like all the sciences, derives its distinctive quality as a rational attempt to understand a part of our total human experience from its employment of scientific method—in its case, the method distinctively appropriate to theological investigation. In the twentieth century that method is taken for granted by theologians—at least as theology is now-adays taught in the theological faculties of British Universities—and it is rarely submitted to critical scrutiny or to comparison with the methodology of other scientific disciplines. Ever since the rise and general acceptance of the methods of literary and historical criticism in the nineteenth century, it has come to be assumed that there is such a thing as theological scientific method and that every student of theology nowadays knows what it is. Yet outside the theological faculties and colleges the workers in other scientific fields have scarcely a notion that such a thing as theological scientific method exists at all.

The student of Christian apologetics is, however, compelled to raise the question of the nature and implications of the method of theological science, precisely because he is concerned to establish the validity of theological knowledge. There are many thoughtful people who to-day deny the possibility of a genuine theological knowledge and (which comes to the same thing) disallow the claim of theology to be a science. Just as in the eighteenth century a thinker like Hume by his criticism of the category of causation engendered skepticism concerning the possibility of scientific knowledge within the sphere of the natural sciences themselves, so in the twentieth century many thinkers who criticize the category of revelation have helped to undermine belief in the possibility of our knowledge of God, or of a scientific theology. Just as Kant set himself to answer the question, How is natural science possible? in his *Critique of Pure Reason*, so also the Christian apologist must critically examine the human mind and its workings with a view to establishing not only the possibility, but even the necessity, of theological science. In the eighteenth century and in more recent times the great majority of scientific workers have ignored the doubts and questionings of Hume and his successors; they have simply pushed on with the study of the natural sciences and have been rewarded with spectacular results. To those engaged upon the actual work of scientific research and discovery it would have seemed foolish to doubt whether scientific knowledge was possible when practical proofs of its validity were being piled up year by year. Similarly theologians to-day have many proofs of a pragmatic kind within their own experience and within the Church, so that to them it seems unnecessary to ask whether a scientific theological know-ledge is possible: they are in daily contact with such knowledge. But the student of Christian apologetics, with his eye upon the task of constructing a convincing apology for the twentieth century, is bound to attempt the task of showing that there is a theological method which is nothing less than the application of scientific method as such within the sphere of theological existence, and that as a result of it a valid theological knowledge is possible. Apologetics involves a critique of "the theological reason".

So long as theologians continue to make little effort to under-stand the nature of their own theological method or to convince other people of its validity; so long as they are content to leave unanswered the fundamental questions which the modern mind asks concerning the nature of theological truth, they will be unable to make effective contact with the mind of a generation which has come to believe that the only kind of knowledge which can properly be given that title is scientific knowledge. The modern mind has come to believe that knowledge is to be defined as that which either can be demonstrated (as in mathematics) or can be shown inductively to be reasonably certain through the application of the scientific method (as in the empirical sciences). Some Christian thinkers have thought that it is necessary to attack this assumption and to maintain that there are other kinds of knowledge besides scientific knowledge, such as religious or artistic knowledge. This was chiefly because scientific knowledge had commonly come to be equated with knowledge obtained through the natural sciences, and scientific method *par excellence* was held to be the method of the natural sciences. That method aimed at complete objectivity, impersonality and the extrusion of all values and value-judgments. The personal standpoint or faith of the observer must be rigidly excluded from his work. It was widely held that even the human sciences, even history itself, must qualify as sciences by adopting the scientific method as it was thus understood within the natural sciences.

But in the twentieth century there has been an important change of outlook amongst scientists themselves, which has resulted chiefly from the rise and general recognition of the human sciences (*Geisteswissenschaften*) as over against the natural sciences. Within the human sciences there has been a notable breakaway from the main assumption of positivism, that is, in a word, that the methods of natural science are the only valid scientific methods and that these methods are of universal applicability. This has followed upon the general rejection of the categories of the physical sciences as the categories of science *par excellence*, and upon the growing insistence that the human sciences have the right and the responsibility of formulating their own categories by the methods appropriate to their own enquiry. Theologians, of course, have always claimed this right, insisting upon using such categories as that of revelation regardless of what naturalistic philosophers may have said; but others, including many historians, did for a long time incline to the view that the methods of natural science were to be identified with scientific method as such, and that therefore even history must be modelled upon the pattern of the physical sciences. Thus, they tended to accept the category of cause and effect and to look for "facts" which could be "classified" or generalized according to the familiar methods of the more abstract natural sciences. To-day hardly anyone adopts this kind of historical positivism as a satisfactory account of the nature and purpose of history, and the assumptions of scientific naturalism are widely rejected by the workers in all the human sciences.

One way of stating the difference between the outlook of to-day and that of the older naturalistic period is by saying that the knowledge which is sought in the human sciences is not now an impersonal, "objective" knowledge, from which all value-judgments have been carefully excluded. It is recognized that in the more concrete or human sciences, including history and theology, the standpoint of the observer and his personal judgment cannot and should not be extruded in the name of science. There can be no impersonal, "objective" knowledge of historical and theological truth, because our knowledge of human existence is different from our knowledge of the external world which the natural sciences investigate. In the concrete sciences our personal *existence*, our whole being, is bound up with and, in an important sense, included in the object of our study. It is, of course, true that even in the natural sciences there can be no knowledge that is absolutely independent of any act of faith, or of assumptions which are incapable of scientific proof; but the *existential* character of the more concrete or human sciences greatly enhances the importance of the personal act of judgment or of faith which is involved in any study of them. The impersonal methods of natural science are seen to be out of place in them; there is a subjectivity in the study of the human sciences which is indispensable to them, and without which truth is not attainable in them, and yet this does not mean that they do not have their own valid standards and requirements, or that they are merely impressionistic, or that they are "subjectivist". We must learn to understand that there is a difference between subjectivity and subjectivism.

Thus, a consideration of scientific methodology to-day shows us that the ideals of the natural sciences are inappropriate—at least in precisely the same sense—in the human studies. We call the latter "existential", and in so doing we indicate that the "impartiality" and "detachment", which are so valued in the natural sciences, are neither possible nor desirable in the more concrete sciences. But this recognition of the existential character of the human sciences (including history and theology) does not commit us to the acceptance of the philosophy known as existentialism, or the philosophy of subjectivity. In so far as the existential philosophers have helped our generation to recognize what we have called the existential character of the human sciences, we owe them our grateful respect; but it does not follow that in this aspect of the truth about the nature of human knowledge we are to find a final clue to the ultimate truth about the deeper questions of philosophy. Indeed, the standpoint of this book will be seen to be incompatible with an existentialist philosophy, *qua* a final philosophy, which we cannot but regard as one of the current forms of irrationalism which the disillusionment of our times has rendered popular. It is significant that its prophet and precursor was the melancholy Kierkegaard and that it should have flourished in Germany after 1918 and in France after 1940. Moreover, like every other philosophy which does not derive its key-category from the biblical revelation, it is compatible both with a Christian and with a non-Christian interpretation: Jaspers and Marcel have followed Kierkegaard's hint in utilizing it in the service of religion, but Heidegger and Sartre have found it compatible with atheism and nihilism. Those insights into truth which render existentialism plausible as a philosophy are, of course, much older than Kierkegaard; they were already present, for example, in the subjectivist side of St. Augustine's theory of knowledge (though this was only one side of it) or in the limpid self-knowledge of Pascal. These insights, ignored during the long reign of rationalism and naturalistic philosophy, equally uncongenial to St. Thomas as to Voltaire, to Descartes as to Herbert Spencer, and proclaimed only by lonely prophets such as Pascal or Kierkegaard, are to-day meeting with a more general recognition of their truth; to-day the long domination of rationalism and naturalism seems to be passing, and our generation is perhaps ready to learn certain truths in the sphere of Christian epistemology from the subjectivist-objectivity of St. Augustine. Prominent amongst these truths, at least as far as theologians are concerned, is St. Augustine's view of general and special revelation.

A consideration of the existential character of our knowledge in the fields of the human sciences helps us to see why it is not nowadays necessary to claim that there are other kinds of knowledge besides scientific knowledge. A few years ago the late Canon B. H. Streeter and others who were concerned with Christian apologetics thought that it was incumbent upon them to urge that there were two kinds of knowledge, that given through the empirical sciences and that which comes by way of poetry, art and religion. When Streeter worked upon the task of "reconciling" science and religion, the view was still prevalent in this country (for the work of Dilthey in Germany was hardly known here) that the methods of the natural sciences were to be identified with scientific method as such, and that any study which claimed to give us knowledge must be conformable to the presuppositions, aims and methods of natural science. The study of organic life, of mind and of society, of history and of religion and ethics, must be conducted along the lines which had deservedly attained such high prestige in the physical sciences; and philosophy itself was nothing more than the universal application of the methods of natural science. The temper of the age was naturalistic or positivistic, and even those who rejected naturalism or positivism as a philosophy were bound to come to terms with it. In order to be considered scientific, biology had to be mechanistic, the social studies naturalistic and history positivistic. Theologians for the most part ceased to think of theology as a science, because the naturalistic assumptions of science in general seemed to rule out their claim to be scientists at all. If science was naturalistic, historians might accept the position and make their submission, but theologians met the situation by ignoring science and its claims altogether and developing their own scientific method without reference to what was happening in the scientific world as a whole. The few theologians who faced the challenge deemed discretion the better part of valour and modestly claimed that there were other kinds of knowledge besides scientific knowledge. This type of apology, however, did not prove very effective in a positivistic age, since the admission that religious or artistic knowledge was not scientific was sufficient to condemn it as knowledge altogether.

To-day the situation is completely changed or is rapidly changing, although the old naturalistic assumptions still dominate the minds of many who are out of touch with recent discussion. The workers in the human sciences are claiming freedom from dictation by physical categories and methods and are giving more attention to the personal or existential aspect of their sciences. Historians are no longer afraid of value judgments. The existential philosophers and novelists have called attention to the fact of subjectivity. Many scientific humanists are themselves putting forward the claim that science is concerned with ethics and can indicate the nature of ethical progress. The sociologists of knowledge have demonstrated the personal and subjective factors intruded into all our thinking by the fact of social conditioning, and the insights of Marxism in general have helped to break down the old-fashioned rationalism. In this they have been seconded by the "new" psychologists. In the following chapters we shall have occasion to criticize the conclusions of existentialists, scientific humanists, Marxists and Freudians; but we must make it clear that while we reject their systems as complete and final answers to philosophical problems, we recognize and gladly acknowledge the value of their insights. Christians in this generation have much to learn from all of them, and the first task of Christian apologetics is not to refute the Marxists and the rest but to understand what they have to teach and to accept and build upon the truth which they have seen. One of the truths which we must learn from the Marxists and the Freudians concerns the importance of the personal and subjective factors in our knowledge, and not only in the spheres of economics and society. Christian apologists as yet scarcely seem to have begun to appreciate the significance of Marx and Freud as allies in the struggle against rationalism and positivism, the two great untruths which have infected so much of modern thought, and which have so effectively closed the doors of many minds against the entrance of Christian truth. There is much in modern thought with which the student of Christian apologetics can make contact and which forms a starting point from which discussion with non-Christians can begin. There is one question which theologians have in common with the workers in all the human sciences: how is knowledge possible in history and the human studies, that is to say, outside the sphere in which the method of the natural sciences can effectively be employed? Neither Dilthey nor Collingwood succeeded in doing for historical science what each had hoped to achieve, namely, to construct a critique of the historical reason, to do for history (or, more broadly, the human sciences) what Kant attempted to do for the physical sciences—to show how knowledge is possible in historical (and human) studies.

Thus, one of the perplexing yet absorbingly interesting questions which confront modern thought is to show how knowledge is possible outside the sphere of the natural sciences. Obviously this is no less vital a question for theologians than for the workers in any of the other human sciences. The theologian shares to-day with many Christian and non-Christian humanists a well-founded apprehension concerning the fate of a civilization in which skepticism, ethical relativism and nihilism follow in the wake of the age of rationalism and positivism. The Christian shares with every kind of humanist the aim of showing that in our knowledge of man, of history and of society there is a subjectivity in which values are a matter of obligation, in which personal judgment is not merely impressionist and fanciful, and in which there is a difference between sense and nonsense. The problem is that of realizing the objectivity of value through the subjectivity of knowledge. It is not the purpose of this book to put forward a solution to this problem, or to construct a Christian epistemology or philosophy. The most that we can do is to show reason for thinking that the theologian has a special contribution to make towards the modern discussion of the problem of knowledge, since the problem is not a new one in the history of Christian thought, although it assumes a new and urgent form. Our situation to-day is not so unprecedented as those who know little about the history of thought are inclined to imagine; there have been moments in the past when Christian faith has been confronted by naturalism, skepticism and relativism, in which it has been able to create the necessary conditions of understanding. We shall be able to point out certain grounds for believing that Christian faith can again to-day perform its ancient office of restoring man's lost rationality by offering him something better than rationalism.

There may be some who read these pages for whom "science" still means "natural science" (or, even more simply, "stinks"), who will consequently be surprised and shocked to hear theology described as an empirical science. The fact that there are many people who are unaccustomed to thinking of theology as a science indicates, on the one hand, how little the significance of the nineteenth-century revolution in theological method has been understood, and, on the other hand, how strongly the naturalistic or positivistic view of the essential nature of science still dominates opinion, even now that the human sciences have come of age. But careful reflection upon the subject will show that the study of Christian apologetics to-day must necessarily be concerned with the question of the method of theology in relation to scientific method in general. The permanent thing about science, as Dr. A. D. Ritchie has said, is its *method*, not its theories or conclusions. Scientific theories and conclusions have no permanence, and the Christian apologist who conceives it to be his duty to "reconcile" the latest scientific theories with Christian truth is beginning at the wrong end of the argument. The proper starting point of Christian apologetics is scientific methodology. To-day there exist sciences (including theology) which yield empirical knowledge and which nevertheless do not and cannot employ the methods of the abstract natural sciences. The Christian apologist must show that theological scientific method as applied to the facts of Christian existence to-day—to the facts of the existence of the Church and her Bible—yields a body of knowledge which requires and validates, at the scientific level, certain strictly theological categories, such as that of revelation. Theological existence must be shown to be unintelligible in terms of any non-theological categories, and theological method must be seen, *qua* scientific method, to involve the employment of these categories.

Three possible objections to the foregoing statement may perhaps be anticipated here. First, some may object to our speaking of theology as one of the "human sciences". It may be briefly replied that, though theology might be styled a "divine science" in respect of its aim or of its subject matter, nevertheless in respect of its *method* (which is the important matter in speaking of it as *science*) it is truly human, and subject to all the limitations and imperfections of our fragmentary human knowing.

Secondly, it may be objected that the claim that theology is a science, yielding scientific knowledge, does away with the necessity of faith and attempts to offer us *gnosis* in its place. Such an objection completely misunderstands what we have called the existential nature of the knowledge that is available through the historical and human sciences. In these studies personal judgment, the estimate of values, discrimination and the venture of faith are all-important. In this they differ from the more abstract sciences. In all of them there is an important sense in which faith precedes reason and is indeed a condition of rationality, and this is especially true in the spheres of theology and philosophy.

Thirdly, it may be objected that what we have said implies that the centuries of patient and devoted study of theology before the nineteenth-century revolution in theological method were of little value in the promotion of true theological understanding— a conclusion manifestly preposterous. But no such conclusion is involved in anything that we have said above. Although theology as an empirical (non-deductive) science is no older than the nineteenth century, it does not follow that therefore all theological works written before that date are "unscientific" and of small value. Here one of the most important distinctions between the abstract natural sciences and the more concrete or existential human sciences is clearly seen. Empirical theological science to-day does not stand in relation to pre-critical traditional theology as, for example, chemistry stands in relation to alchemy. In the

BCA

abstract sciences yesterday's theories have only "a mere historical interest"; but in the concrete sciences, and also, of course, supremely in philosophy, the history of the science, as with the history of philosophy, is an essential part of it, and it is incomprehensible without it. No one can understand what theology is about until he has learnt something of the history of Christian thought. In theology it does not follow that what is newer is *ipso facto* more true or more profound. Thus, the contrast between the natural and the human sciences is at this point most remarkable. An undergraduate studying natural science at Oxbridge to-day does not read Newton, and a Professor of Chemistry from Redbrick would have much to teach Roger Bacon. But in the human sciences the situation is very different, in so far as these sciences are something more than the amassing of quantities of "facts". It is doubtful whether Freud would be able to teach St. Augustine much beyond a list of jargon-terms for processes with which Augustine was very well acquainted. In all concrete studies the moderns have much to learn from the ancients.

Thus it happens that when the writer, observing an honourable and gracious tradition, comes at the end of his Preface to acknowledge his indebtedness to other writers, he finds himself more deeply aware of his obligation to the older than to the more recent doctors and thinkers of the Church. There is one figure amongst the great names of the past, whose thinking upon the question of the nature of Christian truth has a peculiar relevance for the circumstances of our day, which in many respects are so akin to those of his; and to him the writer's indebtedness will appear throughout this book. Amongst the many modern authors to whom a special obligation is due, it would be too invidious to select some names and too burdensome to the reader to mention all. The extent of the writer's indebtedness will, it is hoped, be readily apparent, since he has attempted to make due acknowledgment both in the text and in the footnotes. The consideration of such a theme as ours necessarily involves an entering in upon other men's labours, and, as Coleridge has said, even a dwarf sees far when he has the shoulders of giants to mount on.

ALAN RICHARDSON.

THE COLLEGE,
  DURHAM.

# CHAPTER ONE

# CHRISTIAN APOLOGETICS AND PHILOSOPHY TO-DAY

## § 1. *The Nature and Necessity of Apologetics*

AN APOLOGY in the original meaning of the word is a defence; it is primarily the defendant's answer to the speech of the prosecution. It has often been pointed out that the very first preaching of the Christian faith opened with words of apology in this sense.[1] There is necessarily a defensive element in all Christian preaching, and it is often impossible to say precisely at which point defence passes over into counter-attack. Apology in its Christian meaning implies the defence of Christian truth. It meets an accusation, explicit or unexpressed, by stating the facts of the case and pointing out the rational conclusions to be drawn from them, as St. Paul did when he made his defence before Agrippa.[2] Particular apologies are works written to repel a specific charge or line of attack upon Christianity, and in this wide class of Christian literature we find such writings as the Apologies of Justin Martyr or Aristides, Origen's *Contra Celsum*, Aquinas's *Summa contra Gentiles* or Bishop Butler's *Analogy of Religion*. Apologetics, as distinct from apology, is the study of the ways and means of defending Christian truth. It is not the task of apologetics, as a theological discipline, to meet a particular attack upon Christianity or to add one more volume to the library of Christian Apologies. Apologetics deals with the relationship of the Christian faith to the wider sphere of man's "secular" knowledge—philosophy, science, history, sociology, and so on—with a view to showing that faith is not at variance with the truth that these enquiries have uncovered. In every age it is necessary that this task should be undertaken; in a period of rapid developments in scientific knowledge and of vast social change it becomes a matter of considerable urgency. Thus, apologetics as a theological discipline is a kind of intellectual

---

[1] Acts ii. 14f.     [2] Acts xxvi. 1f.: ἀπολογεῖσθαι.

stock-taking on the part of Christian thinkers, who may be described as attempting to reckon up their assets in the light of contemporary philosophical thought and scientific knowledge. Hence, also, apologetics is primarily a study undertaken by Christians for Christians; and in this respect it is to be distinguished from the task of apology, since an apology is addressed to non-Christians. Apologetics is thus a necessary preparation for the work of an apologist, or, more simply, it is a part of the essential training of Christian preachers, evangelists and teachers. It may well be true that there exist honest enquirers, who would gladly acknowledge themselves Christians if their doubts could only be removed, who would be helped by overhearing the discussion of apologetics amongst Christian thinkers; and in this way apologetics may indeed fulfil a secondary function by helping such enquirers.[1] If any enquirer finds himself reading this book, he may indeed gain reassurance from the fact that it was not primarily written for him.

A distinction is sometimes drawn[2] between general religious apologetics and Christian apologetics in particular, and this

[1] Some writers have understood the primary aim of apologetics to be what we have described as its secondary aspect. Thus, A. B. Bruce in *Apologetics; or Christianity Defensively Stated* (Edinburgh, 1895) writes: "Apologetic . . . is a preparer of the way of faith, an aid to faith against doubts whencesoever arising, especially such as are engendered by philosophy and science. Its specific aim is to help men of ingenuous spirit who, while assailed by such doubts, are morally in sympathy with believers. It addresses itself towards such as are drawn in two directions, towards and away from Christ, as distinct from such as are confirmed either in unbelief or in faith. Defence presupposes a foe, but the foe is not the dogmatic infidel who has finally made up his mind that Christianity is a delusion, but anti-Christian thought in the believing man's own heart. 'A man's foes shall be they of his own household.' The wise apologist instinctively shuns conflict with dogmatic unbelief as futile. He desiderates and assumes in those for whom he writes a certain fairness and openness of mind, a generous spirit under hostile bias which he seeks to remove, a bias due to no ignoble cause, animated even in its hostility by worthy motives" (p. 37). This is finely said, and any serious student of apologetics will be in sympathy with Dr. Bruce's aim. But it is unsatisfactory as a statement of the nature of apologetics as such, because it confuses the task of apologetics with that of apology. Apologetics is related to apology as, let us say, homiletics is related to preaching.

[2] See, e.g., D. S. Adam, art. "Theology" in Hastings's *Encyclopaedia of Religion and Ethics*, Vol. XII, pp. 297f.

distinction will help to define the limits of our subject more precisely. General religious apologetics deals with such matters as the defence of the religious or theistic view of the world, the arguments for the existence of God, the answer to the problem of evil, the counter-attack upon atheistic or agnostic views, and so on; it is akin to what used to be called "natural theology" and to what is nowadays sometimes called the philosophy of religion. It endeavours to treat of these matters without the help of a special revelation. Christian apologetics, in the narrower sense which that expression carries when it is used precisely, is concerned with the implications of the Christian revelation for the rational understanding of the world and of our existence in it. It seeks to show that revelation, as Christians understand it, is not merely compatible with the exercise of reason, but is actually a help and guide to the human reason in its attempt to understand; and, moreover, that revelation is not a figment of the imagination of Christians, but that it is a category based upon observable facts and recognizable experiences, when they are correctly interpreted. It is with Christian apologetics, as distinct from general religious apologetics, that we shall be chiefly occupied in this book; we shall deal with problems of general religious apologetics only in so far as they have an important bearing upon the more restricted questions of Christian apologetics. There are certain important considerations arising from the modern discussion of the nature of scientific truth, of ideological presuppositions and of historical investigation which must be examined before we shall be ready to turn to the proper questions of Christian apologetics, since they have an obvious bearing upon our manner of approach to the latter. The proper questions of Christian apologetics, with which we shall be specially concerned, include the nature of revelation in general and of the Christian revelation in particular, the validity of the traditional arguments of Christian apologetics from miracle and prophecy, the inspiration and authority of the Bible, and the relationship between faith and reason.

It is true to say that apology, and therefore apologetics (though the word belongs to the modern period), have always found an honoured place in the central line of development of Christian theology down the ages. But there have been certain periods in which both the art and the theory of apology have been somewhat neglected. The need for apology is not obvious in an age in which the State orders all its subjects to be baptized in infancy and sends to the stake anyone who ventures to express religious doubts. Yet it is remarkable how conscious the great theologians —even the most allegedly "dogmatic" amongst them—have been of the need for the apologetic element in their presentation of the faith. Theologians of the very highest rank, such as Origen, Augustine and Aquinas, are also the Church's leading apologists. A surprisingly large proportion of the first book of Calvin's *Institutes* is devoted to apologetic and proof from reason: the young humanist scholar of the Renaissance who became the leader of the Reformation never misses an opportunity of pointing out the errors of classical humanism. A few theologians, such as Luther, have entertained so low an estimate of the powers of the human reason that they have seen little purpose in addressing themselves to it; faith, they have claimed, requires no justification at the bar of reason.[1] But such an extremist position is not

[1] Karl Barth in our day would seem to suggest that apologetics is not a legitimate activity for Christians because it begins by assuming that reason is competent to discuss the possibility and even the content of revelation, or at least it presupposes that reason creates the needful "point of connection" between God and man: "faith must take unbelief seriously and itself not quite seriously, and therefore secretly or openly ceases to be faith." Barth likes clear-cut distinctions: reason is always "faithless reason", and so faith is necessarily the contradiction of reason; the only true apologetic is the confrontation of unfaith by faith, and the latter is God's work as the former is man's. God's Word needs no defence by man, and only unfaith would think of defending it. He quotes Luther with approval: "We must take care not to . . . defend the Gospel so that it collapseth. Let us not be anxious: the Gospel needeth not our help, it is sufficiently strong of itself. . . . 'Tis a small thing that this puny breath should range itself against the sophists; what would this bat accomplish by its flapping?" (K. Barth, *Doctrine of the Word of God; Church Dogmatics*, Vol. I, Part I, Eng. trans. by G. T. Thomson, Edinburgh, 1936, pp. 30–3). Richard Hooker, whose view of the relation of faith and reason is set out in *The Laws of Ecclesiastical Polity*, Bk. III, Ch. viii, dealt firmly with the strictures upon reason of the sixteenth-century Puritans, who had been influenced by the Continental extremists. "A number there are," he says, "who think they cannot admire as they ought the power and authority of the Word of God, if in things divine they should attribute any force to man's reason. For which cause they never use reason so willingly as to disgrace reason" (*loc. cit.*). *Plus ça change plus c'est la même chose*. British theology must perform again in the twentieth century the task which Hooker so ably undertook in the sixteenth.

representative of the general or classical attitude of Christian thought; even Tertullian appealed to the conscience of the Roman ruling class,[1] and even on occasion, when it suited his purpose, argued that Christian teachings were very like those of the heathen poets and philosophers.[2]

In our own times it has become fashionable in certain quarters to question the value or even the legitimacy of Christian apologetics. It is said (not indeed untruly) that it is the task of the believer to confront unbelief with the Gospel challenge, to convict of sin and utter the message of repentance and renewal. To criticize or attempt to make rational judgments upon God's revelation is presumptuous, and if men could thus rationally criticize and evaluate it, it would obviously not be divine. (This is essentially the same argument as was formerly used by those who objected to biblical criticism.) Our task, it is said, is not to argue about God's existence but to confront men with His judgment and mercy, not to discuss whether God has given a revelation but to tell men what it is. Now it is true that the apologist must not substitute argument for preaching; it is equally true that a large part of the apologist's task is to declare plainly what the Gospel is, removing the misconceptions about it which abound in men's minds and are often the chief obstacles to Christian belief. Furthermore, the student of apologetics must not assume that men can be converted to Christian faith by means of rational argument alone or indeed by any human means: God, who gives the revelation, gives also the faith by which it is received and the light by which it is understood; faith, as we shall consistently maintain, is always the gift of God. It is doubtless true, and much to be regretted, that a good deal of modern preaching has lost the confident ring of authentic Christian proclamation and has often adopted an "apologizing" tone:[3]

---

[1] *Apol.* IX.          [2] *Ibid.*, XLVII.

[3] The popular confusion between "apology" and "apologizing" (in the modern sense) may claim royal patronage. When in 1796 Bishop Richard Watson (1737–1816) published *An Apology for the Bible,* George III commented: "Apology for the Bible! Apology for the Bible! I did not know that the Bible required an apology." (Overton and Relton, *The English Church from the Accession of George I to the End of XVIII Century,* p. 260.) Bishop Watson also addressed an *Apology for Christianity* (1776) to Edward Gibbon in answer to the attack on Christianity in the *Decline and Fall* (Ch. XV), still beloved of the rationalist press.

"one rather feels . . ." It is not difficult to understand why a reaction in favour of a more authoritative declaration of the Gospel should have set in with the decay of the liberal theology in recent years.[1] But these are not reasons for doubting the value or legitimacy of apologetics.[2] The real basis of the rejection of apologetics as a theological discipline is to be found in a particular theory of the relation between reason and revelation, the theory that they are irreconcilable opposites, and that there is no "point of connection" in man's reason or conscience to which revelation can appeal. This theory runs counter to the main current of Christian thought upon the subject; there is nothing in the Bible and little in the teaching of the great doctors of the Church to support it. It is, in fact, no older than Luther; indeed, it is hardly accurate to say as much as this, since Luther did not work out careful theories on philosophical questions.[3]

[1] It is, however, astonishing to read in the Editors' General Introduction to the *Library of Constructive Theology* that "the time has gone by when 'apologetics' could be of any great value". The words read like a condemnation in advance of most of the books in the series. But the next sentence indicates that the writers hold a dubious notion of what apologetics is: "Something more is needed than a defence of propositions already accepted on authority." Christian apologetics is, of course, not the defence of propositions already accepted on authority, but the defence of the proposition that there is an authority in or behind revelation, or that there is an authoritative revelation.

[2] On this matter see Leonard Hodgson, *Towards a Christian Philosophy* (London, 1942), pp. 11–19; *Democracy and Dictatorship in the Light of Christian Faith* (London, 1935), p. 30; John Baillie, *Our Knowledge of God* (Oxford, 1939), pp. 14–16; and H. F. Lovell Cocks, *By Faith Alone* (London, 1943), pp. 118f.

[3] Luther's repudiation of reason apart from revelation may be illustrated by the following quotation: "The natural wisdom of a human creature in matters of faith, until he be regenerate and born anew, is altogether darkness, knowing nothing in divine cases. But in a faithful person, regenerate and enlightened by the Holy Spirit, through the Word, it is a fair and glorious instrument, and work of God. . . . The understanding, through faith, receives life from faith; that which was dead is made alive again" (*Table-Talk*, Hazlitt's trans., CCXCIV). In what he affirms—namely, the empowering of the reason through faith in Christ—his teaching is wholly true to the thought of Augustine; but the contrast between Augustine's view and that of Luther may be illustrated by the following passage from Augustine, who, though his main emphasis is upon the fact that faith precedes reason in the understanding of truth, nevertheless clearly recognizes that there is a sense in which reason precedes faith, since the Word cannot even enter into an irrational creature, and hence that reason is a necessary "point of connection" between man's soul and the divine Word: "Perish the

## § 2. The "Point of Connection" in Reason and Conscience

Against all such theories the discussion of apologetics involves the recognition that there is a "point of connection" between the minds of believers and those of at least some unbelievers. Dr. Paul Tillich points out that apologetics implies a willingness to defend oneself in the face of an aggressor before a mutually acknowledged criterion.[1] For example, when Stoic teaching about the Logos was widely accepted, it was possible for the early Apologists to defend their conception of Christ as the Logos-incarnate before those who were ready to admit the validity of a Logos-philosophy. There is, of course, always the danger that the Christian apologist may go too far in the direction of his opponent's categories and fail to show that the Christian faith always transcends and to some extent negates the categories of all non-Christian thinking; but, at least, there is a "point of connection", a starting-point for discussion. Apologetics thus implies that there are distinctions within unbelief itself, even though they are hard to define. There is first the seriously-minded humanist, who believes in values

notion that God hates in us that in which He has created us superior to other living creatures! Perish the notion, I say, that we ought to believe that we need not accept or look for a reason for what we believe, since we could not even believe if we had not rational souls (*animas*). In certain things pertaining to saving doctrine, which we are not yet capable of perceiving by reason but shall be some day, faith precedes reason (*fides praecedat rationem*); and this faith cleanses the heart, so that it may receive and endure the great light of reason. The prophet thus speaks quite rationally when he says, *Nisi credideritis, non intelligetis*—'If you will not believe, you shall not understand' (Isa. vii. 9, LXX). The prophet here distinguished between faith and reason and counselled us that we should first believe, so that we might come to understand the thing which we believe. Hence it is seen to be reasonable that faith should precede reason. For if this precept is not reasonable, therefore it is unreasonable—which God forbid! If therefore it is reasonable that faith should precede reason to bring us to certain great matters which cannot yet be understood, then undoubtedly, in however small a degree, reason, which persuades us to it, is likewise antecedent to faith (*procul dubio quantulacumque ratio quae hoc persuadet etiam ipsa antecedit fidem*). Hence the Apostle Peter warns us that we should be prepared to answer everyone who asks of us a reason for our faith and hope (1 Pet. iii. 15)" (*Ep.* CXX, 3, 4). The continuation of this passage gives a complete vindication of Christian apologetics.

[1] *The Interpretation of History* (New York, 1936), p. 43.

and searches for them, and who in the modern world is himself the product of generations of Christian teaching and of a Christian culture and civilization; secondly, there are the convinced believers in some non-Christian philosophy of life, such as Marxists or Mohammedans; and thirdly, there is the class of people who are apparently indifferent to all questions of truth and value, and who are so interested in themselves and their worldly needs and pleasures that they care for none of these things. Perhaps there is a fourth class—namely, those who deliberately and cynically despise all truth and value and exalt self-aggrandisement (whether nationalistically as in Nazism or individually as practical atheists) to the point of religious devotion; these are the real perverts, and Christian truth is the only effective prophylactic against such ultimate *corruptio optimi pessima*. As regards any particular specimen of these third and even fourth classes, it would probably be going too far to say that there is absolutely no "point of connection" with him or her; but in practice it is clear that apologetics will provide no useful approach to such people in general. Only the uncompromising confrontation with the disturbing Gospel proclamation is likely to have any effect upon them.

But the case of the two former classes is altogether different, and the great Christian apologists of the past have frequently addressed themselves to such. Justin Martyr's appeal to the understanding of the philosophers of the second century is a good illustration from the ancient Church of an apology addressed to the first class; and Aquinas's *Summa contra Gentiles* may be instanced as an outstanding example of apologetics for the second class, since St. Thomas starts from those rational principles which his oponents already acknowledge: the Aristotelian philosophy is a mutually acknowledged criterion.[1] The study of apologetics

---

[1] It is not suggested that St. Thomas wrote for Mohammedan or Jewish readers rather than for Christians; he knew that his readers would be mostly Christians. But this fact illustrates the nature of Christian apologetics, which in one of its aspects is the thinking out of the Christian position in the light of criticisms made of it by unbelievers. St. Thomas wishes to show how reason apart from revelation, such as even Mohammedans must follow (the "mutually acknowledged criterion"), refutes the errors of the heathen and leads up to Christian truth. Cf. *Summa contra Gentiles*, Bk. I, Ch. ii: "Some of them (the heathen), like the Mohammedans and pagans, do not agree with us as to the authority of any Scripture whereby they may be convinced, in the same way as

will obviously be of great value to Christians who are anxious to make an approach to the members of either of these classes. Those who have never studied the implications of the Christian faith in the light of such truth as may be found in the case of the humanist or the Marxist are unlikely to make a successful defence of Christianity against the humanist or Marxist attack, and will be unequipped to mount a powerful counter-offensive. The humanists' high regard for truth and value and the Marxists' eagerness for social justice alike prove to be highly significant "points of connection", and there is thus in each case a mutually acknowledged criterion, however small may be the area of agreement when the discussion begins. Wherever reason and conscience are found to be at work, the task of Christian apologetics becomes important. This view of the validity and urgency of apologetics is grounded upon the whole understanding of the relation between revelation and reason which underlies and, it is hoped, becomes explicit in the argument of this book; and it is in harmony with the thought and the practice of the great theologians of the Church from St. Paul's or St. John's day to our own.[1]

Both the secular humanism and the Marxism that we encounter to-day have been deeply influenced by Christian teaching and ideals.[2] To this extent they have already been touched by the revelation of the truth in Jesus Christ. Since, as we shall maintain, all revelation is "saving" revelation, they cannot be said to be totally "godless" (whatever they may call themselves) or totally bereft of the illumination of the Sun of Righteousness. In so far as they see truth at all, they see it through the shining of the

we are able to dispute with the Jews by means of the Old Testament, and with heretics by means of the New: whereas the former accept neither. Wherefore it is necessary to have recourse to natural reason, to which all are compelled to assent. And yet this is deficient in the things of God."

[1] St. Paul's alleged repudiation (in 1 Cor. i and ii) of his method of approach to the philosophers of Mars Hill (Acts xvii. 22–34) is too uncertain to argue from. His attitude towards the reason and conscience of the pagan world is more clearly expressed in Rom. i-iii, of which due note is taken throughout the argument of this book; Rom. i. 20 in particular became the foundation-text of "natural theology", especially in the Middle Ages. If one required a concise biblical proof-text for the sanction of Christian apologetics, one could always turn to 1 Pet. iii. 15.

[2] For Marxism in this connection, see Alex. Miller, *The Christian Significance of Karl Marx* (London, 1946).

Source of Light, which alone renders possible man's knowledge of truth. But their vision is cloudy and distorted; it is only an imperfect seeing, as of those who see men as trees walking. The touch of Christ's hand has begun but has not finished its healing work upon their blind eyes. The task of Christian apologetics may be described as that of preparing to bring their eyes to be touched again by the hand of Christ, so that they may see all things clearly. The gift of sight is always a miracle of divine grace; but this does not mean that Christians may sit still and take no trouble to make ready the way of the Lord. "The fact that it is God that giveth the increase is no reason why we need not plant and water."[1]

The nature of the Christian apologist's task has changed considerably since the opening of the twentieth century. The late Archbishop Temple has described how at Oxford in the decade before 1914 it seemed that the task of the Christian apologist was to work out a Christo-centric metaphysic in terms of an idealistic philosophy which was still widely accepted by thoughtful people.[2] The influence of such teachers as Edward Caird, Josiah Royce and Bernard Bosanquet was still strong. Even in 1924 Dr. Temple believed that a very slight touch to the intellectual balance might make the scales incline towards the acceptance of such a Christo-centric metaphysic, since the spiritual and even theistic philosophy of the Oxford idealists was still the dominating outlook.[3] To-day there is no dominating outlook and no widely accepted philosophy. Professional philosophers often seem to spend their days discussing whether metaphysics is possible at all. According to one current view, all statements about values are meaningless noises; according to another, philosophy itself is nothing more than the product of economic forces. It thus comes to be widely held that certainty is attainable only within the sphere of the empirical sciences. No knowledge is possible except scientific knowledge, and the only task that remains for the philosopher as such is to expose all propositions or views which cannot be demonstrated by means of the scientific method. It is hardly surprising that many would-be

[1] St. Augustine, *In Ps.* CXIX, *Serm.* xxxii. 4.
[2] Art. "Theology To-day" in *Theology*, Vol. XXXIX, No. 233, November, 1939.
[3] *Loc. cit.*; see also Preface to *Christus Veritas* (London, 1924).

philosophers, discouraged by such a limitation of their proper vocation, hasten to discard their philosopher's gown for a party-shirt and to assert that their function is not to explain the world but to change it.[1]

In the ancient world philosophers often wore a distinctive dress, as ministers of religion do nowadays, because they believed that they had, as philosophers, a vocation and mission to instruct men concerning truth and the good life. There were, of course, plenty of sophists and skeptics; but there were also many who, though perplexed and saddened by the irrationality of mankind and the apparent futility of things, nevertheless maintained their personal belief in reason and conscience, and therefore regarded philosophy as a way of life, to be handed on to those who could receive it as a matter of obligation. There is a pathetic nobility in the creed of a Marcus Aurelius:

> "If Providence watches over all and may be inclined to mercy, render thyself worthy of celestial aid. But if leaderless Chaos be all, rest content that in the midst of this storm-swept sea Reason still dwells and rules within thee. And if the tide swirl thee away, let it take thy flesh and spirit with all the rest; for Reason it cannot take. . . . If there be a God, all is well; if Chance governs all, see that it governs not thee."[2]

Belief in the objectivity of value is the condition of the progress or even of the continuance of civilization. Skeptics have undoubtedly a wholesome and necessary function to perform, which is primarily that of awakening men of faith from their dogmatic slumbers; yet not only philosophy but even civilization itself would perish if the generality of men ceased to believe that truth is knowable and moral values binding. Likewise, if in the realm of aesthetic judgment there are no objectively valid standards,

---

[1] Cf. R. G. Collingwood, speaking of the teaching of philosophy at Oxford in recent years: "The pupils, whether or not they expected a philosophy that should give them, as that of Green's school had given their fathers, ideals to live for and principles to live by, did not get it; and were told that no philosopher (except of course a bogus philosopher) would even try to give it" (*An Autobiography*, Oxford, 1939, p. 48).

[2] *Meditations*, 12. 14; 9. 27.

there can be no intrinsic difference between a Beethoven sonata and tickling one's ear with a feather provided that one likes both these forms of pleasurable enjoyment. If there is nothing objectively good, there is no moral difference between Socrates and Himmler —only, at most, a kind of sociological difference.[1] We all know that such statements are nonsense, even if we cannot immediately articulate our reasons for knowing it. It is notoriously difficult to uphold by logical argument against a clever skeptic the conception of the objectivity of truth and of aesthetic and moral values;[2] and yet it would be a gross error to assume that mankind as a whole is ever for one day left in doubt upon this all-important question. The fact that there is from time to time in the history of civilizations a momentary failure of nerve on the part of intellectuals, especially in times of crisis and change, should not obscure from us the broad truth that mankind down the centuries has never doubted that there are objective standards of truth, beauty and goodness, existing independently of any individual's predilections and hesitations. The fact that from time to time there has been a widespread *"trahison des clercs"* on the part of those who ought to have been the leaders of civilization should not lead us to suppose that civilization itself could continue if the *communis sensus* of mankind ceased to bear witness to the objectivity of value. When Arthur Koestler and others declare that they do not know whether ethical absolutes exist but that it is necessary for us to believe *as if* they do, they are acknowledging that civilization depends upon belief in the objectivity of value and that the preservation of civilization is a valuable end of

---

[1] "If one way of life is no better than another, then no way of life is valuable at all" (Michael Roberts, *The Recovery of the West*, London, 1941, p. 138. The whole argument of Chapter 6 is highly relevant to this discussion).

[2] St. Augustine's argument concerning the logical impossibility of a thoroughgoing skepticism still remains valid: "Everyone who knows that he is in doubt about something knows a truth, and in regard to this thing that he knows he is certain. Consequently everyone who doubts if there be truth has in himself a true thing which he does not doubt; nor is there any true thing which is not true by truth. Consequently whoever for whatever reason can doubt ought not to doubt that there is a truth" (*De Vera Relig.*, xxxix. 73). It is questionable whether Descartes improved upon this form of the argument in his restatement of it in the shape of his *Cogito, ergo sum*: "I think, therefore I am" is not so fruitful a proposition as "I doubt, therefore truth is."

human striving. There is here a "point of connection" from which discussion can start.

## § 3. *Are Scientific Ethics and Philosophy Possible?*

The modern scientific humanists are seriously concerned about the well-being and progress of civilization and culture, and they have for the most part recognized that it is necessary to establish the real existence of ethical and other values upon the firm ground of ascertainable knowledge. Since, however, for them that alone is knowledge which is demonstrable by means of the scientific method, it is argued that science itself can and must determine what are the true ethical values. Thus, we find Mr. C. H. Waddington, who dismisses belief in God as a mere projection of the "super-ego", seeking to establish the validity of ethical values by "scientific" means: science can show us what is the direction of evolution and also what is "good", that is, what ethical principles and types of action will contribute towards the progress of society in this direction.[1] "The scientific attitude" is thus asserted to be a more secure basis for ethical values than is the religious attitude. Most philosophers would probably consider that Waddington's argument involves the fallacy of assuming that the direction of the evolution of society as a whole is objectively good on the grounds that goodness is the direction taken by the evolution of society, and that therefore the argument tells us nothing at all; but, be that as it may, we have here an interesting and instructive illustration of the need, which is felt by all who take morality seriously, of establishing the objectivity of moral value as a part of the structure of the universe itself. This is the testimony of scientific humanism to the reality of ethical values beyond and apart from the mere prejudices and conveniences of individuals and groups. The very category of evolution, which has so often been used to prove the relativity of moral values, is employed by this theory to establish their permanent validity and to assure us of what they are.

The significance of Waddington's argument, if it could be considered sound, would be that it would establish the validity

[1] Cf. C. H. Waddington, *Science and Ethics*, London, 1942, opening essay.

of man's (that is, Mr. Waddington's) ethical judgments on a basis of scientific knowledge and would thus enable us to dispense with any form of faith. But it seems more probable that the argument itself is based on an act of faith, namely, the assumption which underlies all forms of scientific humanism, belief in "progress", the opinion that the later stages of evolution are "better" or "higher" than the earlier. The truth, however, appears rather to be that no philosophy or view of the nature and purpose of the world and man can in fact be built without an act of faith, and that scientific method does not and cannot, without the introduction of a "faith-principle", which science itself does not provide, attain the status of a *Weltanschauung*. Some of the admissions of our scientific philosophers in their moments of candour are very illuminating: "I don't believe in the absolute truth of Marxism in the way that some people believe in dogmas", writes Dr. J. B. S. Haldane; "I only believe that it is near enough to the truth to make it worth while betting my life on it as against any rival theories."[1]

Scientific humanism is attractive to many earnest seekers after ethical values, particularly social righteousness, because it claims to offer a scientific basis for morality, thus avoiding the shifting sands of metaphysics and religion. Everything to-day seems uncertain to the secular humanist except the scientific method: the logical positivists have taught that ethical statements have no verifiable meaning; psychoanalysts have argued that men's ethical ideals are merely the products of their early sexual reactions; anthropologists have emphasized the relativity of all social ethics, varying as they do from culture to culture and from age to age, and the Marxists have insisted that our ethical notions are merely the epiphenomenal by-products of economic tendencies.[2] Those who have lost their foothold on the solid rock of revealed religious truth and who consequently find themselves standing on the quicksands of the age of relativity naturally draw much comfort and reassurance, if they take morality seriously, from the theory that ethical values can be discovered and guaranteed by means of the scientific method. Yet even they are not able to dispense with the necessity of faith: they believe that the direction

[1] *Science and Everyday Life*, Pelican Edition, 1941, p. 191.
[2] Cf. C. H. Waddington, *op. cit.*, pp. 9f.

of evolution is towards the good, and that by studying the direction of evolution within society as a whole it is possible to determine scientifically the nature of goodness. But the whole argument is based upon the initial act of faith, and close enquiry reveals that this faith is after all nothing more than the present-day version of the Victorian faith in "progress".

Modern scientific humanism is a revised version of the evolutionary naturalism of Herbert Spencer, who held that better conduct is conduct which comes later in the course of evolution and is more complex than conduct of an earlier kind. To-day complexity is abandoned as a criterion of progress in ethics: the totalitarian state is more complex than nineteenth-century social structure, but no humanist would maintain that it is better. The criteria of ethical progress in the theories of the scientific humanists seem to be drawn in the first place from biological science, for example, complexity of structure or adaptability to environment. Adaptability to environment is not nowadays more acceptable to the scientific humanists than is complexity of structure, for a jellyfish, though less complex, is as well adapted to its environment as an ant or a man; and we find that a more widely accepted criterion is that of control of environment. If control of environment is taken as the criterion, then the ant or the man is obviously more progressive than the jellyfish, and the direction of evolution may be scientifically determined. Thus, the category of progress is said to be validated in biological science by the emergence of living creatures which attain greater control over (and hence to some extent independence of) environment. Apparently by way of *analogy* from biology the scientific humanists pass over from the biological study of organisms to generalizations concerning the direction of evolution (including that of man and society) as a whole, and assume that man's increasing control over environment (by means of science and scientific planning) is the index of progress in ethics. But obviously this is the very point which requires proof—especially on the threshold of the atomic age! Man's chief problem is not, after all, his control over his environment but his control over himself, and the assumption that such self-control can and will be achieved by better education, social planning or changes in the ownership of the means of production is just as much an act of faith as any of

Ccᴀ

the so-called assumptions of religion and cannot be demonstrated by any known scientific method.

If one uses words accurately, scientific method is a term which can be applied only to matters which are susceptible of being tested by actual experiment and thus of truly scientific verification, and it is apparent that the employment of scientific method can never by itself give us possession of metaphysical truth; there is no purely scientific *Weltanschauung*. "The scientific attitude", or scientific humanism, is not science but philosophy. In other words, philosophy will never be rendered obsolete by advances in scientific method, however remarkable they may be. The broadest categories of science, when applied analogically outside the particular scientific field of their origin (such as the biological category of control of environment) cannot be validated by scientific methods; they can never be more than analogies when they are applied to society or to the universe as a whole. One cannot test the direction of the evolution of society as a whole by any controlled experiment such as scientific method presupposes. Biological categories, for example, cannot be judged more than assumptions or acts of faith when they are extended beyond the working fields of biological experiment and verification. Impressed by the inclusiveness or the significance (to use a question-begging epithet) of a particular category within his own field of research, the scientist not unnaturally passes it on to the philosopher as a "key-category" which may be judged by him to possess universal significance or validity; but when the matter passes beyond the competence of scientific method, that is, beyond the possibilities of controlled experiment, it is misleading and inaccurate to continue to speak of it as a *scientific* category and to imagine that science has superseded the functions of the metaphysician altogether. The philosopher must not lightly abdicate his responsibilities; he must continue to press the question about the justification of categories drawn from some particular field of experience or research—biological, sociological, economic, and so on—when they are extended analogically and used to express statements about the universe as a whole, or the external world, or human destiny, or ethical values.

## § 4. *The Nature and Necessity of Philosophy*

Scientific humanism is not, of course, the only method by which men have tried to arrive at ultimate truth without recourse to an act of faith. Modern philosophy began with the attempt of Descartes to remove all presuppositions which were not either self-evident or demonstrable by reason, and this has remained the goal of all forms of rationalism since his day; in this respect empiricist philosophies have been scarcely less rationalistic than those which are generally styled rationalist. But to-day there seems to be a widespread recognition that men's philosophical systems are not so completely determined by pure reason as their creators have often imagined. Marx and Freud have marked the end of the era of self-confident rationalism, and this at least is part of their Christian significance for us. It is becoming clearer nowadays that without the introduction of a "faith-principle" no metaphysical system and no *Weltanschauung* can be constructed. Indeed, it is largely because this truth is so clearly seen that philosophers have apparently ceased attempting to construct metaphysical systems and seem to regard their function nowadays as primarily that of epistemological criticism; everyone is nervous about making any kind of "leap of faith" in an age in which all affirmations of faith are regarded as prejudices that must be "de-bunked". In some ages—usually stable periods of gradual and peaceful development—there are certain key-ideas or categories of thought and belief which are regarded as so obvious that they are widely accepted as self-evident; but at other times—periods of crisis or of swift social change—all categories are called in question and there is no dominant or widely accepted philosophy. Every constructive philosophy selects a key-idea or category drawn from some particular science or from some definite field of experience, and this it employs analogically to interpret the whole universe, or reality, or "scheme of things entire".[1] In an age in which there is no dominating category of thought or key-principle of explanation, there is no generally accepted philosophical outlook. All kinds of

[1] Cf. D. M. Emmet, *The Nature of Metaphysical Thinking*, London, 1945. It will be apparent that the argument here is indebted to Miss Emmet's valuable exposition of the view that "metaphysics is an analogical way of thinking" (p. 5).

key-ideas have become the principles of explanation used in the metaphysical systems of the past, from the "water" of Thales or the atoms of Democritus to the Ideas of Plato or the One of Plotinus: from the "flux" of Heracleitus to the "emergence" of Alexander or the "control of environment" of the scientific humanists. Every philosophical system must employ a principle of selection, a value-judgment, or what we have called a "faith-principle", which, however self-evident it may have appeared to the thinker or to the age which first decided upon it, does not appear at all self-evident or self-justifying to other philosophers or to other ages.[1] An act of faith is prior to the construction of a metaphysic or to the acceptance of a philosophy of life.[2] Christian philosophy has given expression to its recognition of this universal truth about human thinking in the classical formula, *credo ut intelligam.* The meaning of this fundamental insight of Christian thought will receive fuller consideration in the following pages, and particularly in the last chapter of this book; we may here briefly characterize it by saying that it implies that reason itself must be "justified by faith", by believing something which is not in fact self-evident or demonstrable to all men in virtue of the fact that they are rational beings. The inexorable law is written over all human efforts to comprehend by reason the nature of the universe or the purpose of life: "If ye will not believe, ye shall not understand."

To those who still labour under eighteenth-century rationalistic notions of the human intellect and its capabilities it will doubtless appear wilfully paradoxical to say that the lack of a commonly

[1] Cf. John Baillie, *The Interpretation of Religion*, 1929, pp. 38f.: "The determining factor in the formation of philosophical systems has again and again been the initial presence or absence of religious faith in the philosopher's heart. . . . What was it, ultimately, that put Leucippus, Epicurus, Hobbes, d'Holbach and Mr. Russell into one camp and Socrates, Plato, Descartes, Berkeley and T. H. Green into the other? We submit that nothing had more to do with it than the initial weight they were willing to give to our ethico-religious insights." Cf. also his *Our Knowledge of God*, Oxford, 1939, pp. 132f.

[2] "Even Hegel, the prince of systematizers, can only make the claims he does make for philosophical reason because he believes that in philosophical reason he experiences the spearhead of universal reason thinking through him. . . . Hegel, like other idealists, did not recognize the analogical character of his metaphysics. He could thus see his system as the complete articulation of the Absolute in conscious thought" (D. M. Emmet, *op. cit.*, p. 205).

accepted philosophical standpoint or of constructive attempts in our day to build metaphysical systems is due to the prevalent skepticism in the "climate of opinion" of the twentieth century, that lack of faith in anything at all, which borders upon the dangerous condition of nihilism. Yet this is indeed the truth about our situation to-day. Reason has been dethroned by the combined operations of the psychologists, sociologists of knowledge, Marxists and logical positivists. Rationality can be recovered only by believing in something; or, to put it in another way, the wholeness of our outlook upon the world and life can be re-created only by the deliberate choice of a key-idea by which our fragmentary perceptions of truth can be integrated into a satisfying world-view. But where are we to discover in the thought of our time a significant key-idea which will commend itself to our generation as self-authenticating and worthy of acceptance? Will it be found in biological categories, or in economic or historical categories, or in religious insights? At least we must be on our guard against the intellectualist fallacy of supposing that a faith or a key-idea can be selected as the result of a purely rational and "objective" examination of "facts"; the process of selecting involves the deepest levels of our being; it implicates our whole self, including all its experiences and "social conditioning". Of course, rational examination, as fully rational as we can make it, is necessary, otherwise our illusions and superstitions would serve just as well as a reasoned belief; but it is not all that is necessary. The poet, the artist and the man of action have all a great deal to do with the philosopher's quest, as Plato has demonstrated for all time. And, of course, religion is also involved, since faith in the sense in which we have been speaking of it is not different in kind from what is meant by religious faith, and it is faith of this kind that is essential to philosophy in its constructive aspects.

One advantage which the Christian apologist possesses in an age which is not dominated by any one type of metaphysical outlook is that he is freed from the temptation of trying to come to terms with the reigning thought-system of the day and consequently of subordinating the distinctive faith-principle of Christianity to that of an alien philosophy. While, for example, philosophical thought was dominated by Hegel, many Christian thinkers were vainly occupied in trying to adapt Christian truth to the prevailing winds of the idealist doctrines; while others, like Schleiermacher and the Ritschlians were provoked into so strong a reaction from all forms of speculative idealism that they sought to discover the basis of faith in feeling or "experience", with results almost equally uncongenial to a true appreciation of the essentially biblical quality of Christian truth. To-day the temptations to accommodate the biblical faith-principle of Christianity to that of any alien philosophy are not strong. A philosophy which merits the title Christian is one which succeeds in consistently interpreting the whole of experience solely by reference to the principle of biblical faith, without subordinating it to alien categories, and doubtless therefore a truly Christian philosophy is always an ideal rather than an actual achievement. Whether such a philosophy can be constructed to-day it is not our business here to enquire, still less to attempt to construct one; but it should be noted that the chaos of philosophical thought at the present time is not in itself a reason for refraining from the task or for deeming it unprofitable, since Christian faith is able to supply the very requirement for successful metaphysical construction which the modern secular mind has lost. The task of Christian apologetics is ancillary to that of Christian philosophy. It is doubtless true that every thoughtful man must be in some sense a philosopher; he must have *some* kind of view of man's place and purpose in the scheme of things. The choice, as it has been well said, is not between being a philosopher and not being one, but between being a good philosopher and a bad one. The important fact to be noticed here is that Christianity does not come to men in the twentieth century, any more than it came to men in the first century, as a fully-fledged metaphysic which they are asked to adopt as the basis of their own philosophy of life. It comes with the offer of the *possibility* of constructing a philosophy; it brings to thoughtful men a faith-principle which (though it is also much more than this) is a master-key, opening the doors of rationality and understanding. Had Christianity come into the world originally as a philosophy, it would long ago have passed into the museum of the thought-systems of the past, or it would have been transmuted into many varieties of philosophical forms, combining and dissolving again in the various shapes which loom out of the mists of men's thought down the ages, as Platonism has done. It came, however, not as a philosophy but as a faith, as the belief that certain actual and historical events provide the key or clue to the understanding of human nature and destiny, and this clue it offers to the metaphysician as the category of interpretation by which he may "make sense" of the universe. As a faith it is compelled to seek in every century a philosophical expression, in which its insights may unify and interpret all the knowledge and experience which that age has garnered—scientific, historical, æsthetic, moral, social, and so on. The relation of Christianity to philosophy can hardly be better expressed than in Whitehead's luminous sentence: "Christianity . . . has always been a religion seeking a metaphysic, in contrast to Buddhism, which is a metaphysic generating a religion."[1]

The task of Christian apologetics in relation to philosophy is the elucidation of the nature of the biblical faith-principle by which our experience is to be interpreted as a whole. Whence is this faith-principle derived? What evidence can be brought forward to commend it to thoughtful people in the twentieth century? How is it superior to other faith-principles, such as those of Marxism or scientific humanism? Can it stand the test of examination in the light of modern scientific method? Is not Christian faith only an aspect of our ideological conditioning? Above all, does it help us to achieve rationality in the attempt to understand our world and our experience in it? These are some of the questions which we shall try to answer in our study of Christian apologetics.

[1] *Religion in the Making*, Cambridge, 1926, pp. 39f.

# CHAPTER TWO

# THEOLOGY AS AN EMPIRICAL SCIENCE

## § 1. *The Sciences and their Categories*

BY THE word "science" is meant the study of observable facts and their systematic classification by means of the making and testing of hypotheses in the light of all the available evidence. It is unnecessary for our present purpose to ask philosophical questions about the precise meaning of such words as "facts", "laws", and so on.[1] It is furthermore unnecessary here to stress the truth that great advances have been made in the modern period in the accumulation of knowledge in the study of several departments of human experience, especially those related to the world of sense around us. The fact that there are several well-established and separate—though, of course, not entirely unconnected—sciences is not without significance: our experience of the world is indeed found to be divided into certain clearly distinguishable parts, and each of these is studied by its own appropriate science. Each of these "natural" sciences possesses not merely its own delimited field of investigation but also its own proper categories or principles of interpretation within

[1] Nevertheless, a few working definitions might make for clarification. Science is concerned with generalizations, which are reached by means of induction, which is of the essence of scientific method, since the object of science is to acquire knowledge of general laws by the observation of things experienced. "Laws" are simply generalizations of high probability, "hypotheses" are generalizations of lower probability, and "theories" stand somewhere between the two (see A. D. Ritchie, *The Scientific Method*, 1923, p. 156). All these terms are used quite loosely in general scientific discussion. "Categories" are principles of interpretation of a rather broader kind than hypotheses, and may perhaps be best described by illustrations from particular sciences; thus, *mechanism* is a physical category, *organism* a biological, and so on. Categories drawn chiefly from the biological sciences which figure largely in philosophical discussion to-day include: complexity of structure, adaptation to environment, progress, the direction of evolution, and so on. Psychological categories include personality, purpose, the subconscious mind, projection, and so on. Revelation is a category of theological science. It is clear that categories are not susceptible of verification by induction and experiment in the same way or to the same extent as are hypotheses (not to say laws).

that field. Although the several natural sciences may be said in an important sense to use a common "scientific method", yet they are differentiated from one another by means of the categories which they employ. The general acknowledgment of the right of a particular science to use its own categories, and not those dictated by some other science, is one of the ways in which a particular investigation is recognized as being itself an independent science. A science may properly be said to be independent when it has made good its title to employ categories which are not reducible to those of any other science; otherwise it would be merely a subdivision or department of the science whose categories it borrowed.

Those who are familiar with the history of modern science will hardly need reminding that there has been a considerable amount of conflict amongst scientists themselves about which branches of scientific enquiry have the right to be called sciences. Each new science as it has arisen has had to do battle for the title and status of an independent science. Those whose habits of mind have been fixed in the disciplines of the older sciences have often been unwilling to accord recognition to more recently developed studies, such as psychology, economics and the sociological sciences. If it is assumed that the categories of physico-chemical science are to be regarded as the categories of science *par excellence*, it is not surprising that psychology and anthropology should seem scarcely to qualify as sciences. Nor is the reluctance of physical scientists to recognize some of the newer disciplines as sciences based merely upon conservatism; there is a simplicity about the more abstract sciences (like physics and chemistry) which the more concrete sciences of life, mind and society cannot claim. Observation, measurement and experiment in the physical sciences are easier to contrive, and hence in them definite results are more easily attained. In the mental and social sciences the area of disagreement amongst experts is wider and assured results are hard to come by, owing to the very great difficulty of devising experiments by which hypotheses can be conclusively tested. The physical sciences thus have a certain prestige which the younger sciences have not yet attained.[1] If, however, we judge that the

[1] Cf. C. D. Broad, *The Mind and Its Place in Nature*, 1925, p. 666: "Physics and death have a long start over psychology and life".

determined application of the scientific method in any sphere of human investigation is what earns for an enquiry the right to be called a science, rather than the measure of demonstrable and agreed results which it has attained, we shall not withhold the title from the modern studies of mind and society.

The discussion of the question about which sciences may rightly be styled independent sciences is not concerned merely with a matter of terminology. The underlying issue at stake is the question about what we have called the validity of categories. A science is properly independent only when it can successfully defend its claim to frame and use its own categories. Thus, if the *only* valid category of scientific characterization is (as some have held) a physical one, such as that of mechanism, all other sciences will be subdivisions of physics: biology and psychology could be accounted scientific studies only if they would and could employ the category of mechanism as their ultimate principle of interpretation, and their own categories of organism, purpose, and the like, would have to be explained away as inconsistent with the mechanistic hypothesis. By asserting, however, that biology and psychology are independent sciences, the way is left open for each of them to follow the enquiry wherever it may lead, unhampered by the prestige of hypotheses which have been found successful in other fields of research. Some scientists have in the past behaved like imperialists, wishing to annex the territories of other scientists, while making strenuous efforts to preserve their own from falling a prey to a rival scientific empire. Thus, some psychologists, even while resisting attacks from the direction of the physical sciences on their own domains and while they are fighting a hard battle with fifth-columnists—mechanists and behaviourists—within their own citadel, are nevertheless engaged in trying to explain away the categories of theological science by reducing the latter to categories of their own, such as "projections", "father-complexes", "escape-mechanisms", and so forth.

Every empirical science which is prepared to defend its claim to freedom from dictation from without will assert its right to formulate its own categories of interpretation. We shall not expect to find complete unanimity even amongst the investigators within its own field with regard to all its proposed categories, since progress in scientific understanding is made by the constant criticism and modification of hypotheses and categories. But such criticism and modification must come from within and not from without the particular scientific discipline itself, since those who venture to criticize from outside, however eminent they may be in some other field, have not the technical competence to make a judgment: the incursions of eminent biologists into the theological field are usually no more enlightening than those of the theologians into the biological. The discussion of the categories which are necessary to a science is the proper task of the workers within that science itself, and here there will be ample room for divergence of opinion. For example, some biologists would agree and others would disagree with Dr. Julian Huxley, who allows the validity of the category of progress but denies the validity of the category of purpose in biological science; the question is one which biologists alone must decide. But when they have made their decision, they must remember that it is valid only within the sphere of their competence.

## § 2. *The Metaphysical Criticism of Scientific Categories*

So far we have discussed the question of the validity of scientific categories only at the level of empirical science itself. There are, however, other aspects of this question, which are to be discussed at the philosophical level. Sometimes the distinction is overlooked and philosophical questions about validity are discussed as if they could be settled at the level of science. As we saw in the previous chapter, scientific humanism tends to make this mistake. The error arises partly at least because it is possible to go a long way in scientific research—especially in the physical sciences—without becoming aware of philosophical questions; one may traverse vast and fascinating realms within these sciences before the frontiers of metaphysics are reached. A research chemist might spend a long and busy life absorbed in the engrossing pursuit of his investigation without ever having to pause and consider what Hume or Kant said about the category of causation, just as a physical chemist might work for a long time upon the problems of nuclear fission without becoming aware that ethical considerations are involved in the successful conclusion of his labours. Again, it is possible for a scientist to step across the frontier of metaphysics without being aware that he has done so; the boundaries are not, after all, very clearly defined. This happens sometimes when a scientist is so impressed by the "significance" of a category within his own science that he uncritically assumes that it is capable of interpreting all fields of human experience, as when "mechanism" or "evolution" is offered as the key which unlocks all the mysteries of mind or of the world as a whole. There is indeed a sense in which the proper categories of a particular science may be transferred to another, or to philosophical matters, but it is an analogical sense, and the *method* of this analogical procedure is metaphysical and not scientific. A biologist who passes judgments about theological matters, because he thinks that having studied one aspect of reality he is competent to pronounce upon all, is just as much of a charlatan as a theologian who thinks that his study of theology has conferred upon him the capacity to utter the last word upon the theory of the evolution of biological species; but a biologist or a theologian whose proper studies have convinced him that there is peculiar significance in the categories of his own science is proceeding along entirely sound lines when he turns metaphysician and asks whether the insights into the nature of things which his own scientific studies have brought to him within his own limited field do not suggest some analogical insight into the nature and purpose of the world as a whole. Indeed, it is hard to see how any thoughtful person, who is engaged upon the study of some aspect of experience, can fail to ask himself whether his investigations do not suggest by way of analogy some truth concerning the ultimate nature and meaning of things. The really important consideration is whether such a person is truly aware of what he is doing when he thus crosses the frontier between science and metaphysics.

It is clear that the philosopher himself, "the synoptic man", has a very difficult and responsible task to perform in an age of great and rapid scientific advance. Theoretically his task is to take note of all the categories of all the sciences and then to try to select that which seems to him to be the most significant of them or the most embracing, or else to try to frame a new "super-category" which shall take account of all of them, doing injury to none; but while it is easy thus to formulate the nature of the philosopher's task, the task itself becomes in practice daily more difficult and beyond the powers of any one mind, as each of the specialized sciences increases in complexity. Besides all this, the philosopher has other realms to consider besides those of the empirical or positive sciences: there are also the spheres of the normative sciences, of logic, aesthetics and ethics. The task of the philosopher is indeed formidable in the twentieth century, and it is little surprising that many thoughtful people have concluded that, since no individual's mind is capable of apprehending more than a fraction of the accumulated knowledge of mankind to-day, it is wiser to abandon the attempt to construct a metaphysic or total world-view in the grand manner, and so they confine themselves to writing footnotes on epistemological and methodological topics.

Such counsel, however, ignores the actual nature of the human mind, which is endowed with an insatiable thirst for a rational answer to the question about human life and destiny. Apart from the danger that the Dr. Rosenbergs of the world will turn to their own perverted ends the opportunities which the philosophers and "clerks" refuse to seize, civilization will perish unless men have a faith to live by, and man's deepest needs cannot be satisfied if his fundamental questions remain unanswered. Men must and will believe something. Whatever we are told in an age of the breakdown of traditional views and values about the impossibility of giving rational answers to ultimate questions, we shall go on asking them; and some of us at least will go on trying to be as rational as we can in answering them. Here, we readily admit, it is Christian faith which prompts us to attempt to find rational answers, indeed which makes us try to ask rational questions: "ask, and ye shall receive, seek, and ye shall find, knock, and it shall be opened unto you" is a saying which, as St. Augustine so frequently noted, perfectly expresses both the beginning and the ending of the philosopher's quest; man was created rational in order that he might not rest content until he had found the rational answer, or rather had received it.[1] Faith cannot admit

---

[1] The strength of the influence of the traditional Christian teaching, as fixed by St. Augustine at the beginning of the fifth century, is clearly seen in these sentences of John Locke, in which he anticipates the result of his enquiry into the nature of human understanding: "How short soever men's knowledge may

that in the twentieth or in any other century man cannot know the truth which makes him free. Without unduly minimizing the very great difficulty of metaphysical thinking in an age when specialization has reached the degree of complexity of our present developments, it may perhaps be suggested that our situation is not quite so desperate as it might seem. If we think of the philosopher as being confronted with the task of examining every hypothesis and category of all the empirical sciences, and all the problems of the normative sciences, and then having to try to make a super-induction in order to arrive at a super-category which will comprehend them all, we are doubtless viewing the matter in a manner that is formally correct, but we are over-looking the way in which the human mind (including the phil-osopher's) does in fact work. After all, scientists themselves do not arrive at their categories without the employment of their imagination; the logical processes of induction may be set forth later in a formally correct manner, and they may be tested by experiment and proved to be valid, but it is probable that the scientist originally arrived at his hypothesis or category by flashes of insight or "intuitions". The minds of the philosopher and of the scientist are not different in kind or in operation from the minds of the artist, the poet or the man of religion. We are apt to over-look the fact that the scientist and the poet possess the *human* mind in common, and that when we speak of the scientist or the philosopher as using methods of reason and induction while the poet or religious man uses intuition and imagination, we are making a distinction which exists in theory (and old-fashioned theory at that) rather than in fact. The vast accumulations of specialized knowledge in the various branches of science have not been acquired apart from the intuitions of the artist-scientist and

come of an universal or perfect comprehension of whatsoever is, it yet secures their great concernments that they have light enough to lead them to the know-ledge of their Maker, and the sight of their own duties. . . . It will be no excuse to an idle and untoward servant, who would not attend his business by candlelight, to plead that he had not broad sunshine. The candle that is set up in us shines bright enough for all our purposes. . . . If we disbelieve everything because we cannot certainly know all things, we shall do much-what as wisely as he who would not use his legs, but sit still and perish because he had no wings to fly" (*Essay on the Human Understanding*, Bk. I, Ch. I, § 5). Here is Christian wisdom for the twentieth century, as for the fifth or seventeenth.

they do not necessarily inhibit the insights of the artist-philosopher.[1] The powers of induction in the mind of a great scientific genius are not entirely dissimilar to the faculty of a great poetic genius for perceiving all kinds of analogies which ordinary people do not notice without his help. It is the same human mind which is at work in the scientist, the philosopher, the artist and the man of religion. Newton and Plato, Shakespeare and Amos, are all using the same tool, the human mind.

Now, we can recognize but we cannot penetrate the mystery of the human mind's strange faculty for perceiving analogies and formulating categories. The very vagueness of the words which we find ourselves compelled to use when we discuss this subject—"intuition", "insight" and so on—serves to emphasize the grossness of our ignorance here. One thing, however, is not at all uncertain, namely, that scientific induction and metaphysical thinking alike require as the very condition of their existence this kind of insight, this leaping ahead of the evidence to categories which may perhaps later receive experimental verification or which may be incapable of such treatment. In science, no less than in philosophy or religion, *fides praecedet intellectum*. This applies not merely to the process of arriving at such categories as those of "mechanism", "natural selection", or "the unconscious", but also to those very broad and prior categories, without which

---

[1] Cf. A. D. Ritchie, *The Scientific Method*, p. 53: "There is one point I wish to make perfectly clear, on which it is impossible to lay too much stress; that is that the process of scientific discovery, of finding Natural Laws, which is what Induction is, is an Art, in the ordinary sense of the words. It is possible to state rules for extracting the Square Root of a number or for finding trains in Bradshaw, given which anybody not entirely devoid of intelligence can perform the operation in question successfully. But it is quite impossible to lay down rules knowing which anybody can write poems like Shelley or make statues like Praxiteles. So also is it impossible to lay down rules which will enable anybody to make discoveries like Faraday or Pasteur. But strangely enough Bacon seems to have thought it possible, and many later thinkers who ought to have known better seem to have had some such idea at the back of their minds. It is interesting to the Philosopher to try and state the rules that govern the successful carrying out of an artistic process, but the rules are of no help to one who has not got the artistic faculty and are unnecessary to one who has it."

there could be no science, and yet which cannot be proved, such as the principle of the uniformity of nature.[1] Science itself, including its most distinctive and valuable feature, the inductive method, is based upon an act of faith, and this faith is not formally different in quality from the faith about which the religious man speaks. Without the formulation of categories and hypotheses the progressive arrangement of the observations of phenomena in that kind of ordered whole which we call scientific knowledge does not take place, and yet the actual discovery of categories is in the first place the creative act of an original mind and is akin to the creation of a work of art or to the insight which in religion is described as prophetic genius. We can no more tell whence Faraday or Einstein derived their creative insights than we can say whence Shakespeare derived his tragic conception of *Macbeth*; the most we can do is to describe the general situation of the world of science when Faraday or Einstein went to work upon it; or we can discuss the condition of the drama when Shakespeare came to Southwark, or the sources which he used when he sat down to write *Macbeth*. The difference between Holinshed's *Chronicle* and Shakespeare's *Macbeth* will always remain to convince us that we know as little about the workings of the creative genius of the human mind as we do about its origins. We are, in fact, confronted by mystery, and the rationalist attitude to mystery is simply to ignore it: "Where I find mystery," said Albrecht Ritschl, who had not shaken himself so free from the habits of rationalism as he supposed, "I say nothing about it." This attitude persists to-day in a largely unconscious way in the minds of many people, long after the rationalism of the eighteenth-

---

[1] Cf. F. R. Tennant, *The Nature of Belief*, 1943, pp. 41f.: "Inductive science is founded on an act of faith, and belief in its deliverance has a subjective cause. It has sometimes been said that 'where reason ends, faith begins'; but the truth turns out to be that where faith ends reason begins, so far as generalized knowledge of the world is concerned." Cf. also R. Hooker, *Laws of Ecclesiastical Polity*, Bk. III, Ch. viii: "As though there were any kind of science in the world which leadeth men into knowledge without presupposing a number of things already known. No science doth make known the first principles whereon it buildeth, but they are always either taken as plain and manifest in themselves, or as proved and granted already, some former knowledge having made them evident."

century type[1] of which it is a survival has been discredited. There is no science which can explain the mystery of the existence of science itself.

The task of examining the validity of the categories which are presented by the various sciences, evaluating them and co-ordinating them into a system is the work of the metaphysician; he must select from among them, or perhaps substitute for them, a key-category for the interpretation of our experience as a whole. This, at least, is one way of describing the metaphysician's proper work. Whether he will succeed in this task amidst the somewhat confused conditions of thought in our times is not a question upon which we are called to express an opinion here.[2] In any case scientists (including theologians) have never been hesitant about exercising their right of veto and rejecting the conclusions of the metaphysician, when these conclusions appear to do less than justice to the categories which have been deemed to be of great importance in this or that scientific field. The theologian, like the worker in any other field of empirical science, will be quick to point out the failure of any philosophy which does not take into account in its wider characterization of reality those categories of our experience which the study of his science has shown him to be significant.

[1] Cf. Edmund Burke, *A Vindication of Natural Society*: "A good parson once said, that where mystery begins, religion ends." Also Mark Pattison, *Essays and Reviews*, p. 297: "The defect of the eighteenth century theology was not in having too much good sense, but in having nothing besides."

[2] Miss D. M. Emmet's valuable discussion of this question in *The Nature of Metaphysical Thinking* (Chapter IX) concludes that "the most a philosophical theory may do is to express a few features, in a selective and probably distorted composition, yet in a way which may bring out some significant characteristic" (p. 216). A metaphysician penetrates beyond the limits of empirical investigation by means of the analogy provided by the form of experience which he has taken as his clue. "His view seeks to express some characterization of reality, but necessarily with omission of a vast range of detail, and necessarily also with some distortion due to his selective judgment of what is important." Just as a Fougasse cartoon can convey certain important characteristics of a whole subject through a very few lines, so a metaphysical view conveys its characterization of the real. "There is distortion; there is a high degree of selectivity; there is certainly the artist's personal way of seeing; yet the result conveys an important character of the situation" (p. 204).

## § 3. *The Subject-matter of Theological Science*

There is to-day a growing recognition of the truth that theology is an empirical science, properly so called.[1] By theology we here mean the study of Christian existence in history and to-day, that is, of all that appertains to the believing and witnessing Christian community, the Church, both in the past and in the present. Thus, theology is a different science, though a related one, from either the psychology of religion, which is a branch of psychology, or the comparative study of religion (*Religionsgeschichte*). Like any other science, theology deals with the facts of human experience; it does not (as many apparently suppose) deal with hypothetical objects, or things about which there is a reasonable possibility of doubt. The science of theology is rendered necessary by the existence of the Church, just as the existence of physical objects makes necessary the science of physics.[2] The metaphysician may ask questions about the ultimate nature of physical objects, but his questions arise only "after physics"; similarly the philosopher may ask questions about the ultimate nature of the Church, or of theological existence in the widest sense, but his questions properly arise only after the theologian has made his scientific investigation of the *data* which the existence of the Church provides.[3] The conclusions of the scientist, whether he be physicist or theologian, become *data* and starting-points for the philosopher; and both physicist and theologian must try to conduct their investigations, so far as they can, without any prior philosophical assumptions in their minds.[4] The fact that the

[1] *Vide* Canon Leonard Hodgson, *Theology in an Age of Science,* Inaugural Lecture, Oxford, 1944.

[2] Cf. A. N. Whitehead, *Religion in the Making*, p. 47: "The dogmas of religion are the attempts to formulate in precise terms the truths disclosed in the religious experience of mankind. In exactly the same way the dogmas of physical science are attempts to formulate in precise terms the truths disclosed in the sense-perception of mankind."

[3] The word "Church" is used here and generally to denote the whole believing, worshipping and witnessing Christian community throughout the world, in all its historical continuity across the centuries and in all its historic denominations.

[4] It is, of course, impossible to do this in any literal sense, and it is unlikely that a mind which contained no metaphysical notions (assuming such a mind to be possible) could ever arrive at the wider categories of science. Dr. Ritchie's

physical world or the Church exists *in some sense* is sufficient reason for the scientific mind to go to work upon it, and the *datum* of theology is just as truly "given" as is the *datum* of physics: there *is* a believing and witnessing Church. It is just as truly *there* as was the large stone that Dr. Johnson struck his foot against to refute Berkeley's theory of the non-existence of matter. Of course, after it has been subjected to the scrutiny of its own appropriate science, namely theology, the Church might turn out to be something rather different from what the man in the street takes it to be, just as Dr. Johnson would have been surprised if he could have heard the account of the large stone as it would now be given by a physicist.

The task of theology, then, arises because of the existence of the worshipping and witnessing Christian community, and theology is the science which seeks to formulate categories by which the phenomena of Church-existence may be understood. Before the rise of modern inductive science, theology was studied, but it was held to be a deductive science, and its method was to attempt to deduce necessary conclusions from the revealed truths contained in Holy Scripture, which was thus additional knowledge, based on revelation, to the knowledge which was derived from the natural reason itself. It was inevitable that in the modern period the methods of inductive science, which had proved themselves so valuable in other fields, should sooner or later be applied to the study of theological matters, and during the last hundred years theology has been increasingly studied by the aid of the inductive method, with results which (as in other fields of investigation) have entirely justified the use of that approach. In particular, the study of the Bible by means of the methods of historical and literary criticism has proved very

words are applicable to the theologian as well as to the physical scientist: "The man of science and his commonsense forerunners brush aside a vast number of perplexing problems when they desire to disregard metaphysics and go straight to work on particular parts of the physical world. Their conception of the physical world is already saturated with metaphysics and metaphysics of the most dangerous sort, unconscious metaphysics inherited from our forebears and worked out in extreme youth. Lurking in the background of any description of what we see and touch and hear is some theory and some assumption as to the nature of things; the scientific man's escape from metaphysics is largely illusory. He has simply repressed it" (*The Scientific Method*, p. 6).

fruitful and has brought a new understanding in this as in every other branch of historical theology. But historical theology is not the whole of theological science. If there were to-day no living Church, all theological study would be of the type known as historical theology, that is, the investigation of the beliefs, cultus and behaviour of the Church which existed in former ages; such study would be purely "academic", like the scholar's study of the ancient mystery-religions to-day. It might conceivably be for a few such scholars a deep and moving study, even an "avenue to truth" for them: it is said that a distinguished Semitic scholar died with the name of Tammuz on his lips. But it could have no living meaning for ordinary folk, who have neither time nor inclination for historical research. There is, however, a living Church, and therefore theology is the study of present facts, as well as of historical ones; its primary *datum* is the living faith and witness of the contemporary Church. These cannot be understood except in the light of their history, and so theology must include historical theology, while at the same time it is more than a branch of historical science. The study of theology cannot be "merely academic", because it is the study of a living faith which in its most important aspects can be understood only by those who have experience of it; it is necessarily an "existential" study, because in it the investigator is personally involved, either positively or negatively, in the living-believing-worshipping-witnessing complex of relationships which he is investigating.[1] As in all the more concrete sciences, the personal "perspective" of the investigator enters into his work as itself an object of study, and this makes impartiality or detachment more difficult to attain and constantly raises the kind of question which rarely arises in the more abstract sciences.

We have compared the study of theology with that of physics, as both alike grounded upon the desire to understand better a given part of our human experience. A better parallel, however, in some of its aspects, might be afforded by a comparison of

[1] Heim's explanation of the modern continental use of the word *existentiell* runs: "A proposition or a truth is said to be existential when I cannot apprehend it or assent to it from the standpoint of a mere spectator, but only on the ground of my total existence." Karl Heim, *God Transcendent*, Eng. trans. by E. P. Dickie, London, 1935, p. 75n.

theology with political science. We find ourselves confronted by a given reality, which demands and deserves investigation; in the one case it is the Church, in the other case the State. As regards the latter, we are confronted by the existence of government, or of political authority, in every human social grouping. The investigation of this empirical reality is a proper object of scientific study, even though in the nature of the case its inductions are very much more complex and therefore more difficult to establish than those of the physical sciences. Since all people in every society are either governors or governed (or in some societies both), there is a necessarily existential quality of political investigation which renders "scientific disinterestedness" much harder to attain, perhaps impossible to attain in any complete sense, but not for that reason less desirable as an ideal. It is doubtless true that the scientific study of politics, abstractly conceived, does not and should not lead one to take up any particular attitude towards the State, or to join any particular political party; yet it is probable that the student will not be able to refrain from defining his own personal attitude towards a number of political views and policies, and he will be more clearly able to see and to avoid at least some of the errors of political judgment which result from thoughtlessness or the uncritical acceptance of propaganda. The disinterested scientist and the member of a living political society are, after all, one and the same person, and they can hardly avoid one another's company when they live at such close quarters. In a similar way it is doubtless true that the study of theology does not of itself compel the student to take up any particular attitude towards the Church and its proclamation; yet it is likely that such study will enable him to see more clearly what is involved in the Church's existence and to define on a well-considered basis his own attitude towards it; at least he will have a better chance of ridding himself of those prejudices based on ignorance, which, as in other spheres, darken the minds of those who have never given serious consideration to the fact of the Church's existence. Because of the complex, concrete and existential nature of their categories, in comparison with those of the physical sciences, it is more difficult to draw a clear dividing-line between the boundaries of the political and theological sciences on the one hand and of philosophy on the other; yet there is, of course, an important distinction between them, and so far as possible it must be kept clear.

The view that theology is an empirical science still wears to many eyes the aspect of novelty. Many theologians, although they are well accustomed to employing scientific methods of study in their work, know very little about science outside their own sphere, which they rarely think of under that description; and many scientists at work upon the "natural" sciences know very little about theology as it is developed to-day by modern critical methods. This is an age of specialization, in which one half of the world knows little about the other half. The natural scientist is often unaware that a revolution has taken place in theological method during the last hundred years, and he supposes (if he thinks about the subject at all) that the theologian still lives in the world of St. Thomas Aquinas, when all science was deductive science. It is true that from the days of the formation of the canon of the New Testament to the end of the eighteenth century or later the accepted view of theologians generally was that the articles of Christian faith were deducible by reason from explicit and infallible statements contained in the Bible. On this matter Calvin would not have dissented from Aquinas. The traditional Christian position, both Catholic and Protestant, was that the divine scriptural revelation allowed of the deduction of clear-cut truths, and theology was thus the deductive science of revelation. This conception of theological science survived until long after the rise of the inductive method in the modern period and its successful application in the physical sciences; it should be noticed that it was not displaced by any influences from the direction of the natural sciences but by a movement from within, namely, the discovery by theologians themselves of the categories of modern historical and literary criticism. The nineteenth century will, one may surmise, be reckoned as one of the greatest periods in the history of Christian thought, in which a Copernican revolution was achieved by the introduction of the inductive scientific method into the whole area of theological study. The consequences of this revolution include a complete re-interpretation of the entire conception of revelation. The question which above all others must be investigated by Christian apologetics to-day is whether the study of theology as an empirical science

validates the category of revelation as an indispensable characterization of the facts of which the theologian has to take
cognizance. Theology, then, is the investigation at the level of
empirical science of the facts involved in the existence of the
believing, worshipping and witnessing Christian community by
means of the formulation of categories which shall be adequate
to the proper understanding of these facts. We can put the
matter in another way by saying that the task of Christian apologetics in the twentieth century is to demonstrate that the
Christian faith can bear scrutiny in the light of modern scientific
method, that is, by the scientific method appropriate to it, which
is theological method.

## § 4. *The Independence of Theological Categories*

There are three principal ways in which theology to-day may
be said to make good its claim to be reckoned as an empirical
science. The first is its independent use of its own proper categories of scientific investigation; the second is its employment of
the scientific method, and the third is the spirit of its approach
to its subject-matter. Each of these points must be briefly
considered.

In the first place, then, theology makes use of its own categories
of scientific classification and interpretation. If it did not do so,
if it were compelled to borrow the categories of another science,
it could not be called an independent science; it would then be
merely a sub-division of the science whose categories it borrowed.
We have already noted that in the history of modern thought
there has been a constant struggle on the part of each new science
as it has arisen to secure the recognition of its right to use its
own categories. Psychology, for instance, is not a sub-division of
an all-embracing physical science, because its categories are not
reducible to those of the physico-chemical sciences. Theology is
likewise not a branch of any other science; it is not a branch of
psychology, because it is much more than an examination of the
phenomena of religious experience; nor is it a department of the
comparative study of religion, since it uses categories (like that
of revelation) with which many students of the comparative study
of religion are apparently able to dispense. Psychologists, social

scientists and others have, of course, often put forward the claim
to be able to handle all the *data* of theological existence by means
of their own categories, and if such claims could be sustained,
the proper categories of theology could have no independent
validity; and it is precisely this kind of claim, usually put
forward by those who have not themselves had any training in
modern theological method, that Christian apologetics must be
ready to rebut. The theologian, like any other scientist who has
become convinced of the validity of the categories with which he
works, will be at pains to demonstrate that the subject-matter
with which he deals cannot adequately be subsumed under the
categories of any other science; but, of course, he will agree that
many of the phenomena which he investigates may also be
studied from a different angle by workers in other fields, and he
will welcome all the light which these parallel researches can
shed. The territories of the different sciences overlap, or, more
accurately, two or more sciences often look at the same phenomena
from their own distinctive points of view. The psychologist and
the anthropologist, for example, take cognizance of some of the
same facts as the theologian studies, and there need be no conflict
but rather a helpful co-operation between them, so long as one
science abstains from upholding dogmatically hypotheses which
stultify the categories of the other.

Theologians themselves do not as yet always perceive the
importance of the recognition of theology as an independent
science. Some theologians have been and apparently still are
prepared to accept the reduction of their science to the status of
a satellite of psychology. Throughout the nineteenth century
theology tended to be unduly deferential towards her assertive
sisters among the sciences. The late Dr. H. R. Mackintosh has
said that Schleiermacher, whose notable work on *The Christian
Faith* was published in 1821, opened the greatest century in
theology since the fourth; but, if that is so, we venture to think
that it is because during the course of it, after an uncertain and
roundabout journey, theology came to understand more clearly
her own true nature and task. Schleiermacher himself, and a host
of his followers, have tended to ignore what we have judged to be
the irreducibility of theological categories, such as that of revelation, and to turn theology into a branch of some other science;

they have regarded theology as the investigation of human spirituality, or of the soul's experience of spiritual life in the Church. They have defined theology as "the interrogation of the religious consciousness with a view to discovering what religion is."[1] Such a definition degrades theology to the status of a branch of the psychology of religion; it becomes merely the systematization of the beliefs of a given church at a given time; such a task could be performed for our own times by the mass-observers! The theologian's function would be little more than that of the production of a series of reports like *Doctrine in the Church of England,* each of which would be more or less out of date by the time that it was printed. This is, of course, not at all what we meant when we said that the task of theology is to study the *data* supplied by the existence of the believing and witnessing Church. Theology will deny the validity of its own special categories and abdicate its rank as an independent science, if it surrenders to the view that Christian truth is evolved out of man's own religious consciousness, and thus renounces the historic conception of a given revelation. Theology as a science stands or falls with the category of revelation; if there is no distinctively Christian revelation in history, the special categories of theology will not be needed, and in the place of theology the scientific study of religion could be more competently undertaken by the psychologists, sociologists and anthropologists. The century of theological activity which Schleiermacher opened, it is worthy of remark, explored every conceivable method of interpreting the phenomena of Christian existence by means of non-theological categories; but it closed with the confident re-assertion of those categories and the renewed insistence upon the independence of theology. The century of Protestant theology that Schleiermacher inaugurated came to an end with the publication of Karl Barth's *Epistle to the Romans* in 1919.[2] The wheel had come full circle.

[1] J. Baillie, *Interpretation of Religion,* 1929, p. 14; cf. W. Temple, *Nature, Man and God,* pp. 44f. If the task of theology be that of "formulating the deliverances of religious experience", it is not difficult for skeptical and critical minds to raise serious objections to it; see, e.g., J. L. Stocks, *Reason and Intuition,* Oxford, 1939, pp. 220ff.

[2] H. R. Mackintosh (*Types of Modern Theology,* 1937, p. 60) stated that Schleiermacher's *Christian Faith* is, next to the *Institutes* of Calvin, the most influential dogmatic work to which Protestant theology can point. Some will

## § 5.  *The Method and Spirit of Theology*

The second reason which may be given for regarding theology as an empirical science is its use of scientific method. We have already noted the significance of the substitution of the method of induction for the older conception of theology as a deductive science, which took place in the nineteenth century. The theologian collects and systematizes the facts of Church-existence, including, of course, the historical facts connected with the origin and growth of the Church. By every device of modern historical and literary criticism he seeks to determine the nature of these facts, upon which the Christian faith was founded and through which it is expressed, and, having performed this task in the sphere of historical theology, he then goes on to ask what categories —such as those of divine revelation or inspiration—are necessary for the interpretation of those facts and of the facts of Church-existence to-day. The latter part of his task is the discipline traditionally known as dogmatics, the attempt to formulate the doctrines that arise from the facts thus examined in the full light of our modern knowledge. That this part of the task of theology very quickly approaches the boundaries of metaphysics, or of the philosophy of religion, need not disconcert us; we would naturally expect it to do so, since, if theological categories are held to be necessary, they must obviously have a high significance for the philosophical understanding of the world and its meaning. The relatively existential character of the human sciences, as distinguished from the natural sciences, means, as we have already noted, that their frontiers with philosophy are sooner reached and are less well defined.

In the field of historical theology, however, it is easier to keep clear of metaphysical questions than in that of dogmatics, although, of course, it is impossible to avoid raising these questions in the course of the investigation. In the various branches of

hold that the publication of Barth's *Church Dogmatics* now proceeding may necessitate the revision of such a judgment. It is too early yet to say, but it is obvious that a revolution has taken place in Protestant theology since 1919. For Barth's conception of dogmatics as a science see his *Doctrine of the Word of God; Church Dogmatics*, Vol. I, Part I, Eng. trans. by G. T. Thomson, Edinburgh, 1936, pp. 1–17 and 315–30.

historical theology—literary and historical biblical criticism, including textual criticism, church history, patristic studies, linguistics, and so on—it is possible for scholars who have no personal interest in the Christian faith (in the sense of dogmatics) to work alongside believing Christian scholars in the tasks of scientific research. Eminent names will at once occur to the mind. Cardinal Newman remarked that it was a melancholy fact that the greatest of all ecclesiastical historians was "the infidel Gibbon". Yet even here, as in all historical matters, the influence of the investigator's acceptance or non-acceptance of dogmatic categories (or of the Christian faith) is very considerable in determining the weight which he gives to this or that piece of historical evidence, or deciding whether this or that event ever took place at all. This is a difficulty of all historical research, which almost amounts to a scandal in the eyes of those whose acquaintance with science tends to be limited to the physical sciences and who have been brought up in the simple belief that "it's no use arguing about facts". In the historical sciences, as we shall notice more carefully in a later chapter, it is possible for two competent investigators to arrive at opposing interpretations of the facts, and indeed even to disagree about what are and what are not facts. For this reason it is not possible to separate historical from dogmatic theology in any hard-and-fast way, since historical theology is always likely to be affected by dogmatic interpretations —whether those interpretations are inspired by Christian faith or by some non-Christian view of things. It is no objection, as we shall see, to the view that theology is a science that its account of the facts with which it deals is to some extent conditioned by the categories that the investigator adopts; this is true of all the sciences, but it is more obvious in the more existential ones, because in these the whole being of the investigator is personally involved, as it never could be in the more abstract natural sciences. The physicist or biologist who denies the validity of theological categories does so not because he is a scientist but because he is not a Christian man. Meanwhile the theologian will go his way, revising and modifying, enlarging and deepening, the categories of his science, according as his study of the facts directs him; he will follow the argument where his reason leads him.

This brings us to the third reason why theology is to be regarded as a science, namely, because of the scientific spirit in which the theologian approaches his task. An objection will occur to many minds at this point.[1] A scientist, it will be said, is one who comes to his subject with an open mind, without having his conclusions prescribed for him; but a theologian is usually a Christian before he begins his work; his dogmatic interest takes precedence over his scientific judgment. Now the notion of an open mind requires careful scrutiny; it will not be found that the natural scientist is in a very different position from the theologian, if we take into account the more definitely existential nature of theological science. The notion of the open mind does not and cannot mean that the scientist should come to his study with his mind a *tabula rasa*, or in a complete state of Cartesian doubt. Science in any form would be beyond the capacity of anyone who even approximated to this condition.[2] Scientists must approach their work with certain categories and convictions in their minds: they must believe in the unity and uniformity of things, in the value of knowledge, the importance of their subject, and so on. The scientist does in fact come to his task convinced (from whatever reasons) that his subject is worth studying, that there is a "real" object to be studied and valuable knowledge to be gained by studying it, that there are connections to be traced and meanings to be discovered, whether or not there are practical and useful results to be obtained. Moreover, he does not begin his study with the assumption in his mind that all the conclusions reached by his predecessors in that field of research are just as likely to be wrong as to be right, and that therefore he must begin again at the point where Newton began, or Bacon, or Thales. He accepts, for the time being at least, the authority of tradition; he learns what has been thought until now, before he presumes to doubt it. Yet when it is naïvely stated that the theologian does not have an open mind in approaching the objects of his study, it seems to be assumed that he ought to begin his study of theology unconvinced that there is in it anything worth studying, and ready to believe that all the theologians of the past and of the present have been pursuing a will-o'-the-wisp. No one is likely to contribute greatly to the advancement of knowledge who has doubts about

[1] See, e.g., J. L. Stocks, *op. cit.*, pp. 218ff.
[2] Cf. A. D. Ritchie, *The Scientific Method*, p. 104.

the value of his science or the validity of its categories. Whatever an open mind may mean, it cannot mean one thing for natural scientists and another for theologians.

The theologian, like every other scientist, must come to his work with a high regard for its dignity and value, a deep sense of vocation, lofty standards of intellectual integrity and an earnest desire to know the truth. A survey of the history of Christian thought shows that the great theologians of the past have been men of this calibre. An important *datum* for the theologian to-day to note is that not one of them has ever found that his allegiance to the Christian faith has inhibited his reason or prevented him from following the truth wherever it has led, though sometimes it has made him critical of the empirical church or church-order of his day and has thus led him to become a reformer. The Greek Fathers, though remaining loyal to the central core of Christian belief, nevertheless allowed themselves considerable latitude of interpretation and speculation in their expression of theological truth. Even those theologians who have come to be popularly pictured as pillars of conservative dogmatism were in their own day regarded by their contemporaries as dangerous innovators, to be treated with wariness. St. Thomas Aquinas, the "Angelic Doctor", throughout his short working lifetime had to contend boldly for the new Aristotelianism against the traditional Platonic Augustinianism, and "Thomism" was opposed not only by Franciscans like St. Bonaventura and John Peckham, but even by members of St. Thomas's own Dominican order like Robert Kilwardby. Luther and Calvin were bold pioneers of new outlooks in theology before they became the respectable fathers of "Lutheranism" and "Calvinism". However safely traditionalist a great theological teacher may appear to a later age, it is certain that in his own day he was not regarded as a reliable guide for seekers after orthodoxy. Anyone who will take the trouble to do so can readily assure himself that the great figures of classical Christian theology were men dominated by a passionate desire to know the truth and to teach it in spite of all consequences.

Since the theologian must come to his subject with a high regard for its dignity and value, it follows in practice—if not absolutely in theory—that he will be a convinced member of the believing and witnessing Christian community. Where else will he acquire the sense of the dignity and value of his science, save in the Christian Church? Apart from his life in the Church, he will have no direct knowledge of the *data* of his enquiry. It is not an accident but a practical (though not perhaps a theoretical) necessity that theologians are Church-members. There are, of course, many scholars engaged upon the scientific study of some branch of historical theology who sit loose to the obligations and responsibilities of Church membership, or who even stand outside the Church altogether. But dogmatic theology is essentially the concern of the Church, for a dogma is, quite simply, an ecclesiastical definition. Such definition is the outcome of the theologian's labours. This point is very important and it is frequently misunderstood. It is the theologian who formulates the definitions or dogmas of churches, and it is a mistake to think of dogmas as imposed upon theologians by an extra-theological authority. A dogma is an articulation of what the Church believes, and it is the task of the theologian to articulate what is implicit in the existence of the Church. Only those who possess what we have called existential knowledge of the Church's faith and life are in a position to articulate its true meaning. This truth has long been perceived by Christian thinkers, whose general attitude might be summed up in the words of St. Anselm: "The right order of proceeding is that we should believe the deep things of the Christian faith before we presume to discuss them by means of our reason."[1] A man who has no personal understanding of faith or grace would be unlikely to succeed as a dogmatic theologian, though he might become a distinguished scholar in some branch of historical theology, including the history of dogma. The situation is not radically different from that in other sciences: a flat-earth enthusiast might conceivably pass an examination in astronomy (that is, in what he would conceive to be the wrong-headed theories of the pseudo-astronomers), but it is improbable that he would contribute much to our knowledge of the stars.

The theologian's task is consequently not one which can be performed in its entirety by the scholar in his library. The primary *datum* of theology is the faith, worship and witness of the living Church. The science of theology is rendered necessary by the fact that to-day the authentic declaration of Christian

[1] *Cur Deus Homo*, Bk. I, Ch. 2.

truth is proclaimed—by word and sacrament, by pastoral ministry and healing care—throughout a Christian community that has but recently become world-wide. The vigour and growth of the Church during the last century and a half have been as remarkable as they have ever been in any age of the Church since that of the apostles themselves; and the awakening consciousness of the essential unity of the severed branches of the one Church has impressed upon many thoughtful people the significance of what Archbishop Temple has called "the great new fact of our time". These things, and many others, such as the arising of the "confessing churches" and their witness in the face of the new paganisms of the twentieth century, are empirical *data* for the theologian. It is just this kind of knowledge which the person who stands outside the Church usually lacks. Moreover, he also probably knows nothing of the advances made in the study of historical theology during the last hundred years, and so he remains unaware that he lacks the necessary materials out of which a rational theological judgment can be made. Yet the facts which constitute the empirical *data* of theology, both historical and contemporary, are not hard to ascertain; they are not esoteric or mythical; they are well documented and accessible to the inspection of any interested enquirer. It is a characteristic of Christian faith that the events to which it calls attention have not been done in a corner.

It remains perhaps to be added that, just as the Church and its witness and life are necessary to theology, so also theology is necessary to the witness and life of the Church. The Church exists to proclaim the truth in word and deed, and Barth is right in saying that the Church's proclamation is the raw material of dogmatics.[1] Theology is the discipline by which the Church corrects and sets in order its proclamation. A church which loses interest in theology will soon lose interest in its proclamation, and will thus be well on its way to becoming an "institution" which survives merely by means of the momentum of its own machinery, until it finally runs down.[2] The revival of theological

---

[1] *Doctrine of the Word of God; Church Dogmatics*, Vol. I, Part I, Eng. trans., p. 84.

[2] Cf. K. Barth, *op. cit.*, p. 85: "How disastrously must the Church misunderstand herself, if she can dream that theology is the business of a few theorists

interest and study which has taken place in recent times is a sure token of the vitality of the Christian Church and is itself another *datum* for the theologian.

specially appointed for the purpose, to whom all the rest, as vigorously confident practical men, are to listen incidentally with half an ear, so that on their side they may make it a title of honour to live 'quite untheologically' for the demands of the day."

# CHAPTER THREE

# CHRISTIANITY AND IDEOLOGY

## § 1. *The Meaning of "Ideology"*

THE LACK of a common faith and outlook in Western civilization in the twentieth century and the decay of the traditional system of beliefs and values have been noted by many thoughtful people, both Christian and non-Christian alike; and they have usually viewed our present situation and future prospects with considerable misgiving.[1] Although it is true that, as we have remarked above, there is to-day no widely accepted philosophical outlook amongst our contemporaries, as there used to be, for instance, in the Middle Ages or indeed until the close of the eighteenth century, this does not mean that there are in our times no general assumptions about the world and life embedded in the modern mind. On the contrary, such assumptions exist and are none the less potent because the majority of men are unaware of them. These assumptions become doctrines which gain widespread acceptance, not because people have made any conscious and determined effort to articulate and understand them, but because the general pressure of social development predisposes men to accept them uncritically as though they were self-evident truths. As T. E. Hulme pointed out in a well-known passage, "there are certain doctrines which for a particular period seem not doctrines, but inevitable categories of the human mind". People "do not see them, but other things *through* them".[2]

---

[1] Amongst those who have written about the need for a "new faith" see John Strachey, *A Faith to Fight For* (1941), and E. H. Carr, *Conditions of Peace* (1942). Strachey notes the weakening of that "Protestant, Puritan faith, which was young and strong three hundred years ago", but adds that "it is turning out that there is more in that faith that is still sound and valid for our day than some of us had realized" (p. 139); Carr thinks that "it is not inconceivable that the new leadership for which the world craves may arise from within the Christian Church" (p. 116).

[2] *Speculations* (ed. Herbert Read, 2nd Ed., 1936), pp. 50f.

Like the idea of "progress" in the Victorian Age, they are spectacles through which everything else is seen. It is a noteworthy fact that these assumptions become most prominent in the mind of society at those periods of history in which skeptical rationalism has most completely succeeded in destroying the traditional religious beliefs of the people: the Greece of Socrates's day and the Europe of our own provide outstanding illustrations. These assumptions, based not so much upon rational reflection as upon the general social drift and economic development of the times, are properly called "ideological". The word "ideology" is nowadays used in several different senses, and in this chapter we shall consistently try to give it one meaning, the only one, in fact, which it can usefully carry.[1] Although it implies the holding of a definite attitude towards the questions of human life and destiny, ideology differs from philosophy in that, since it is accepted uncritically and is not articulated intellectually, it is in no sense the product of conscious reasoning; it operates at the level of group-suggestion rather than at that of individual thinking. In so far as it is articulated at all, the task is performed by demagogues and journalists.

Ideology, then, is the product of "social conditioning" rather than of deliberate religious or philosophical teaching, or even of political propaganda, though the latter is often designed to make cunning use of it. Those who have called attention to ideological elements in human thinking have stressed the fact that a man's ideological standpoint will vary according to his position in society: that of the industrial worker will differ materially from the outlook of the *rentier* or the big industrialist. This truth is so obvious and has been so much emphasized in recent years that we need dwell upon it no longer. It is more important for us to notice a point which is less frequently perceived, namely, that although there are significant variations in ideological outlook resulting from the relative position of the various groups or "classes" within society, nevertheless in any given age there are certain ideological assumptions which, despite modifications, tend to pervade the whole of society from top to bottom. We

---

[1] " 'When *I* use a word,' Humpty Dumpty said in a rather scornful tone, 'it means just what I choose it to mean—neither more nor less'." *Alice Through the Looking-Glass*, Chap. VI.

may take as an example one of the characteristic assumptions of the twentieth century, the belief that "science" and scientific "planning" are able to change human nature, to develop and perhaps even to perfect it. This assumption has taken the place of the Victorian belief in universal progress,[1] since that notion could hardly have survived unchanged the major disasters of the twentieth century; it seems to have adapted itself to the more chastened mood of our times, and, since it is no longer possible to think of progress as automatic and inevitable, it is now assumed that there is nevertheless an endless possibility of progress through the scientific management of human affairs. Man possesses the means by which his own nature can be perfected and his prosperity assured in the resolute application of scientific method to all the problems of human life. Thus, there appears in this ideological commonplace the contemporary expression of man's perennial "natural religion", his faith in himself, which, according to the insight of biblical religion, results from his glad acceptance of the Serpent's lie: "Ye shall not surely die . . . ye shall be as God, knowing good and evil."[2] This will doubtless be the form in which the new "post-war liberalism" will express itself in the popular mind for some time to come—until the next international crisis or "economic blizzard" brings men face to face with reality once more.

This widespread contemporary belief in the efficacy of scientific "planning" provides a convenient illustration of what is meant by an ideological notion, when words are strictly used. It arises from the general social and economic developments of our time: the necessity of planning in war-time and in the post-war age

[1] It is not perhaps sufficiently widely acknowledged that many Christian preachers and thinkers in Victorian times did not share the belief in inevitable progress. Robertson of Brighton made some remarkable prophecies of disaster, and at the time of the Great Exhibition was uttering warnings to counteract the current optimism. When the Regius Professor of Divinity at Oxford spoke such words as the following, the scientific naturalists doubtless regarded his views as "old-fogeyism": "I do not know whether modern civilization may or may not have a decline as well as a progress, a fall as well as an uprise: but if it be so, it will be because Christianity has been overpowered, and unbelief taken its place, and let loose the base herd of human passions from their foul den" (R. Payne-Smith, Bampton Lectures, 1869, p. 31).

[2] Gen. iii. 4f.

has accelerated the general recognition that in a highly industrial-
ized civilization a planned economic order is essential. Nothing
but such planning can assure the well-being of "the common
man", and then only if it is undertaken by disinterested and
rational beings, and not by self-interested monopolies and parties.
In the popular mythology "Science" becomes the *deus ex machina*
which steps in to perform a saviour's rôle. The element of
irrationality in all ideology is well illustrated by the fact that
even on the threshold of the atomic age the belief in "Science"
as the new and popular divinity is hardly shaken by the ambiguous
quality of its latest gifts to mankind: "Though he slay me, yet
will I trust him."[1] The element of illusion enters into the notion
in proportion as it comes to be believed that the "planners" will
assuredly act from purely rational and altruistic motives, and it
strengthens its grip on the popular imagination in proportion as
the insights of the Christian religion lose their hold upon the
masses. When belief in man's sinfulness and in his need for a
supernatural redemption is weakened, ideological notions arise
to fill the vacuum thus created and to reassure men that the
problem of human destiny has been satisfactorily solved. And it
is to be noted that this kind of ideological assumption, though it
manifests itself in different forms in the various classes of society,
pervades the whole community at every social level. The Tory
expatiates on the advantages of planning, which can make the
world safe for individual initiative, while the demagogues of the
left exhibit socialism as both the means and the goal of the
ideally planned society. Meanwhile popular "scientific" writers
come forward to demonstrate how "the scientific attitude", when
it permeates the minds of the planners, will not only happily
transform the conditions of human living but will even enrich
and redeem human nature itself. Thus a popular ideological
prejudice becomes the key-category of a fashionable materialistic

[1] For a scientist's protest against the popular idolization of "Science" see
A. S. Nash, *The University and the Modern World* (London, 1945), Chap. I. "That
science is becoming a kind of established religion for the masses is to be
expected when it has its endowed institutions to which rich men leave large
sums in much the same spirit with which the mediaeval merchant endowed
chantries and when, amid the ritual of after-dinner speeches, science is thanked
for increasing the happiness and well-being of mankind as if it were a benevolent
deity" (p. 44).

philosophy, and multitudes of half-educated men and women in a banausic civilization accept an ancient superstition as the latest conclusion of modern science.

In order to guard against misunderstanding, we should perhaps interrupt our argument at this point to make it quite clear that we are discussing the question of ideology and not the merits or demerits of social planning; the latter has been chosen only as a prominent contemporary illustration of the former, as it manifests itself in the modern mind. As to the value of social planning itself we express no opinion, save to remark that, judged from a Christian point of view, the supreme value of a rationally planned society, if such could be achieved, would be that it would make it easier for people to believe in God. It is unplanned, "capitalistic" society, of which the law is every man for himself and the devil take the hindmost, that engenders atheism. It is one of the most curious ironies of the history of thought that Karl Marx should not have perceived that in his rejection of religion he was actually swallowing the most pernicious poison of the capitalist system which he detested, its practical atheism. For the social system which Marx condemned was the concrete embodiment of the view that there is no God or that God does not care about the fate of the weak and helpless ones, the dispossessed and disinherited. A rationally planned society would ideally be one in which human life was lived on the assumption that the end of human existence was true community and brotherhood, and in which society was organized as if the Christian Gospel were true; it is in this sense that a planned society would make it easier for men to believe in the God of Christian faith. And yet, such is the power of the human mind to pervert the truth, the ideal society, if it were achieved, would tempt men to believe that *they* were rational and that *they* alone had achieved this salvation: the comfortable classes are not usually noted for the depth of their religious faith and insight. But we must return to our argument.

## § 2. *Is Christian Faith Ideological in Origin?*

It is important that those who are concerned with Christian apologetics in the twentieth century should give careful consideration to the question of ideology. The neglect of this subject by Christian writers gives an opportunity to anti-Christian propagandists to exploit an unreal advantage. They are enabled to impress upon the immature the view that religious belief itself is intrinsically ideological in origin. Religion is represented as being nothing more than the epiphenomenal and transitory product of an unequal and undeveloped social order, arising from the unfulfilled desires which such a social order fails to satisfy; it will therefore pass away when a just and mature order of society has been achieved. The classless society of the future, it is said, will have no need of religion. The facts, however, do not support this familiar contention. Ideological notions are strongest amongst people who have lost their traditional religious faith, and they provide a kind of pseudo-religion to take its place. Ideology may well be defined as religion-substitute. The fact that religious faith always expresses itself in the particular ideological forms current in any given period is no reason why we should confuse religion with ideology; and, even though it requires a penetrating and candid investigation to distinguish between the genuinely religious and the merely ideological elements in the outlook of a particular period or individual, this does not mean that religion itself is an aspect of ideology. The core of religious belief is not ideological, whatever may be said of the soft pulp in which it is often wrapped up. Nothing but ignorance of the history of the Christian faith could allow anyone to suppose that Christianity itself is in origin ideological; but unfortunately it is of the facts of history in general and of Christian history in particular that the modern "sociological" writers are most sadly ignorant. There has been a certain hard core of Christian belief and experience which has persisted in the Church from the first to the twentieth century; certain quite specific and precise affirmations have been made about God, Christ and human nature and destiny by the Church in every age. These affirmations are recognizably the same in every century; they have persisted through many different types of social system and have survived all the ideologies which these systems in their turn have cast up. The ideologies of Christian people have varied from time to time and from place to place, but there is a fundamental and invariable identity of Christian faith which has sought to express itself through them all. The social expression of the

Christian religion has varied considerably along with the variations of social custom and economic structure; but it is not true to say that the central affirmations of the Christian faith have themselves changed with changing social and economic developments. The truth is that both in intention and (to a far greater extent than is recognized by those who have not studied Church history) in actuality the Church as a whole has consistently maintained the faith of the New Testament. We may perhaps adapt Whitehead's *dictum* and say that Christianity is not an ideology generating a religion, but a religion in search of a social expression. The view that the Christian religion is itself the product of ideological factors cannot be maintained in the light of a study of the history of the Church and of her theology. What common ideological factors could account for this impressive unity of the faith down the ages, if we have regard to the vastly different social and economic conditions of the various periods of Christian history? What similar social and economic factors could have produced the same ideological reactions in, let us say, St. Paul, St. Athanasius, St. Augustine, St. Francis of Assisi, St. Thomas Aquinas, Luther, Hooker, Bunyan, Pascal, Joseph Butler, John Henry Newman and William Temple? These men did not have a common ideology, they had a common religious faith. The attempt to explain the Christian religion by any theory of "social conditioning" is probably the most preposterous of all methods which have ever yet been tried as a means of discrediting Christianity, but it is widely successful in an age which knows almost nothing of history.

Amidst the very great religious confusion of our times an ability to distinguish between the religious and ideological elements in our outlook and in that of other people is a part of the essential equipment of the student of apologetics. But many people to-day, particularly amongst the older generation, find the word "ideology" and the conception which it represents equally distasteful. This is partly because the term has become a journalistic catchword, often used to convey political abuse or to cover emptiness of thought. It is also partly because left-wing political writers have given it its popular vogue. But it must be conceded that Marxist thinkers have rendered a real service by their relentless insistence upon this aspect of human irrationality. Whether we like it or not, the word ideology stands for something that is important in all human thinking, implying as it does that all men are to some extent "conditioned" by their social environment and that every philosophical, historical and theological judgment is liable to distortion by ideological factors, of which the thinker is unaware. The real question here is not whether men are or are not thus socially conditioned, but how far they are thus conditioned; and to this question we cannot now return an answer in any detail, beyond pointing out that if there are aspects of man's knowing and believing which are not wholly determined by ideological factors (such as his religious faith), then it is clear that he must possess the means of making judgments that are not wholly the result of his social conditioning. To be aware of the existence of the ideological element in thought is the first step towards escape from its dangers. To understand the conception of ideology is to realize why the eighteenth-century conception of reason as a faculty by which men arrive at objective and rational judgments has been abandoned nowadays by almost all thinkers. To learn, even though it be from Marx and his followers, that man's reason is, like his will, "fallen" and the prey of his own self-interested motives, is to re-learn a fundamental truth of the biblical conception of man, which St. Augustine and many Christian thinkers before and even after the Renaissance knew quite well.

## § 3. *The Validity of the Conception of Ideology*

Why, then, should the conception of ideology have been so lightly regarded and coldly shunned by so many Christian thinkers in recent times? Perhaps it would be helpful if we turned aside once more from our argument and looked at the origin and history of the term which has come to stand, almost accidentally, for so important an idea. The fact is that the word "ideology" has come down in the world. It began life as the quite respectable name for the study of the origin and nature of ideas, until its meaning was somewhat narrowed down and it came to designate a particular type of epistemological theory associated with the names of Condillac and Destutt de Tracy in eighteenth-century

France. According to this theory all ideas are derived from sensations—a theory which has quite aristocratic relations in the history of thought, for St. Thomas Aquinas and John Locke had held similar views. De Tracy wrote a work called *Les Éléments de l'Idéologie*, and towards the end of the eighteenth century articles appeared in the learned reviews bearing such titles as "The Ideologists of Paris". But evil communications corrupt good manners, and the word has never recovered caste since Napoleon became its patron. He gave it a new meaning, using it in a derisive sense to denote the impractical ideas and ideals of theorists, visionaries and utopians. It was thus opposed to all that was realist and practical in politics. Disinterested altruism, for instance, was mere "ideology", and the only thing that really mattered in the world was the power which could be put behind self-interest. The ideals of 1789—equality, liberty, fraternity— were mere "ideology"; they could have no influence upon the course of power politics. "The advocates of liberty and of progress", wrote Emerson in 1847, "are 'ideologists', a word of contempt often found in his [Bonaparte's] mouth." It is hardly surprising that, having been introduced into a wider society under such patronage, the word should always afterwards have carried an unfavourable sense.[1] It next passed into use amongst Marxist writers, who shared with Napoleon a contempt for the power of "mere ideas" and who represented themselves as being the political men of action.[2] Although their own devotion to the Scribbler in the British Museum belied their theory, the extremists soon came to accept the view that all human religious and philosophical thinking is merely an epiphenomenon arising from the economic system or, more precisely, from the type of the means of production, temporarily in being. In this extreme form the conception of ideology reduces the effectiveness of ideas in

[1] It is interesting to note that during the *Essays and Reviews* controversy the word "ideological" was used by the conservatives to imply mere "spiritualized" or symbolic, as against literal, truth. Thus, for example, Bishop Samuel Wilberforce wrote in 1861: "They ideologically suggest that, when it is asserted that our Lord miraculously fed the multitudes . . . no more is meant than that. . . . He fed the souls of thousands with edifying moral discourses."

[2] See Karl Mannheim, *Ideology and Utopia* (London, 1936), p. 64.

human affairs to zero,[1] and we are left asking how we could ever know that Marxism itself represents the final truth and not a mere passing ideological by-product of a fleeting period of economic evolution. When the harnessing of atomic energy has brought about the greatest change in the means of production that has ever yet taken place in man's history, it is improbable (if the Marxists are right in their view of the dependence of theory upon economic practice) that the economic interpretation of history will appear as satisfying as it did to its nineteenth-century originators. Undoubtedly such extremism is untenable and has brought the whole conception of ideology into disrepute. When extreme theories are advanced and pushed to the point of absurdity, the truth which they contain is apt to be overlooked; and it was easy for "liberal" thinkers to smile at the crudities of Marxism and thus to ignore the whole question of "the sociology of knowledge" and to avoid the problem of how far their own thinking might be "conditioned" by their social position and outlook.

It is not possible within the limits of this chapter to undertake the kind of twentieth-century "enquiry concerning the human understanding" which is needed to determine the issue between

[1] This is, of course, the authentic Marxian position. Cf. Karl Marx's preface to his *Critique of Political Economy*: "In the social production of their means of existence men enter into definite, necessary relations which are independent of their will, productive relationships which correspond to a definite stage of development of their material productive forces. The aggregate of these productive relationships constitutes the economic structure of society, the real basis on which a juridical and political superstructure arises, and to which definite forms of social consciousness correspond. The mode of production of the material means of existence conditions the whole process of social, political and intellectual life. It is not the consciousness of men that determines their existence, but, on the contrary, it is their social existence that determines their consciousness" (*Handbook of Marxism*, ed. E. Burns, 1935, p. 371). Also F. Engels: "According to this conception, the ultimate causes of all social changes and political revolutions are to be sought, not in the minds of men, in their increasing insight into eternal truth and justice, but in changes in the mode of production and exchange; they are to be sought not in the philosophy but in the economics of the epoch concerned" (*op. cit.*, p. 279). For the testimony of two notable thinkers of our day to the power of ideas in human affairs see the concluding pages of A. N. Whitehead, *Science and the Modern World* (Cambridge, 1933), and of J. M. Keynes, *General Theory of Employment, Interest and Money* (London, 1936).

the extreme theories of the "sociologists of knowledge", who hold that all religious and philosophical thinking is in the last resort merely "ideology", an epiphenomenon of social and economic development, and the rationalists or "liberals", who maintain that the human mind is capable of laying aside the prejudices of social conditioning and can proceed by reason, whether deductively or inductively, to an impartial or objective verdict upon religious, philosophical and historical questions. The principal problem with which we are attempting to deal in this chapter is whether the modern conception of ideology is a category by means of which the independent validity of theological categories can be dispensed with, or, more simply, whether religious faith can be explained away in terms of social conditioning. Our answer to this question has already been given in outline, and, if we attempt now to sketch in some of the details of that answer more definitely, we may perhaps be able to give a few tentative indications of the form which a solution of the problem at issue between the "sociologists" and the "rationalists" might take.

According to the classical line of Christian teaching concerning the capabilities and limitations of our human reasoning powers, both the view of the sociologists of knowledge and that of the rationalists are wrong in their extreme forms. Perhaps it would be better to say that the Christian understanding of human nature both agrees and disagrees with each of them in certain material respects. On the one hand, it agrees with the upholders of the "sociological" point of view in believing that self-centredness is a characteristic of all men and is a factor which distorts men's vision, so that they tend to see things, not as they are, but in relation to their own private interests and fortunes. Man imagines that he is the centre of the universe: this is his original sin; and the result is that he loses the capacity of seeing things in their true proportion or perspective. Thus, he becomes the willing victim of his own illusions, and he identifies whatever makes for his own private profit with moral causes and public good. F. H. Bradley in a well-known epigram declared that metaphysics is the finding of bad reasons for what we believe upon instinct; if this were the worst that could be said about the frailty of the human intellect, man's predicament as a rational animal would not perhaps be desperate. But a more honest judgment would be that men's philosophy very often turns out to be the finding of bad reasons for whatever ideological prejudices self-interest has engendered in their minds; men's reasons so often turn out to be rationalizations, and not "reasons" at all. "The heart is deceitful above all things and is desperately sick";[1] this is the biblical insight into man's endless capacity and predilection for self-deception. No part of human nature escaped the consequences of the Fall of Man, and his reason did not remain unimpaired; and Christians cannot but see in the facts adduced by the sociologists of knowledge ample testimony to the truth, in one of its aspects, of the biblical estimate of human nature. To this extent the Christian view is in agreement with the findings of those who have called attention to the very considerable part played by ideological factors in all human thinking. To this extent, therefore, it is in disagreement with the liberal-rationalist assumption that human reason is an effective instrument by which objective philosophical, ethical and historical judgments can be made.

But, on the other hand, the classical Christian view of human reason would find itself in sympathy with the rationalist criticism of the extreme form of the sociological theory. Where everything is relative, nothing can be known to be relative; unless there is somewhere a fixed point of reference, there is no criterion by which movement can be measured. Unless something can be known to be true, the conceptions of error, subjectivity, illusion, deception and ideology can have no meaning. The theory that all knowledge is socially determined (and not merely that it is socially conditioned) is self-stultifying; it is a variant of the statement that no truth can be known to be true, including this one. If all judgments were in essence ideological, men could never have detected the existence of ideology. Against every form of irrationalism and skepticism, the classical tradition of Christian thought down the ages has maintained that truth is knowable. To believe anything else is theoretically possible, but not practically; it is not possible to discuss or even to deny the knowability of truth without in fact believing in it. But it *is* belief; and belief of this kind is indispensable to rationality.

[1] Jer. xvii. 9.

Proof and certainty are dispensable to rationality, but belief is not. This is a point of the deepest epistemological significance, and it is overlooked in almost all non-Christian theories of knowledge, as indeed it has been overlooked by many thinkers whose intention was to take a Christian view, especially in recent times. And it is just here that the Christian view is in disagreement with the rationalist view of how the human mind comes to the knowledge of truth. The Christian takes belief seriously; the rationalist tries to dispense with it. The Christian says that without believing there is no knowledge; the rationalist says that where there is believing there cannot be knowledge. The rationalist holds that the faculty of human reason is capable of knowing truth directly or indirectly by virtue of its own intrinsic nature; and indeed some Christian thinkers, such as Aquinas, have come near to accepting this position, at least for purposes of apologetics and in certain well-defined areas. But, if we may take St. Augustine as representing the main line of Christian approach to this question, we may say that the Christian view does not encourage man to believe in the unaided power of fallen reason to arrive at objective judgments of truth, especially in existential matters.

Here we must briefly anticipate the argument and conclusion of this book as a whole; the following sentences may not perhaps appear to be immediately self-authenticating, since they depend for their validity upon considerations which will be brought forward in the following chapters. Man comes to the knowledge of the truth, not by the untrammelled exercise of his reasoning powers, but by accepting or being given the faith which enables him to use his reason aright; reason cannot work until it first makes an act of faith, and it does not work correctly—that is, rationally—unless it makes the *right* act of faith, unless it has faith in the Truth itself. Reason does not precede faith, as rationalism supposes, but faith precedes reason. St. Augustine describes how, as a young man desirous to know the truth, he had for a time been misled by the promises of the Manichees, who claimed that they could make clear the truth without recourse to any venture of faith; they opposed their rationalism to the teaching of the Catholic Church, which declared that men must have faith before they can reason correctly.[1] After faith had

[1] *De Utilitate Credendi*, 2.

come to him, Augustine saw clearly that all forms of rationalism were in error, as indeed he had formerly suspected because of the failure of the Manichees to make good their promises. Let no one imagine that St. Augustine's position is irrationalist: he is expressing the central affirmation of Christian thought upon this subject, and it is an affirmation based on Christian experience down the centuries. Faith is caused by the shining of the Sun of Truth upon the eyes of our minds, and this is what makes men rational. One cannot see the sun unless its light shines on the eyes; and it is not otherwise with truth. The extreme exponents of ideologist theories and the liberal-rationalists are alike in error in overlooking the indispensable part which is played in human knowing by the element of faith; the ideologists equate it with "wishful thinking" and the rationalists with mere "opinion", but in reality it is neither of these things. It is the key-category of epistemology and the very condition of the knowledge of the truth; objectivity is impossible without it, however paradoxical such a statement may sound to the ears of those brought up in rationalist traditions. Faith, in the sense in which Christianity understands it, is neither ideological in origin nor irrational in operation; it is not opposed to reason, but complementary to it; it is as necessary to the activity of reasoning as is the presence of light to the activity of seeing.[1]

## § 4. *Christianity and its Social Expression*

In essence and in origin, then, Christian faith is not ideological, but to assert this is not to deny that in any given age it expresses itself in the ideological forms of the times. The content of faith

---

[1] Cf. St. Augustine, *De Utilitate Credendi*, 22–5, also *In Joan. Evang.* XXIX, 6: "Understanding is the reward of faith. Therefore seek not to understand that thou mayest believe, but believe that thou mayest understand"; or *ibid.*, XXVII, 9: "We believed that we might know; for if we wished first to know and then to believe, we should not be able either to know or to believe"; also *Serm. (de Script. N.T.)* CXXVI, i. 1: "The mysteries and secrets of the Kingdom of God first seek for believing men, that they may make them understand. For faith is understanding's step, and understanding faith's attainment (*meritum*). This the Prophet expressly says to all who prematurely and in undue order look for understanding and neglect faith: 'Unless ye believe, ye shall not understand' (Isa. vii. 9, LXX)."

is not socially determined, but its expression is socially conditioned. Christianity, being a religion in search of a social expression, is compelled to express its insights into the truth in the thought-forms of the day, and these thought-forms are largely ideological in origin. When faith is strong, it takes the thought-forms and moulds them to its own requirements, but when current ideologies dominate men's minds, there is a serious danger that Christian truth will be obscured or adapted to the prevailing categories which men see things through. The process of disentangling the complex of genuinely religious factors from the ideological elements with which they are combined and through which they seek to express themselves is one which calls for all the knowledge, skill and insight which the historian can bring to his research when he sets out upon the study of a particular age or civilization. Over-simplified solutions are certain to be false; finality can never be reached upon such questions as these. Who will ever be confident that he has spoken the last word concerning the tangle of economic motives, nationalist aspirations, intellectual re-awakening and genuinely religious conviction which produced that tremendous re-orientation of the European mind which we call the Reformation? Too often the different aspects of historical development, such as the economic or the religious, are studied in separate compartments; in particular the history of Christian thought has all too frequently been written in abstraction from the broad current of social, political and economic history with which it is so closely interrelated. We have learnt from writers like Max Weber and R. H. Tawney to understand something of the correlation of religious and economic factors in the history of certain periods; we have been made aware that there is an important connection between religious and ideological factors in the mind of the sixteenth and seventeenth centuries, that an Arminian theology is better suited to the social ideals of the older landed aristocracy, while the vigorous and expanding bourgeois classes found more adequate expression for their ideological standpoint in the theology of Calvinistic Puritanism. There are many questions which we should like to put to the historian. Why should an Empire, a whole civilization, suddenly become engrossed in a bitter theological controversy over an iota and take sides in a dispute concerning the Catholic *versus* the Arian Christology? What were the sociological conditions which formed the background of the revolution in theological thought, of which Albertus Magnus and Thomas Aquinas were the prophets, by which an epoch of Platonic-Augustinian thinking was brought to an end and a new age of Thomistic-Aristotelian theology was inaugurated? What religious and intellectual satisfaction did the new scientific Aristotelianism bring to the restless bourgeoisie of the nascent capitalism of the thirteenth century, discontented alike with the established feudal order and with the old Platonist modes of thought, and attracted towards the naturalism of Averroes and the sectarianism of Peter Waldo? It was Lord Acton who said that not the Devil but St. Thomas Aquinas was "the first Whig". Is it true that the original "Thomism" was the first attempt ever made to present "the relevance of Christianity" to the *intelligenzia* of a rising middle class?[1] Again, we should be grateful to the historian if he would tell us more about "the social origins of the denominations", for it would seem that differences between denominations within Christianity are often largely ideological, even though the denominations themselves persist centuries after the original ideological impulses which expressed themselves in religious forms and theological systems have spent their force. Perhaps the real differences which divide churches from one another would be brought more clearly into the light of day if ideological considerations were studied by those interested in problems of Church unity as intently as are theological matters.[2] Or again, it seems to be clear that, though

[1] On this question see the suggestive essay on "The Significance of Mediaeval Christianity" in *The Vitality of the Christian Tradition*, ed. George F. Thomas (New York, 1944).

[2] As an illustration of this type of problem we will cite the judgment of a contemporary historian upon the Oxford Movement in one of its aspects. After remarking how in the early nineteenth century there had been little or no doctrinal difference between most Anglican clergy and most dissenting ministers, Mr. Ensor proceeds: "The vantage ground which they [the Anglican clergy] enjoyed over these rival practitioners was legal, since the state inflicted heavy civil and educational disabilities on the latter and their flocks. But between 1828 and 1871 all these disabilities were repealed, and in the latter year even the ancient universities were thrown open. Unless Anglicanism developed some convincing doctrinal difference, its clergy would have difficulty in maintaining any exclusive professional position. Here the new movement [then called

religious insights inspire men to work for social amelioration, the Church's "social gospel" is itself usually coloured and conditioned by the direction of social development, so that, as has been said by critics, the social teaching of the churches tends to be "parasitic" upon the actual process of events rather than the prime cause of them;[1] or, to put this point in another way, the implications of the Christian Gospel for society, though they have been inherent in the preaching from the beginning, are not perceived until the course of social evolution itself makes them apparent. Why did not the implications of the Gospel in the matter of slavery become generally apparent to Christians until the eighteenth or nineteenth century? It may be true that, as A. N. Whitehead has said, "the progress of humanity can be defined as the process of transforming society so as to make the original Christian ideals increasingly practicable for its individual members". He adds that in the present state of society "a literal adherence to the moral precepts scattered throughout the Gospels would mean sudden death".[2] Christians in society in general, as distinct from a few prophets and fanatics here and there, seem to be safeguarded from this catastrophe by their inability to see the social implication of the Gospel until the course of social evolution brings it home to them.

These questions will serve to illustrate the complexity of the problem concerning the relation between religion and ideology, and they should serve to warn us against any premature attempts to reach solutions by means of categories which are too narrow to embrace the great variety of factors involved. The evidence, in so far as it can be sorted out in the present state of our knowledge, does not suggest that the category of social conditioning or of

Ritualistic] came directly to their aid. By placing again in the foreground salvation through grace, grace received through sacraments, and sacraments only valid if administered by episcopally ordained clergy, it supplied exactly what the profession needed. Hence it is not surprising that, though the bishops were cold to it and the laity, as a rule, fiercely hostile, the rank and file of the clergy, including many of the ablest, came round to it more and more" (R. C. K. Ensor, *England, 1870–1914*, Oxford, 1936, p. 141; so also G. M. Trevelyan, *English Social History*, London, 1944, p. 564).

[1] Cf. Bishop H. Hensley Henson, *The Church of England* (Cambridge, 1939), pp. 157–63.

[2] *Adventures of Ideas* (Cambridge, 1933), p. 18.

ideological self-interest is adequate to account for the phenomena of Christian belief. The fact would seem to be that *some* apparently religious beliefs owe their origin, or the strength of the conviction with which they are held, to ideological causes rather than to genuinely religious insights, and so may be said to be socially conditioned;[1] but the question then arises whether such beliefs ought to be called "religious" at all. Social prejudice does not become religious belief simply because men work it into their religious devotions and sing hymns about "the rich man in his castle, the poor man at his gate". The fact that ideology disguises itself under the forms of religious faith does not mean that religious faith itself is ideological in essence. Nor does it imply that Christianity can be explained away as "mere ideology", because Christian faith must necessarily express itself in the terms and thought-forms of the particular social organization and outlook of the period in which it is preached and lived. Theologians have long ago noted and commented upon this truth. The bright shining of the Sun of Truth must veil itself in the mists of human ways of thinking, or else our eyes would be blind with excess of light: we have our treasure in earthen vessels. We need only to call to mind the various theories of the Atonement which have been current in different ages of the Church's history. Each has clothed itself with the ideas of the type of society of its own period. Thus, the Ransom theory suggested by Origen was favoured by theologians throughout the period in which men's minds were dominated by the view of "rights" (including the "rights" of the Devil) upheld by Roman law; St. Anselm's Satisfaction theory was thereafter prevalent in the Middle Ages, when social thinking expressed itself in terms of the honour or

[1] For an example see E. W. Watson, *The Church of England* (2nd Ed., Oxford, 1944), pp. 18f.: When in the early Middle Ages the see of Rome rose to pre-eminence, "there grew up a system of ecclesiastical order, with the Bishop of Rome at the head of the hierarchy, and as both he and the other bishops were concerned with religious matters, this hierarchical arrangement came to be itself regarded as having a religious sanction. Then came theological explanation of the observed facts. Just as the astronomers of those ages were quite right in their observations of the stars, but erred in the hypotheses they framed to account for the facts, so it was with the theologians. They worked out their hypothesis to account for the Pope's position in Christendom, and have ended by putting it into their creed. . . . When the Roman Church appealed to some secular potentate for help it made St. Peter write in his own name."

satisfaction that should be rendered to one's overlord in feudal society; in the Reformation period, when forensic ideas of sin as the transgression of law were dominant, the various Penal theories were put forward; and finally Moral Influence theories of the Atonement were congenial to an age of toleration and universal suffrage, when persuasion and education had taken the place of compulsion and dictation as ideals of society. The expression of the Church's faith in the Atonement wrought by Christ changes with the changes of social structure and outlook; and yet it would be absurd to overlook the plain fact that it is one faith which is seeking to express itself under many forms. Origen and Anselm, Luther and Rashdall, are men of their own times; moreover, they are essentially teachers and preachers, striving to make clear the meaning of the Christian faith in the redeeming work of Christ to the men of their own day; and so they use the forms of thought which would be understood by the men of their own times. Yet each of them has drawn his inspiration not from the categories of the thought of his own day but from the classical witness of the apostles which is contained in the New Testament; and this brings us back to the central fact, that there is an identity of faith which underlies all its expressions, and that this "hard core" of faith is not itself ideological in essence. It is the ideological elements in the expression of Christian truth which arise and decay again, dissolved in each new period by "the acids of modernity", not the "hard core" of the faith itself. All forms of theological modernism—whether the modernism of Aquinas or the modernism of Schleiermacher or Rashdall—are in a sense accommodations of the original and enduring Gospel to contemporary thought-forms, including ideologies; and their value from the theological point of view depends upon whether they have successfully used the contemporary philosophical and ideological complex of forms for the expression of the New Testament faith or alternatively have subordinated the Gospel to the "climate of opinion" of their day. But in this sense every living theology must be modernist; a religion which expresses itself only in the forms of an age that is past is already dead, and the faith of a living Church must be expressed in living forms, even though it be an ancient and indeed a timeless faith.

## § 5. *Christian Faith and Worship as beyond Ideology*

We do not wish to suggest that even the New Testament itself is free from all ideological content, since no religious faith can be expressed save against some local and temporary social and economic background. Even the parables of Jesus presuppose a particular historical social background, yet few would venture to assert that their religious insights are derived from the ideological attitudes of the inhabitants of Palestine in the first century A.D. Such a proposition is too absurd to require serious refutation, yet it would presumably have to be maintained by anyone who tried to hold the extreme form of the sociological position. All great literature, such as the plays of Sophocles or Shakespeare, for example, has a social background by which it is to some extent conditioned; yet literary and dramatic genius are not to be explained away by the hypothesis of ideology, nor is religious insight. The Bible as a whole has demonstrated during the course of many centuries an ability to create and express the religious convictions of men who have held widely differing ideological notions in widely differing periods of economic development. Biblical insights have in fact assisted in the dissolving of many ideologies and social patterns and in the bringing to the birth of many new ones. This is because the Bible itself is the vehicle of a truth which is beyond all ideologies and which is the solvent of all the imperfect forms of social evolution. Within the period of the biblical history itself, the biblical faith expressed itself in many widely different social forms. Yet there is an identity of faith which runs all through the Bible and underlies its many expressions, and which has likewise persisted through all the centuries of Christian history. From the far-off nomadic days, when Jehovah was the Shepherd-King of the tribe, through all the vicissitudes of the settlement under the Judges as an agricultural people in Canaan, beyond the establishment of the monarchy and the palmy days of the great Empire of David and Solomon, to the bitter trials of invasion and exile, to the period of subjection to the imperial powers of Persia, Greece or Rome— through all these vast and literally epoch-making changes, the fundamental identity of the biblical faith persists. What common ideological factors underlie all these different phases of biblical

history? Of course, we see the biblical faith evolving and the
conception of God and His dealings with men becoming purer
and deeper; yet from the days of Moses and the desert wanderings
onwards to the coming of Jesus and His Church, and on again to
the days of the world-wide Christian Church of the twentieth
century, the same essential biblical faith in God as King and
Father still endures, and the same estimate of man as a being
whose deepest need is religious, rather than social or economic or
political, still persists. The Bible remains the norm of Christian
faith and the standing refutation of all theories about the deriva-
tion of religion from ideology. In it the same recognizable
conception of God appears throughout, though expressed under
widely different social and political forms; if in the early days
God appears in the garb of a monarch of the "oriental" type, He
is nevertheless still the Shepherd of His chosen flock; when later
He comes to be known as the Lord of the whole earth, He
remains still the faithful Keeper of the Covenant with Israel;
when He manifests Himself as the Judge of the nations, of
Babylon or Rome or Judea, He is still also the loving God whose
mercy is being revealed in the fulfilment of His purpose of
salvation by means of His chosen instrument, the Old Israel or
the New. New forms, new social and historical circumstances,
arise and pass away, but ever and always behind and beneath them
all there is the revelation of the one unchanging and eternal God.
No hypothesis of ideological conditioning is able to account for
the persistent unity of the biblical theology over a thousand years
of change, or for the unity of Christian faith in which it has been
continued for nearly two thousand years more. There was born
a faith in God and a religious view of the world when, three
thousand years ago, a slave tribe came out of Egypt: that faith
and that religious view remain to-day, vastly deepened and
enlarged, as the faith and view of a world-wide Church. Theological science must find categories which can help us to understand this unique phenomenon of history; it cannot be understood
by means of the narrower categories of the social sciences. There
is a knowledge of God, it would appear, that is prior to and
independent of all social conditioning, and which itself is a
factor that conditions the growth and decay of social systems and
their ideologies.

An important consideration which is understood only by those who stand within the fellowship of the Christian Church is the remarkable experience of the transcending of ideological limitations which takes place in Christian worship. Non-Christian writers are able to argue that ideological influences are determinative of all experience chiefly because they choose to ignore those elements in human experience which do not support their theories. There is, however, in the experience of Christian worship a means by which Christians themselves can put ideological theories to a practical test. This is especially true of liturgical worship, for no one would deny that the danger of "free" or non-liturgical worship is that it may so easily degenerate into the expression of social and ideological aspirations rather than of genuinely religious adoration. Like the New Testament itself, or like great literature, the forms of liturgical worship are amazingly independent of ideological elements; the ideological expression is doubtless apparent here and there, but it is so clearly irrelevant. One of the great advantages of using ancient liturgies and classical forms of worship is their power to liberate the worshippers from ideological preoccupations. The ideological element which obtrudes itself into worship is forgotten and left behind as the generations rise and pass away, leaving behind only the enduringly religious deposit of the worship of previous ages. The anti-Christian "sociological" writer may be relied upon to quote "God bless the squire and his relations" and to assume that his case is proved up to the hilt; it is noticeable that he does not attempt to prove his argument from the *Te Deum* or the *Gloria in Excelsis*. The great Christian hymns and acts of worship have a timeless quality which enables them to give expression to the religious sense of men in every age. The Bible itself is the clearest proof of this, particularly in its use in Christian worship. The Psalms, for example, have been used by the protagonists on both sides of many an embittered ideological dispute. Religion unites: ideology divides. Archbishop Laud in the Tower, awaiting execution, expresses his inner faith and consolation by making prayers out of those very Psalms which were the treasure and inspiration of Milton, Cromwell and Bunyan.[1] The truth is that in Christian worship, especially in its biblical and liturgical forms,

[1] Cf. R. E. Prothero, *The Psalms in Human Life* (London, 1903), pp. 180ff.

the worshipper partakes of an experience which transcends ideology, in which conservative and revolutionary can lose themselves and kneel as brethren side by side, because they have been enrolled in the worshipping communion of saints of all the ages. Such worship is truly Catholic, and one of the meanings of the word "catholic" to which more attention might well be given in our day is "supra-ideological".

To enter into liturgical worship means to identify oneself with the Church's adoration that belongs to every century and to all lands. In the *Book of Common Prayer* we have a standing refutation of all theories which confuse religion with ideology. The very title signifies the universality of Christian worship in space and time. It is true that here and there we may detect the ideological flavour of the periods in which some of its parts were written; we catch, for instance, a reminiscence of the feudal system in the Collect for St. Michael and All Angels' Day, or a hint of a forgotten ideology in the "Duty towards My Neighbour" in the Catechism, and there are the various State prayers and services for State occasions. But for the most part the book is astonishingly free from those social presuppositions which one might have expected would have made it more acceptable in the sixteenth and seventeenth centuries than in the twentieth. It gathers together a rich store of the liturgical treasures of the ancient and the mediaeval Church and combines them into its peculiarly biblical-Anglican synthesis which altogether transcends the limitations of time and place. It is noticeable that most appeals for the revision of the Prayer Book are based not on the grounds that it confronts us with the ideology of the past but on the grounds that it does not express the "social consciousness" of the twentieth century. Doubtless there are occasions when it is right and proper to express the ideals of the Christian social conscience in the Church's worship; but to endeavour to incorporate these ideals into the liturgical structure of worship is like trying to mix oil and water. Christian worship is not the same thing as the expression of ideological aspirations, and Christian faith cannot be subsumed under sociological categories.

The conclusion of the matter is that there is no such thing as a "Christian ideology". There may be a Puritan ideology, or a Laudian ideology; there may be a liberal-Christian ideology or a Catholic-Fascist ideology, but there is no Christian ideology as such, for Christianity is not ideology. It would be less inappropriate to speak of a Marxist or a Fascist ideology than of a Christian ideology, for the political religions and philosophies have more obviously sociological origins. But it is unhelpful to speak of what are, after all, definite philosophies as ideologies, since, if we use terms strictly, ideology means those presuppositions which are not as yet articulated into definite theories and systems. These presuppositions afterwards become rationalized into systems and philosophies, but when this has happened there is little point in confusing issues by continuing to speak of them as ideologies. Marxism as a philosophy required the social conditions of the nineteenth century before it could come to birth, and when those conditions have finally passed away—as under an efficient system of parliamentary or democratic socialism, if such could be established—Marxism as a philosophy would be nothing more than a museum-piece: hence the hatred of Marxists for democratic socialists. Fascism, too, required the special social and political conditions of the twentieth century before it could rationalize the frustration and disillusionment of nationalist sentiment into a philosophical system generating a religious fervour; and Fascism also as a way of thought will disappear when the causes of its underlying ideology have been removed. But a study of Christian origins demonstrates conclusively that Christianity did not arise as the rationalization of any ideological motives in the first century and so become, like Marxism and Fascism, a philosophy generating the religious fervour which feeds on ideological aspirations. It is true that it arose in history, in a particular time and place, and that it was founded upon certain specific historical events; but they *were* events, not social movements or aspirations; and thus Christianity is founded upon history and fact in a way that the political faiths are not. What is involved in the recognition of Christianity as an historical religion will be the subject of the following chapter.

# CHAPTER FOUR

# THEOLOGY AND HISTORY

## § 1. *Christianity as an Historical Faith*

THE EMPIRICAL Christian Church shares many features in common with other forms of human organization, but it is distinguished from all of them by its inner principle of existence. Its outward form has varied considerably from age to age and from place to place, but its constant factor has been that inward faith in God which, as we have noted, has persisted from the earliest days of its life. It is this enduring inward faith which makes the world-wide Church of the twentieth century continuous not only with the Church of the Apostles but also with the people-Church of the ancient Hebrew nation. There is, despite all variations of expression and presentation, a fundamental unity of faith in God as righteous and merciful that has persisted from the days of Moses and the desert wanderings of Israel. It would be more accurate to say that there has existed a people in a continuing covenant-relationship with the God of biblical faith ever since the day at Horeb when Jehovah spoke with Moses "as a man speaketh unto his friend".[1] During the period of three thousand years and more which separates Moses from our own day, the covenant-people have existed; their distinctive trust in God has not been outgrown or altered beyond recognition, although, of course, it has been deepened and widened. Evolutionary theories, though containing an element of truth, have spoken about a "progressive revelation", and have done much to obscure the essential fact of the unity of faith that runs all through the Bible and all through the Christian centuries, because they have tended to suggest that that which comes later in time is something quite other and "higher" than that which comes earlier. It is true that men's *ideas* of God change and "progress", and it is possible to trace the development of the intellectual formulation of ideas about God; but we are here speaking of a deep-seated belief in

[1] Exod. xxxiii. 11.

God, an attitude of faithful trust in and dependence upon God, which is essentially a relationship with God, rather than the entertaining of an idea about Him. This is what all forms of rationalism fail to understand about the inner meaning of the biblical faith. The relationship of men to God remains fundamentally the same, although the intellectual formulation of it changes considerably as the thought of mankind evolves from age to age. But the evolution of ideas must not be confused with the evolution of the relationship itself. The covenant-relation of man with God is the unifying factor of all the long biblical-Christian history, and it is at least as old as Moses; probably it is older than Moses, but we may leave that question to the experts in the origins of Semitic religion.

This distinctively biblical covenant-belief in God did not arise because the Hebrews first thought out an idea about God and liked it so much that they decided to accept it, although this rather absurd suggestion seems to be approved by all rationalistic writers—doubtless because that is the way they imagine that they have themselves come to accept their own metaphysical beliefs. On the contrary, the Hebrews found themselves believing in God, involved in a certain relationship with Him, because of certain great historical experiences through which they as a nation had passed. In other words, the biblical covenant-belief in God is a distillation from the history of the people of Israel. Biblical *ideas* about God are a further distillation from this covenant-belief in God; the believing relationship precedes the ideas. The Hebrews were not given to the habit of sitting down and formulating their ideas about God (or about anything else) in any deliberate and systematic way. They showed the world not how to argue about God or construct a theistic philosophy but how a people could enter into a covenant-relation with Him. This relationship was the distinctive and enduring feature of their history. It is because of this entirely unique origin of the faith of the Bible and of the Church that theology can never be merely a department of the science of the comparative study of religion, since science is not interested in a class of one. It is the unique existence of a believing covenant-people through many centuries and to-day that makes necessary the science of theology. It is because this covenant-faith was in some sense *given* in a long course of historical events that the question of history becomes so important for Christian apologetics. If it had been merely a matter of ideas about God, theology would have been merely a department of philosophy or of the philosophy of religion; but the covenant-relationship with God is a matter of historical fact, and therefore its investigation necessarily involves a process of historical research. It becomes a duty of the highest importance for the theologian to examine, with all the help which modern historical method can lend him, the nature of those historical events amidst which this covenant-belief came into being; we must look at the facts in order to see what kind of induction must be made from them. The Christian faith is thus an historical faith, in the sense that it is more than the mere intellectual acceptance of a certain kind of theistic philosophy; it is bound up with certain happenings in the past, and if these happenings could be shown never to have occurred, or to have been quite different from the biblical-Christian account of them, then the whole edifice of Christian faith, life and worship would be found to have been built on sand.

The critico-historical method of biblical research which was developed in the nineteenth century has given to us in the twentieth century a new form of the question about the truth of the biblical record of historical facts. The question is no longer whether every detail of the biblical history is literally and minutely true—whether Shem was a hundred years old when he begat Arpachshad and lived five hundred years more after that, whether Joshua made the sun stand still, or whether Herod Agrippa I was smitten in Caesarea by an angel of the Lord and was eaten by worms. Our question now is whether the modern scientific study of the facts of biblical history justifies the Church's view that the only satisfactory interpretation of those events is that they happened according to the will and through the power and guidance of a divine Being, whose character and purpose is revealed to us in them. Can the events of the Exodus from Egypt, or those of the extended period of crisis which culminated in the Exile in Babylon and the Return, or, above all, the events associated with the life and death and resurrection of Jesus Christ be so accounted for by the modern historian that he has no need of that hypothesis?

## § 2. *The Character of Historical Thinking*

Just as theology is not to be reduced to the status of a department of philosophy or of the comparative study of religion, so also theology is not simply an aspect of the study of history. The historian, *qua* historian, cannot pronounce the final verdict upon the truth or falsity of Christianity. The reason why he cannot do so is that the classical Christian position is not the affirmation that certain historical facts are themselves the revelation of God, although some Christian writers in recent times have tended to speak as if they were. As we shall see more fully later, the Christian understanding of historical revelation is that it was given through certain historical events as interpreted by the faith and insight of the prophets and apostles of the Bible. Even if—which is not at all likely—a Christian and a non-Christian historian found themselves in substantial agreement concerning the facts of the biblical history, they would differ so widely in their interpretation of the facts that, when they came to write their respective histories, they would arrive at quite dissimilar conclusions. There is an obvious distinction between the establishing and collecting of facts and the writing of history, and it may be briefly stated in the following way: in the establishing and collecting of facts, it is essential that the personal beliefs and values of the researcher should be excluded from his investigations as far as is humanly possible; in the writing of history the attempt to exclude these personal beliefs and values is not only undesirable but impossible. Unfortunately the distinction between these two aspects of the historian's work has not always been clearly kept in view. We may leave it to those whom it properly concerns to decide whether a university history-teacher ought to concentrate on teaching his pupils the methods of the disinterested establishment of facts, or whether he should try to share with them his own highly personal interpretation of the facts, which is necessarily based upon his whole philosophy of life or his religion; our answer to this question will depend upon what we conceive to be the function of a university in the twentieth century. It is clear that the university teacher cannot produce a number of Macaulays and Carlyles, any more than his colleagues in another department can produce a number of Miltons and Shelleys, but it does not follow from this that Macaulay and Carlyle were not historians any more than it follows that Milton and Shelley were not poets.

The view that Mommsen and Ranke rather than Macaulay and Carlyle are to be held up as models of what a historian should be seems to be no longer the dominant view amongst historians to-day. No longer is the piling up of "facts" regarded as the whole duty of the historian, and "original work" no longer means simply the unearthing of details which had not previously been noted in monographs and learned journals. More than thirty years ago Dr. G. M. Trevelyan, who has done as much to recreate the habit of reading history as any other writer of our day, criticized the conception of history as a "science", which had been so largely responsible for breaking down the well-established Victorian tradition of the reading of "literary history" amongst the educated public. "The public," wrote Dr. Trevelyan, "hearing on authority that they [*sc.* the "literary historians", such as Carlyle and Macaulay] had been 'exposed' and were 'unsound', ceased to read them—or anybody else. Hearing that history was a science they left it to scientists."[1] When history became the amassing of facts and the production of vast "synthetic histories" of the Cambridge type, a series of volumes of this kind would be read only by specialists; as far as the educated public is concerned, it is indeed "bought by the yard to decorate bookshelves, but is regarded like the *Encyclopaedia Britannica* as a work of reference; its mere presence in the library is enough".[2] Though the writing of literary history, which involves interpretation and a personal point of view, is no longer despised by historians to-day, our generation remains lamentably lacking in historical knowledge.

[1] G. M. Trevelyan, *Clio, a Muse* (1913); p. 171 in Longmans' 1931 Ed.

[2] *Op. cit.*, p. 174. Similarly A. J. Toynbee (*A Study of History*, Vol. I, 1934, pp. 3f.) speaks of "the subjugation of the ancient kingdom of historical thought by the modern Industrialism of Western life"; upon the subject of "synthetic histories like the several series of volumes now in course of publication by the Cambridge University Press" he says: "Such series are monuments of the laboriousness, the 'factual' knowledge, the mechanical skill, and the organizing power of our society. They will take their rank with the stupendous tunnels and bridges and dams and liners and battleships and skyscrapers, and their editors will be remembered among the famous Western engineers. In invading the realm of historical thought, the Industrial System has given scope to great strategists and has set up marvellous trophies of victory."

The truth is that "scientific history", the establishing and
collecting of "facts", is only a part of history-writing.[1] Of course,
there must be the quarrying of the facts before the edifice of
history can be built, and anyone who aspires to write history in
the literary sense must first have toiled for long hours in the
quarries whence the facts are hewn. No sensible person will
undervalue the unending labour that the search for facts involves
or the assiduity of the workaday scholars who, in Lord Acton's
phrase, "get their meals in the kitchen". Least of all will the
theologian, who knows that the Christian faith is rooted in
history, despise or shrink from the hard grind of historical
theology. Faith cannot be for Christians a substitute for facts,
since it is mediated through them. But "scientific history" (as it
has come to be called) is not the only or the crowning achievement
of the historian. Before history as the full record and interpretation
of the past can be written, the historian must bring to the facts
that he handles a perspective, a point of view, a scale of values.
Without these his work would be mere cataloguing, the arranging
of a card-index, useless for the instruction of wisdom and for the
understanding of our world. It is the historian's personal attitude
which gives his history its abiding value, and in this sense all
history is *somebody's* history: impersonal history is not so much
history as chronicle. If we are to find meaning in history, it must
be Gibbon's meaning, or Macaulay's, or Trevelyan's: there is no
impersonal meaning. What would be the interest or value of
Gibbon without his skepticism, his pessimism, his sense that the
world's great age was over, his view of history as "the register of
the crimes, follies and misfortunes of mankind"? Who would wish
to read a Macaulay who did not passionately believe in toleration
and the absolute value of universal franchise and in things which
were called Whiggism in his day but which are often taught as

[1] Cf. H. W. V. Temperley, *Research and Modern History* (1930), pp. 18f.:
"In my own memory the idea that history is a science has perished, and the
effects of this change of view are already evident. . . . The theory that an historian
could be really impartial seems to us to-day one of manifest buckram. We wonder
that anyone troubled to destroy it. I suppose traditions of science or scientific
impartiality still hung about history and that they have faded away as Clio advanced again into the foreground. . . . Not only do we repudiate the ideal of Ranke
that history should be colourless, new and impartial. We do not even suggest
that it is desirable." Cf. C. Oman, *Memories of Victorian Oxford* (1941), pp. 160f.

being essentially "British" in ours? What makes Trevelyan's *English Social History* a best-seller? Surely not merely its author's vast erudition, for other learned works have dropped still-born from the press; is it not rather his deep love of the "English" values of independence and fair play, his belief in the worth of the individual, his respect for "the common man", his reverence for truth and his noble patriotism? But what made Gibbon a skeptic, Macaulay a Whig or Trevelyan an English humanist? Not the *facts* of history themselves, but rather the perspective from which they look at the facts. Nor is it merely their ideological background, although it is true that Gibbon is rooted in the eighteenth century, Macaulay in the nineteenth and Trevelyan in the twentieth, and each of them is unthinkable in any other century than his own. There is something else, beyond the "facts" and beyond "ideology"; there is the personal attitude, values or philosophy of life of each of the three, or, in a broad sense, their whole religious outlook. Even "the infidel Gibbon" has a religious outlook in this sense. It is this last factor which gives their work its permanent value and which gives each of the three his title to be considered a great historian.

Those who have looked upon history *par excellence* as being of the type known as "scientific history" would have regarded this kind of personal writing of history, literary history, as going altogether beyond the legitimate bounds of the historian's sphere. History, they would have said, is not concerned with values, since history is science; as soon as the historian begins to obtrude his own scale of values into his work, objective history stops and disinterested research is jeopardized, since the investigator will find the "facts" that he is looking for. This, of course, is true. Literary history is "existential" history, and the personal attitude of the investigator is at once bound up with the objects of his study. But it is none the less a necessity for the human mind in its quest for understanding, whatever the academic specialist may say. The understanding of history, as distinct from the amassing of facts, involves faith and therefore it involves taking risks. There is no disinterested platform from which a "safe" and objective understanding of history can be attained. It is worth while pointing out that risks of a different kind will be taken, if the competent academic historian does not seek to put his knowledge at the service of understanding. If he does not concern himself with values in history, others will do so, and they will have a free hand to interpret history to the public at large and to the young. That this is not an imaginary danger is seen by a glance at what happened to history in Hitler's Germany, in the very country in which "scientific history" was born.[1] The fact that academic freedom perished in the country of its origin is not entirely unconnected with the way in which the historians regarded their own proper task; for the nation which does not understand the traditions and values of its own past is likely to fall an easy prey to the distortions of propagandists and scare-mongers who thrive on public ignorance and academic indiffer-ence. The historian's task in education cannot be accomplished by historians who regard history as a science and value-judgments as irrelevant to their work.

Another objection to the attempt to limit the scope of history to the scientific establishing and cataloguing of facts is that this proceeding is based not on the requirements of scientific method as such but on a rather doubtful theory of the nature of human knowing, which assumes that "facts" can be established and classified apart from all value-judgments about them. The theory is the counterpart in the field of history of that naturalistic philosophy which we have already encountered and which is self-styled "the scientific attitude".[2] The truth is that it is not

[1] See art. on "The Teaching of History and Pre-history in Germany", a translation of an official circular issued by the German Minister of the Interior, Dr. Frick, in 1933, containing "guiding ideas" for historical instruction in all German schools, in *Nature*, Vol. 133, pp. 298f. (February 24th, 1934).

[2] This chapter was completed before the publication of R. G. Collingwood's posthumous volume, *The Idea of History* (Oxford, 1946). From our present point of view Collingwood's book is particularly valuable as a critique of naturalistic philosophy or historical positivism, that is, the assumption that the methodology of the natural sciences is to be taken as the pattern of historical thinking (see especially pp. 126–51). But Collingwood, despite his vast erudition and width of view, does not reach a clear and confident understanding of the true nature of history and of its relation as a human science to philosophy. This is perhaps not unconnected with his complete failure to appreciate the biblical and Christian understanding of history; incredible though it may seem in a work of this kind, he dismisses the Old Testament in one page (p. 17) as mere "theocratic history and myth", and there are only two references to St. Augustine (one of them

humanly possible to write a history out of nothing but "facts".
The principles by which they are to be classified must come from
somewhere; and, moreover, there are so many facts that some
selection must be made from them. The process of selection is
accomplished by means of some criterion which is not derived
from the facts themselves. They are judged according to their
significance, and significance necessarily implies the existence of
some scale of value. Out of the millions of facts which might
have been recorded, the editors and writers of the most Brobding-
nagian series of volumes, like the compilers of the most micro-
scopic monographs, must make a selection. Some are included,
some excluded; some are treated in detail, some are mentioned in
passing. But such selection means judgment according to some
scale of significance, and there must always be some principle
according to which the final selection is made. The fact that the
principle of selection is not consciously present to the minds of
the selectors does not mean that it does not exist; it merely means
that it is more than ever likely to be a source of bias and error.
It may be that the most "significant" facts of all are being
unwittingly omitted. This is what frequently happens amongst
those who pride themselves on having reached a "scientific" or
"impartial" view of history.[1]

wrongly indexed). Consequently he never quite frees himself from the naturalistic assumptions which he finds so repugnant. Nevertheless the book is a
notable attempt to take up the question which F. H. Bradley had raised in 1874
in his first published work, *The Presuppositions of Critical History*, and which has
long been neglected by English philosophers. In Germany the task of constructing a Critique of the Historical Reason, such as Collingwood had hoped to
achieve, had been attempted by Wilhelm Dilthey (1833–1911), who perceived
the necessity of undertaking a philosophical enquiry into the nature of historical
knowledge, as distinct from the knowledge of natural phenomena, such as the
revolution in historical method which had been accomplished in the nineteenth
century itself had rendered necessary. See on this subject H. A. Hodges'
important book, *Wilhelm Dilthey: an Introduction* (London, 1944).

[1] Professor John Foster provides us with a convenient illustration of how the
principle of selection works, even in the compilation of a large-scale "synthetic
history" of the modern type: "Take the *Cambridge Modern History*, which covers
the period from the Renaissance down to *c.* 1900. Look up 'missionary' in
Volume XIII, the Index to the twelve which have gone before. You will find
one reference, 'Missionary Ridge; fighting at, 1863'. It is an obscure place in
Tennessee, scene of a skirmish during the American Civil War. Having drawn

It often happens that secularist historians are led to imagine that because they have discarded all forms of religious belief they are therefore able to write "scientific" and "impartial" histories of religious and non-religious matters alike. The non-religious point of view, it is assumed, is truly objective, because all religious "bias" has been laid aside. This is the historian's version of the rationalist fallacy, and it confuses the begging of the question with the solution of it. It assumes that because an historian is not a Catholic or a Protestant, not a Christian or a Marxist, that he will therefore be able to give us a scientific or unbiased history of, let us say, the Reformation or the English Civil War.[1] Actually, of course, whether he knows it or not, he will be writing history from the point of view of some fashionable naturalistic philosophy, and his perspective will be none the less personal and "subjective" because he is unaware that his "scientific view" is not science but philosophy of the materialistic school. The root fallacy here is the not uncommon assumption that the historian must derive the criterion of his judgment, or the scale of values by which he selects and interprets his facts, from the study of the facts themselves: to import anything from outside would be "unscientific". Thus, the late Dr. H. A. L. Fisher in a much-quoted passage near the beginning of his

a blank there, try one of the great societies. I tried 'London Missionary Society'. This is more hopeful; the references are three. Two again concern, not battles, but minor incidents connected with the Boer War. The third looks more impressive. It occurs on a page where the headline runs, 'Niger problem solved —Livingstone'. But mistake it not: it is only the source of the *Niger River*, not the enlightening of the Dark Continent. . . . It is time to protest against a neglect of religious facts which is itself a falsification of history. From 1792 onwards begins the Missionary Awakening. . . . There begins an expansion of the Church which is unequalled in any page of history. The *Cambridge Modern History* gives a whole volume to the French Revolution, and another to Napoleon. But there is no mention of that contemporary movement which is the greatest happening since Pentecost" (John Foster, *Then and Now*, London, 1942, pp. 61f.).

[1] This simple-minded faith still lives in the minds of certain modern historians. For instance, Mr. Trevor-Roper, after dismissing the "prejudices" of various High Church or Dissenting biographers of Archbishop Laud, adds: "Only Gardiner, who treated him [Laud] not as a churchman, but as a protagonist in English history, was able to look upon Laud in that secular spirit from which alone an impartial view can come" (H. R. Trevor-Roper, *Archbishop Laud*, London, 1940, p. 6).

*History of Europe* declares: "One intellectual excitement has, however, been denied me. Men wiser and more learned than I have discovered in history a plot, a rhythm, a pre-determined pattern. These harmonies are concealed from me." True to his old-fashioned liberal tradition, Dr. Fisher suggests that the clue to history, if found at all, must somehow be found within history; the facts themselves must somehow carry their own explanation. So Dr. Fisher is led to confess that he has not been able to find the plot or meaning of history within history. Yet, a few lines further on, still true to another tradition of Victorian liberal thought, he makes the uncompromising statement that "the fact of progress is written plain and large on the page of history". But whence did Dr. Fisher derive the scale of values by which he is able to measure progress in history? Not from history itself, in which he can discern no plot or pattern, but presumably from his whole liberal upbringing and tradition, which he assumes (as all the Victorians did) to be universally valid and apparent to all rational beings. The truth is that the meaning of history must be sought outside history and that the principle of the interpretation of history will not be found within it; an historian who has faith in nothing will find no clues in history. In the understanding of history, as in other matters, faith precedes understanding; and those who bring no faith to history will find no faith-principle in it. If there be a purpose in history, it is discernible only by faith, for, in St. Augustine's language, the "two cities"—*civitas Dei* and *civitas terrena*—"lie confusedly together", and it is only when reason is "purged and instructed by faith" that it can detect and understand the purpose of history, our "journey's end" and "our way unto it".[1] Amongst thinkers to-day St. Augustine's conception of the relationship between faith and history is coming to be widely accepted as near the truth of the matter. Thus, for example, a leading modern writer has said: "It is impossible to interpret history at all without a principle of interpretation which history as such does not yield. The various principles of interpretation current in modern culture, such as the idea of progress or the Marxist concept of an historical dialectic, are all principles of interpretation introduced by faith. They claim to be conclusions about the nature of history at which

[1] *De Civ. Dei.* Bk. XI, Chaps. i and ii.

men arrive after a 'scientific' analysis of the course of events; but there can be no such analysis of the course of events which does not make use of some presupposition of faith as the principle of analysis or interpretation."[1]

## § 3. *Faith and Values in History*

It is, then, impossible to write history in any other sense than that of the cataloguing of facts without the employment of some faith-principle which history itself does not provide; indeed it is scarcely possible to say as much as this, since one cannot even make a catalogue without some kind of scheme of classification and without some purpose at the back of one's mind. In our age the historian, like other men, tends to be ideologically self-conscious; in all probability he has taken part in the enjoyable activity of "de-bunking" other people's pre-suppositions, and he is inhibited from the expression of his own convictions by his fear of the attentions of the "de-bunkers". The writing of history requires courage as well as faith. In previous ages, however, as for example in the nineteenth century, when there still existed a general agreement about the validity of "Christian values", even though Christian dogmas were openly criticized, the historian could write history in the light of certain presuppositions which appeared permanently valid to the great majority of his contemporaries. Thus, as is well known, Lord Acton deemed it to be the historian's duty to pass stern judgments upon the characters of history who passed in review before him, and he reprimanded Bishop Creighton for not having condemned the persecuting Popes (such as Sixtus IV) according to the fully developed morality of the Victorian ethical code. Acton's own view of ethics was assumed by him to be the necessary and incontestable scale of values of all rational beings in any age. "What I have said," he writes in a letter to Creighton, "is not in any way mysterious or esoteric. It appeals to no hidden code. It aims at no secret moral. It presupposes nothing and implies nothing but what is universally

---

[1] Reinhold Niebuhr, *The Nature and Destiny of Man*, London, 1941, Vol. I, p. 151.

current and familiar. It is the common, even the vulgar, code that I appeal to."[1] Importing this rigorous moral standard into his study of history, Acton finds that, since "power tends to corrupt, and absolute power corrupts absolutely," therefore "great men are almost always bad men"; consequently the historian must judge great men as the great criminals they almost always are: "I would hang them higher than Haman, for reasons of quite obvious justice, still more, still higher for the sake of historical science."[2]

In Lord Acton's work, then, we have an explicit example of the importing into history-writing of the moral standards and values of the historian's own age. We are not tempted to adopt towards Acton a supercilious attitude of superior wisdom on that account. It was a sound insight which led him to pass ethical judgments upon the characters of history, and it was almost inevitable that the judgments which he passed should be based upon the accepted standards of the Victorian Age. Only prophetic minds of rare perceptive power are able to transcend the conventional standards of their own day, and even they can do so only to some extent. Moreover, Acton's canons of judgment, though scorned as "bourgeois" by some twentieth-century critics who imagine that they have outgrown "liberal" ethical ideals, are perhaps values which Europe after the Second World War will have to relearn from the Victorians. His error, if we may speak of such a thing at all, was that, in common with most of his contemporaries, he assumed that there was a universal or objective standard of values, and that he knew what it was—"the common, even the vulgar code." It is more apparent to us, who no longer live in a stable society seemingly assured of continuous progressive development, that ethical standards vary from age to age, from faith to faith, and from ideology to ideology. But Acton was doing the true work of an historian in and for his own day. We are not, of course, arguing that there is no such thing as a universal, objective standard of value, but merely that the historian (like other men) must avoid the error of assuming that his own personal scale of values, or even "the common, the vulgar code", can be

[1] See extracts from Acton's letters to Creighton appended to his *Historical Essays and Studies* (ed. Figgis and Laurence, 1907), p. 504.

[2] *Op. cit.*, p. 505.

simply and straightforwardly identified with it. As in all existential matters, self-knowledge is the beginning of sound judgment in the writing of history.

It is because of this endless variation from age to age of ethical standards, philosophical ideas and ideological assumptions that history must be constantly re-written. Even if we could be quite certain that no new facts about a given epoch would ever be brought to light, it would still be true that the "final" and "definitive" history of that period could not be written. History written in the nineteenth century differs from that written in the twentieth century not so much because new facts have been brought to light as because the perspective of the historian has changed. As in all human affairs, the pendulum swings from one side to the other, as each new generation of historians reacts from the ideals and assumptions of its predecessor. This does not mean that there is no such thing as historical truth that is knowable, or that in practice succeeding generations of historians cannot approximate ever more closely to it.[1] But there is no such thing as a final "verdict of history", because every new age will have its own new perspective. When historians tell us that it is still too early to write the history of (say) the First World War or of the Third Reich, they do not merely mean that the facts as yet have not all come to light, but that we are still too near to the facts to see them in any clear perspective. We learn a great deal about previous periods of history by taking note of the perspective in which they themselves saw still earlier periods: we learn much about the eighteenth-century mind when we read Gibbon on the age of the Antonines, or about nineteenth-century ideals when we read Macaulay on the English Revolution; and this, indeed, is one of the reasons why we read Gibbon and Macaulay. There is a sense in which the twentieth century can understand the sixteenth better than the nineteenth century could ever have done. The age of "sweetness and light" had as little in common with the persecuting zeal of religious men in the Reformation period as it has with the fanaticism of our recent totalitarianisms: a work like Lord Eustace Percy's *John Knox* could have been written only by one who was living through

[1] See on this topic G. M. Trevelyan, *The Present Position of History*, Inaugural Lecture, 1927. Reprinted in *Clio, a Muse* (1931 Ed.), pp. 177ff.

the crisis of the twentieth century and meditating profoundly upon its significance.

It is not merely true that we see history from the perspective of our own age, but it is also true that we understand our own age more adequately if we have learnt to look at it in the perspective of history. Sometimes we hear Hegel's remark repeated that the only thing we learn from history is that men learn nothing from history. This statement, fortunately for the human race, is not entirely true. Admittedly most twentieth-century people learn little from history, but that is because they know almost nothing about history. Happily for us there are a few who have learnt from history to see their own age in a truer perspective. It was indeed fortunate for Britain in 1940 that she managed to place in office a Prime Minister who knew something about English history, and that Marlborough's descendant thus called to leadership in an hour of destiny was also Marlborough's historian.[1] Here, as Mr. Rowse points out, is the complete refutation of the view that history is no "use". And if history has its use in practical affairs, experience of the latter is in its turn also useful in the writing of history. The veteran of many campaigns is likely to make a better military historian than the armchair strategist who has never drilled a platoon: "the captain of the Hampshire grenadiers . . . has not been useless to the historian of the Roman Empire."[2] History and life belong together; the personal experience of the searching issues of real life, the problems and values which have been encountered in the actual business of living, are all ingredients in the making of an historian. Thus it comes about that to-day historians no longer conceive of history as merely "the biography of states", or as "past politics", or as "a science: nothing more, nothing less", or as "the record of economic evolution and its implications". The scope of history has nowadays "come to include every aspect of the life of humanity".[3]

Nevertheless history is not philosophy. Great history cannot be

[1] See the essay on "Mr. Churchill and English History" in A. L. Rowse's *The English Spirit* (1944).

[2] Gibbon, *Autobiography* (World's Classics Ed., p. 106).

[3] G. P. Gooch, *History and Historians in the Nineteenth Century* (London, 1913), p. 573.

written without insights which are akin to the insights of poets, prophets and scientists; there must be the leaping ahead to principles, values and inductions, which involves in a true sense a venture of faith. These insights are often the very factors which lead to the making of philosophical outlooks or systems, but they are employed in a different direction. The whole work of the historian becomes *data* for the philosopher rather than philosophy itself. The historian should be a philosopher to this extent at least, that he has learnt to be aware of and to criticize the assumptions of his own thinking and the scale of values and principle of selection which he has adopted. If, like Lord Acton or Dr. H. A. L. Fisher, he remains unaware that his own assumptions and values are not necessarily those of all rational beings, he may still be a good historian but he will be a bad philosopher. Nor is history, even literary history, the same thing as the philosophy of history. Though the insights which the historian brings to his work necessarily commit him (whether he knows it or not) to certain broad philosophical attitudes and to the repudiation of others, his aim is to describe and interpret a period of history rather than to show how all history displays or fits into one all-embracing design or unity. The fascination of the great philosophies of history, such as those of Augustine and Hegel, Marx and Spengler, lies in the grandeur of the answers which they seek to give to man's perennial question about his own destiny. The historian does not address himself to this question, even though his own attitude towards it will affect all his writing of history. The historian neither starts nor ends with a philosophy of history; he studies history for its own sake, and he has no interest in making facts fit into preconceived theories. But this is an entirely different matter from saying that he is able to rid his mind of all its presuppositions when he enters his library or lecture-room.

## § 4. *The Christ of Faith or Historical Skepticism*

It is important that the Christian apologist in the twentieth century should understand the nature of historical study and writing, as this is to-day conceived by most historians. The importance of what we have called a "faith-principle" in the writing of history must not be overlooked, and the older rationalist assumption that historical research can of itself "disprove" Christianity must be exposed as an illusion. In matters which are most highly "existential", where the deepest convictions of the investigator himself are profoundly involved, his view of what actually are or are not facts is to some extent influenced by his personal standpoint of faith. This consideration, as we shall see, is particularly relevant when we ask the question about the historicity of the miracles of the New Testament, or indeed when we discuss the Gospel history in general. It is an official dogma of Marxism that Jesus never lived; Marxist historians have often convinced themselves of the truth of the "Christ-myth" theory, and they quite sincerely believe that they have arrived at this conviction as the result of a completely disinterested and "scientific" examination of the historical facts and sources. We are all familiar with the way in which the various authors of the many "lives" of Jesus which have been written since Strauss published his *Life of Jesus* in 1835, though they all claim to have made an impartial study of the historical facts, nevertheless find just the kind of Jesus in the Gospel history which their personal faith leads them to find. "According to your faith be it unto you." The recognition of this truth has inclined many towards utter skepticism concerning the possibility of our knowledge of the Jesus of history. Such a conclusion, however, is not involved in the considerations which we have adduced concerning the nature of historical study. Because our view of the nature and significance of the historical facts varies according to the perspective from which we look at them, it does not follow that all perspectives are equally false. That perspective from which we see most clearly all the facts, without having to explain any of them away, will be a relatively true perspective. Christians believe that the perspective of biblical faith enables us to see very clearly and without distortion the biblical facts as they really are: they see the facts clearly because they see their true meaning. On the other hand, when once the Christian meaning of the facts is denied, the facts themselves begin to disappear into the mists of doubt and vagueness. The interpretation of the biblical facts, as it was given to them by those who recorded them in the biblical prophetic history and apostolic witness, is necessary to a true seeing of the facts themselves. It should not surprise us that, when once the apostolic interpretation of the Gospel facts was discarded by the biblical critics of a certain nineteenth-century type, the figure of the historical Jesus concerning whom the apostles had borne their historical testimony should vanish in the mists of conjecture. The rejection of the apostolic interpretation by liberal protestants of the Harnack type was inevitably followed by the historical skepticism of Bultmann and the form-critical school. But it was the "liberal" presuppositions of the form-critics that were at fault, not the historical method which they suggested. The contemporary discussion of history and interpretation in the Gospels is showing us quite unmistakably that the two cannot be divorced.[1] Indeed, it is hardly accurate to speak of history *and* interpretation, for what is history without interpretation?

It was perhaps natural that the exhilarating discovery of the historical and critical method of biblical study in the nineteenth century should at first have led to the view that the truth or falsity of the Christian religion could be established beyond the possibility of conjecture by means of the new and scientific methods of investigation. Many people to-day still hold this view, although, as we have seen, it is based on the rationalistic misunderstanding of the nature and limits of scientific and historical method. As soon as the critical method of biblical study had come to be generally accepted amongst scholars, theologians set to work to demonstrate that in the historical facts themselves lay the sure foundations of the Christian faith; others set out with equal confidence to show that the whole structure of faith was precariously based upon the sands of myth and legend. Both sets of investigators, of course, found what they were looking for; and thus at the same time, by means of "impartial" scientific

---

[1] R. G. Collingwood points out (*The Idea of History*, p. 135) that F. H. Bradley's essay on *The Presuppositions of Critical History* (1874) grew out of the situation created by the application of the new methods of historical criticism to the New Testament narratives by the Tübingen school, notably David Strauss and F. C. Baur, which had resulted in an extremely negative conclusion. He adds: "The destructiveness of this result, however, was due not simply to the use of critical methods, but to the positivistic spirit in which those methods were used." A philosophical criticism of the presuppositions of the form-critics leads us to-day to a precisely similar verdict.

research, Jesus was found to be both "solidly historical" and also the legendary cult-hero of a mystery-religion patronized by St. Paul. The error lay in a mistaken understanding of the nature of historical investigation, and in particular in the overlooking of the importance of the element of personal belief as it affects the conclusions of the different investigators. The illusion of having attained an impartial scientific viewpoint is the inevitable penalty of embracing the rationalist theory of the nature of historical research; there are no such things as "absolute perspectives" in existential matters; we see facts not as they are in themselves, but in the light of our own personal categories of belief and interpretation. We do not see history impartially, that is, as God sees it; and the claim of scientific rationalism—whether made by rationalistic theology or by rationalistic unbelief—to give us an undistorted or impersonal vision of the truth of history is but a modern version of the Serpent's lie: "Ye shall be as God, knowing good and evil."[1] The course of the long debate upon the historicity of the Gospel narratives during and since the nineteenth century supplies ample corroboration of the view that the only facts to be seen are interpreted facts. Strauss and Renan, Seeley and Gore, all handled the same historical sources and documents, but they reached surprisingly different conclusions; their view of what constituted the historical facts was determined not by any purely objective and scientific study of the records but by their willingness or unwillingness to believe the apostolic interpretation of the events to which the apostolic testimony bore witness. The type of biblical criticism which believed that by separating the "historical facts" from their apostolic interpretation we could arrive at "what really happened" was nothing but historical rationalism masquerading as liberal theology, and it led inevitably to skepticism concerning the possibility of our knowledge of the historical Jesus. It is clearer to us in the twentieth century that, whatever else it may or may not be, revelation in history is not identical with historical facts; there must be some prior enlightening of the eyes of the mind before either the facts or their meaning can be seen in their true perspective; it is clear also that, when this enlightening comes, both the facts and their meaning are seen together and are not seen apart from each other. But this is no new conclusion.

[1] Gen. iii. 5, R.V.

From the days of the earliest of the evangelists, St. Mark, it has been known to Christians that the mystery of the person of Jesus cannot be penetrated by our natural eyes but only by the eyes of Christian faith.

Thus, Christianity is an historical religion in the sense that it arises out of a prophetic interpretation of certain events in history. To say that Christianity is an historical religion means much more than to say that it has had a long history, for so have other religions, such as Buddhism or Confucianism; yet these are not what is meant by historical religions, since they do not derive their key-categories from the interpretation of any historical events. The Christian interpretation of history is derived from the Bible, which is essentially a book of history; that is to say, the Bible is a record of historical events whose meaning has been interpreted in terms of the activity and will of God through the insights of the prophets and apostles. This chain of prophetic and apostolic interpretation, which brought the Bible into being, goes back at least as far as Moses, who interpreted the events of Israel's exodus from Egypt in the light of his understanding of God's purpose. Taught by the insights of the prophets and apostles of the Bible, prophetic minds all down the Christian centuries have endeavoured to understand the events of their own day in the light of the biblical conception of God's righteousness and forgiveness. St. Augustine's *City of God* is the outstanding example of a Christian apology directed towards the interpretation of the historical situation of a particular age, but it possesses an enduring interest for every generation of Christians because it shows how the biblical-prophetic insights can become the key-categories of a total philosophy of history. Christianity is not itself a philosophy of history; it is rather the source of insights into the meaning of historical events which yield key-categories for the constructing of philosophies of history. It is no part of the task of Christian apologetics to attempt to construct a philosophy of history; the task of Christian apologetics in relation to history is merely the humbler one of demonstrating the superiority of the biblical-Christian view of the nature of history and historical investigation over the various rival views, such as that of scientific rationalism. Those who have studied this aspect of Christian apologetics must then go on to perform two other tasks, which are both urgent in our day: first, they must show that the prophetic and apostolic interpretation of the events of both Old and New Testament history is the only one which can "make sense" of the historical evidence, without explaining it away or reducing us to utter skepticism; and secondly, they must show how the events of our own contemporary history are best understood in the light of the Christian faith in God's judgment and mercy in history. We need particular apologies directed towards both these ends to-day. But the question which arises immediately out of the considerations brought forward in this present chapter is that of the grounds for the Christian belief that a revelation of God's character and purpose has been given in the events of history. Before we enquire into the nature of a special revelation in history, however, we must first consider whether there are grounds for believing that there is given in human life a general or non-historical revelation of God outside the sphere of biblical and Christian history altogether.

# CHAPTER FIVE

# GENERAL REVELATION

## § 1. *The Traditional View: Natural and Revealed Knowledge of God*

FROM THE days when the canon of the New Testament was finally determined in the ancient Church until the rise of biblical criticism in the nineteenth century, the traditional Christian view of the nature of divine revelation was that it consisted of truth supernaturally communicated to men in propositional form. This divine truth, which was beyond the possibility of discovery by the unaided human reason, was contained in the Scriptures of the Old and New Testaments. The Bible was thus the only source-book for our knowledge of revealed truth. Its supernatural origin was attested by miracle and prophecy—that is, by the miraculous occurrences which accompanied the events which its writers described, and by the fact that these writers were able to predict events which came to pass centuries after their own day. The task of the theologian was therefore to discover the meanings of the scriptural words—their literal, allegorical, moral and anagogical meanings—and then to arrange these meanings and present them in the form of a complete system of dogma.

But in addition to the "revealed truth" given in the Scriptures and organized in the structure of dogmatic theology, there was according to the traditional view another source of the knowledge of God, namely, man's natural reason. Natural theology, as distinct from revealed theology, consisted of those truths about the divine Being which could be discovered by the unaided powers of human reason. This kind of knowledge of God, it was held, was accessible to pagans as well as to Christians, and indeed, after the days of Albertus Magnus and St. Thomas Aquinas, it was generally conceded that Aristotle was the great master of this type of knowledge of God. But this natural knowledge of God, it was held, does not give to man all that he needs to know;

it is not *saving* knowledge, and it cannot satisfy the craving of the human soul for that measure of truth which is beyond the natural capacity of the human mind. The full Christian knowledge of God and of His redemptive activity on man's behalf, as expressed in such doctrines as those of the Incarnation and the Trinity, can be learnt only from revelation and is not ascertainable by the natural reason. Man is an *ens incompletum* and therefore stands in need of the divine grace.

The foregoing account of the nature of the relation between the natural and the revealed knowledge of God presents in very broad outline the traditional Christian view as it came to be formulated by St. Thomas Aquinas in the thirteenth century. Certain modifications of this general view would have to be noted, if it were necessary for our purposes to discuss its presentation in the theologies of individual Christian thinkers. We need not now, however, do more than note that this broad statement represents the general view of Christian theologians from the thirteenth until the nineteenth century. The Reformation did not materially alter the mediaeval standpoint, though here again certain modifications of the view would have to be noted in the case of a few individual thinkers, such as Luther, if it had been necessary for our purpose to recapitulate the development of the doctrine of revelation in its details. To complete our broad general survey we need mention only the two main divergent tendencies. On the one hand, some Reformation theologians and their successors came to minimize the value of natural theology because they were so convinced of the overwhelming importance of the revealed truth contained in the Bible.[1] On the other hand, with the rise of rationalism in the modern period, thinkers like Lord Herbert of Cherbury took the alternative course of minimizing the value of revealed theology because they had come to think that reason could discover and establish all that men needed to know concerning the divine nature and purpose, until at last the deists

[1] The Reformers, of course, rejected out of hand the view that there was a *penumbra* of revealed truth alongside the Bible in the unwritten traditions of Christ and His Apostles, handed down by continual succession in the Catholic Church. This view was explicitly reaffirmed by the Council of Trent, but St. Thomas himself would have agreed with Calvin and the Anglican Articles that nothing was to be received as *de fide* which could not be proved out of the Holy Scriptures.

reached the extreme conclusion that revelation was only a "re-publication of the religion of nature". But both these courses were aberrations from the main path of the development of Christian thought about the nature of our knowledge of God. Generally speaking, it is true to say that the traditional view was re-affirmed by the thinkers in the main stream of development: natural and revealed theology were complementary to each other, and together they comprised the sum-total of our knowledge of God.[1]

This venerable view of the nature of our knowledge of God was rendered no longer tenable in its traditional form by the rise of biblical criticism in the nineteenth century. A hundred years ago Archbishop Trench (as he later became), lecturing in Cambridge,[2] was dimly aware of the gathering storm: "In a time like our own, of great spiritual agitations, at a place like this, of signal intellectual activity, where oftentimes the low mutterings of distant controversies, scarcely heard elsewhere, are distinctly audible, there can hardly fail to be some perplexed with difficulties. . . ." Despite the "distant controversies" already audible from across the German Ocean, the lecturer saw little reason to modify the traditional conception of revealed truth. During the interval of nearly a century between the Hulsean Lectures of Archbishop Trench and the Gifford Lectures of Archbishop William Temple[3] there has occurred perhaps the greatest revolution that has ever taken place in the history of Christian thought, and its consequences for the whole of our understanding of revelation are but imperfectly perceived to-day. The new attitude towards the Scriptures brought about by the application to them of the methods of literary and historical criticism has made it impossible to continue to hold a theory of revelation based upon a view of the Scriptures as the divinely dictated oracles of religious truth. The theologians of the later nineteenth and of the twentieth centuries have been compelled to ask and to answer a new question: If the Christian revelation did not consist in the infallible authority of the divinely given Scriptures, what then

[1] A brilliant account of the traditional conception of revelation and of its breakdown will be found in A. L. Lilley's *Religion and Revelation* (London, 1932).

[2] Hulsean Lectures for 1845 and 1846.

[3] *Nature, Man and God* (London, 1934), Gifford Lectures for 1932–34.

was the vehicle and mode of that revelation? May we regard the content of the revelation as itself remaining unaltered after we have changed our views about the mode of its delivery?

## § 2. *The Inadequacy of the "Liberal" Alternative*

One method of answering these questions was proposed by the theologians of the nineteenth century, many of whom had taken a prominent part in the development or popularization of the new critical approach. It is sometimes called the "liberal Protestant" view, and it finds few supporters amongst theologians of the front rank to-day. It has much in common with the eighteenth century deistical point of view, which, as we noted, tended to make revelation a mere "re-publication" of the truths of natural religion. According to this line of thought, the Gospel merely illustrates—or perhaps even gives the supreme illustration of—universal religious truth. Such truth is, in theory, accessible to all men, irrespective of race, education or century; but in practice it is found to be disclosed in the experience, life or writings of the "religious geniuses" of the world. Amongst these the biblical prophets and apostles were judged to be of the highest rank, and the highest place of honour was, of course, given to Jesus of Nazareth. Hence is derived the supreme value of the Bible as the record of the lives and teachings of these religious giants. But outside the biblical and Christian tradition altogether there were many other great religious teachers, each of whom in his own way saw and proclaimed an aspect of the universal truth. Plato and Confucius, it was urged, have a better claim to be regarded as religious experts than Joshua or Samson. Jesus "fulfils" all that is best in the sacred scriptures of the Eastern religions or in the writings of the Greek philosophers, just as He fulfils the Law and the Prophets of Judaism. There is little difference between the Brahman, Sufi and Christian mystics at their best.[1] In the other great religions there are analogies with every distinctive Christian doctrine. Christianity, purged of its non-essential accretions and dogmatic rigidity, is in its pure and original form, the highest manifestation that has yet appeared of the universal religious consciousness of mankind; and the teaching of Jesus, stripped of

[1] E. Underhill, *Essentials of Mysticism*, p. 4.

HCA

its first-century Jewish envelope and of the theological accretions with which from the time of St. Paul it has been overlaid, is the noblest expression of universal religious truth. The discovery of divine truth is the human counterpart of the divine activity of revelation; and, when the divine initiative in the giving of revelation was strongly stressed, specific acts of revelation in history tended still to be regarded as but striking illustrations of general religious truths: the unsophisticated mind apprehends truth through concrete instances more easily than through general ideas. These specific acts of revelation, as in the biblical history, were but the "speeding up" of the divine "education of the human race" and together they constituted the long process of "progressive revelation".

Now there is indeed much that is true and valuable in this kind of theory of revelation, and many devoutly Christian minds have found it attractive. But its defect is that it does not account for the observable facts of Christian existence. Under the stimulus of the new and exciting discoveries of the comparative study of religions, it clearly perceived the many similarities that undoubtedly exist between Christianity and other forms of religion. It did great service in calling attention to these similarities. But the theory tends to see and to account for only the similarities between Christianity and the non-Christian faiths, and therefore it tends to explain away the inconvenient differences, which also undoubtedly exist. Any theory of revelation which fails to account for the dissimilarities as well as the affinities has failed to account for the facts; it has tried to fit the facts into an hypothesis which is capable of embracing only half of them. Thus, the differences between Christian faith and the non-Christian religions are of such a kind that they cannot be regarded as varying aspects of one universal, many-sided truth; they are so great as to amount to contradictions. How could the Christian doctrines of God or of man be thought to be a "fulfilment" of the Hindu view that personality is essentially negative or evil, or of the Mohammedan view of God which results in a disastrous fatalism or in the conception of Holy War? The resemblances between Christianity and the other religions are often superficial and are easily exaggerated. As a recent writer has expressed it: "The Bhakti tradition in Hinduism—the fervent devotion to a personal god—which seems so near to Christianity is really a little oasis in a desert of pantheism. The Sufi mystic, whose words we hardly distinguish from those of the Christian mystic, has very little contact with Islam, his professed religion."[1] The God of the Bible remains "a jealous God", who will not consent to be represented by false images and conceptions which are unworthy of Him; according to the classical Christian witness down the ages, there can be no worthy representation of God except in Jesus Christ, who alone is the express image of His Person.[2] There is a true sense in which, in Professor Kraemer's phrase, Christ is "the crisis of all religions"; He is the Judge as well as the Fulfilment of every non-Christian religious idea or symbol. The Christian Church historically has not become a kind of "world congress of faiths" or syncretistic union of all the world's religions, as it should have done if the hypothesis which we are considering were able to account for the facts: the world-conference of Christians from many lands and of many denominations assembled at Madras in 1938 was in fact distinctively Christian in membership and outlook, and significantly it discussed the Christian message to the non-Christian world. Such facts are important, since it is the actual believing and witnessing Church as it really exists to-day that we have to explain; it is the actual faith and worship and experience of the living Church which must provide the *data* of theology. The modern view of revelation which we outlined above does not explain the facts of the Christian Church to-day as it demonstrably exists. It is not true that mankind "naturally" (whether by reason or in any other way) arrives at a noble conception of a righteous and loving God, who is apprehended in the sincerity of faith, as a result of following the leading of its own religious consciousness; it is only where the Christian Gospel has been preached that the one true God is known. We must find a doctrine of revelation that will account for the Christian faith not only in its resemblances to but also in its disagreements with all other religious systems, and one which will take due note of the historical fact that Christian faith in God exists only where Jesus Christ has been preached as Lord. The hypothesis of the distillation of the truth about God

---

[1] C. E. Storrs, *Many Creeds: One Cross* (London, 1945), pp. 20f.
[2] Cf. Heb. i. 3, A.V.

and the world from the universal religious consciousness of
mankind does not fit the observable facts; and this is the reason
why it has never been accepted by the leading theologians of the
Church in any age, and why it is dismissed to-day by those who
have studied historical theology. It is demonstrably true both in
history and in the contemporary world that the distinctive values
of Christian faith and worship, of Christian living and pastoral
care, have never been spontaneously evolved where the Christian
Gospel has not been preached. If the knowledge of God which
comes by the preaching of the Gospel of Christ be taken as the
standard of judgment, then it must be conceded that the words of
Jesus have been proved by history to be true: "No man cometh
to the Father but by Me."[1]

§ 3. *The Conception of General and Special Revelation*

We must try to reach an understanding of the nature of man's
knowledge of God which will take due account of the genuinely
religious features of the non-Christian faiths, some of which they
share with Christianity, and which will yet at the same time
adequately comprehend those distinctive elements of the Christian
religion which are not found in any other religious system or
philosophy. It is untrue to the facts to present Christianity as just
one illustration amongst many of general religious truth, even

[1] John xiv. 6; cf. Matt. xi. 27 = Luke x. 22. The question about revelation in
the non-Christian religions has become prominent again in the contemporary
discussion of revelation. Under the influence of Barth it has recently been denied
that the non-Christian faiths are in any sense a preparation for the coming of
Christ: God as revealed in Christ, it is urged, is contrary to the sublimest pictures
men had ever made of Him; God's redemption of the world in Christ cannot
be prepared for or supplemented by any workings of the human religious
consciousness. See Hendrik Kraemer, *The Christian Message in a Non-Christian
World* (Eng. trans., 1938) and the discussion of this thesis in *The Authority of the
Faith* (Tambaram Series, Vol. I). Most popular books on the comparative study
of religions tend to treat the question from the point of view of "progressive
revelation" and are often out of touch with contemporary theological thinking
upon the doctrine of revelation. A notable exception to this statement is
C. E. Storrs, *Many Creeds: One Cross* (London, 1945), which presents a brief but
balanced and scholarly treatment of the differences as well as the resemblances
between Christian faith and the non-Christian religions.

though it be said to be the highest, since that is not how Christianity through all the centuries has understood itself; yet, on the
other hand, it is also untrue to the actual situation to deny that
there is anything of religious truth in the non-Christian religions.
The only kind of theory of the knowledge of God which will
adequately embrace all the facts of man's experience will be one
which recognizes that there are two kinds of revelation or divine
disclosure of truth. There is first *general* revelation, which pertains
to the universal religious consciousness of mankind; and there is
also *special* revelation, which is mediated through particular
episodes at definite times and places in history. The broad distinction between general and special revelation is that the former
is non-historical, in that its content is not communicated to mankind through particular historical situations but is quite independent of the accidents of time and place, whereas the latter
is historical, that is, bound up with a certain series of historical
persons and happenings through which it is communicated to
mankind. This is broadly the distinction between biblical
(Jewish-Christian) religion and the non-Christian religions. The
truth is that only three of the world's religions contain what may
rightly be called an "historical element"—namely Buddhism,
biblical faith of the Jewish and Christian types, and Mohammedanism; and of these Buddhism and Mohammedanism do not
attach dogmatic importance to the historical lives of their founders
in any way that is at all comparable to the Christian conception
of a historical revelation that culminates in the person of Christ.[1]
If we are to do justice to the facts, we must observe that there is
here an important distinction between two different kinds of
facts. Christianity (along with Old Testament Judaism) makes a
claim that is made by no other religion in respect of a revelation
through history, and it is for this reason that Christianity cannot
be fitted into an hypothesis which was designed to account for
the *data* derived from a study of the non-Christian religions;
biblical faith adds to the *data* supplied by the non-Christian
systems a new and distinctive kind of fact, and therefore it
requires an enlargement of the hypothesis which might be judged
adequate to embrace the non-Christian *data*. To the conception

[1] Cf. C. C. J. Webb, *Studies in the History of Natural Theology* (Oxford, 1915),
pp. 23f.

of a general revelation we must add that of a special revelation mediated through history. The modern mind often objects that Christian theologians are unfair to the non-Christian faiths in their insistence upon a unique and crucial distinction between Christian and non-Christian religion;[1] but the truth is that the vital difference between Christian and non-Christian religion is given in the facts of the case themselves, and it is the existence of this distinction and of a revelation through a particular series of historical events which gives to Christian theology its special character and task and which differentiates it from the comparative study of religions as such. If in our attempt to be quite "fair" to the other religions, we try to bring Christianity under the same formula with them, then we shall be ignoring the true facts of the case and attempting to force them into an hypothesis which is not wide enough to embrace them.

We are therefore driven by the facts to accept the view that revelation is of two kinds, general and special. Such a view, it may be noticed at once, has the merit of conserving the truth contained both in the traditional view and in the nineteenth-century reaction from it. It does not explain away the distinctively Christian understanding of a revelation through history, as the nineteenth-century view tended to do; but, on the other hand, it frees us from the traditional conception of revelation as a body of propositional truths contained in an infallible Scripture, from which the nineteenth-century viewpoint had broken loose. Without in any way weakening the claim that we know the full measure of the saving grace of God by Christ alone, it allows us to recognize a genuine revelation of God in non-Christian religions. It has the advantage over the "Barthian" view that it does not have to denigrate the non-Christian systems in order to magnify the Lord of Christian faith, an attitude which surely

[1] Cf. Michael Roberts, *The Recovery of the West* (London, 1941), p. 265: "The main impediment in our time to a rudimentary faith in the historic truth of the Christian story comes, not from the fact that the story was recorded and transmitted in language that paid little heed to the requirements of science, but from a curious and quite unscientific sense of justice. If we admit the claims of Christianity, what grounds have we for rejecting the claims of Buddhism and Mohammedanism? If we suspend our scientific judgment when we read of the Virgin Birth and the Resurrection, what grounds have we for refusing to admit the incarnation of the Buddha?"

betrays the gnawing skepticism which lurks in the very vitals of "Barthianism". In a word, it neither reduces the special revelation in Christ and in biblical history to general terms, nor yet under-estimates the significance of the general religious consciousness of mankind. The genuinely religious gains of the nineteenth-century insights need not be abandoned when we discard the extreme theories of the *Religionsgeschichte* school of thought. As an American theologian has well written: "It should be a primary concern of contemporary theology to re-assert the full Christian idea of revelation in the clearest possible terms, and re-establish its supremacy in Christian teaching, while at the same time making it plain that faith in revelation does not violate that reverence for all truth which liberal Protestantism has—let us hope—made permanently a part of the Christian conscience."[1]

The view of general and special revelation which we have outlined, having come to clear expression again only in quite recent years, is usually accounted modern; but it is fundamentally Augustinian in conception and in this sense is older than the Thomistic division of the field of our knowledge of God into "natural" and "revealed" knowledge, which we have spoken of as the traditional theory.[2] It is gaining increasing acceptance

[1] Walter Marshall Horton in *Revelation* (ed. Baillie and Martin, 1937), p. 242.

[2] Dr. John Baillie (in *Revelation, op. cit.*, p. xviii) writes: "This changed way of regarding the matter was sometimes hinted at by older writers who pointed out that there was a sense in which even natural knowledge could be spoken of as revelation—an internal revelation, as the Reformer Zwingli called it in his *De Vera et Falsa Religione* (1525); but the full development of the usage would appear to be modern." The conception, however, is older than Zwingli, and older even than Aquinas; it is Augustinian. The terms, "general" and "special" revelation, are doubtless modern, but they are merely convenient summaries of St. Augustine's thought about revelation. Thus, B. B. Warfield, writing in the *Princeton Theological Review* for July, 1907 (pp. 353–97), had already used them in his account of St. Augustine's teaching about revelation. See his *Studies in Tertullian and Augustine* (New York and Oxford, 1930), pp. 222f.: "With Augustine . . . all knowledge rests ultimately on revelation. The problem to him was not, therefore, how to supplant a strictly natural knowledge by a strictly supernatural knowledge: but how to restore to men the power to acquire that knowledge which we call natural—how to correct sin-bred disabilities so that the general revelation of God may be reflected purely in minds which now are blinded to its reflection by sin. For this end, a special revelation, adapted to meet the needs of sin-disabled minds, is called in. . . . The intervention of God

amongst theologians to-day as the hypothesis which most fully does justice to all the facts, both Christian and non-Christian alike. According to the traditional or Thomistic view, it is only revealed knowledge which comes to us through the gracious activity of the divine self-disclosure, and it is only through this divine activity of revelation that we possess the knowledge of God's will to save us; our natural knowledge of God is essentially an activity of our human reason, which is capable of discovering unaided at least a measure of the truth about God, but not the knowledge of our salvation by God. According to the conception of general and special revelation, on the other hand, it is maintained that all our knowledge of God is the result of divine self-revelation; indeed, we should rather say that all discovery, all our knowledge of truth of whatever kind, is the result of the gracious and revealing activity of the God of truth. There is no such thing as a purely "natural" or "unaided" knowledge of God or of truth; the hypothesis of general and special revelation compels us to acknowledge with St. Augustine that all human knowledge is to be ascribed to the illumination of God: it is only by the shining of the Sun of Truth that the soul is enlightened to see the light.[1] The existence of a rational part of us, existing independently of God or of faith, is the perennial illusion of all forms of rationalism. Such a conception of the relation of our knowledge of truth to God as the Author and Source of truth is inescapably involved in the deep Christian conviction of the sacredness of truth as such, a conviction which gave birth to and

by a special revelation works, therefore, harmoniously into the general scheme of the production of knowledge of God through general revelation. The conception is that man, being a sinner, and unable to profit by general revelation, God intervenes creatively by special revelation and grace—by special revelation enabling him to walk meanwhile until by grace he is once more prepared to see the Light in its own light. Special revelation, given through the prophets and apostles, is embodied in the Scriptures and brought to bear on man by the Church, in which is found the grace to heal men's disabilities."

[1] St. Augustine was well aware that there was nothing peculiar to Christianity in the ascription of all knowledge to divine illumination. The Platonists, represented in Augustine's day pre-eminently by Plotinus, had recognized this truth; they had failed in their apprehension of it, not because they did not know the world's Creator, but because they had not learned to worship Him aright (*De Civ. Dei*, Bk. X, Chaps. ii.-iv.).

sustains the spirit of modern science, and without which science, properly so called, perishes, as it perished in the Nazified universities of Hitler's *Reich*.

Sometimes it is said that the only sacred thing which a scientist knows is the sacredness of truth; the Christian theologian will discern in the scientist's sense of the *obligation* which truth imposes upon him his personal response to the leading of the God of truth. Since the essence of the Christian understanding of revelation is that all revelation comes from God, if there is such a thing as truth or as the knowledge of God at all, it must come from the gracious and revealing activity of God Himself. All truth is one, and all truth is God's truth, for God, if He exists, must be the God of truth. Hence, if the scientist is devoted to truth, then he is to that extent devoted to God, though he may call himself an atheist. Indeed, for the benefit of logical positivists and others who are doubtful whether the conception of "truth" has any meaning, we may say that in so far as the skeptic or logical positivist is prepared to discuss whether there is any meaning at all in the statements of natural scientists, he is responding to the pressure of God upon his mind, even though he thinks that the term "God" is a word without meaning; the search for the meaning of any words or propositions is in a real sense a part of the search for God, who alone is the ground of meaning. It is true that devotion to truth or the search for meaning is not the whole of any man's obligation to God, and it is also true that a scientist's or a philosopher's knowledge of God, if it stops here, is severely limited; yet the Christian apologist will be quick to perceive that here is a beginning from which such a one may be led on to see that there is a God who has other claims upon him; he must go to such men and say, "Whom therefore ye ignorantly worship, Him declare I unto you".[1] The pressure of truth or meaning upon our minds is nothing other than the impact of God upon us, even though we may not have learnt to call Him by His proper name. It is one of the activities of God in His self-manifestation which is included under the heading of general revelation.

[1] Acts xvii. 23, A.V. Cf. St. Augustine, *Sermon* CXLI: the philosophers have found God as the Truth, but without Christ they will not find the Way to Him. *Veritatem viderunt, sed de longinquo.*

### § 4. The Universality of the Knowledge of God

Thus, if there be any truth at all in the teachings of the philosophers and scientists, it must come from the God of truth Himself. But, beyond this, the conception of a general and a special revelation possesses a decided advantage over the traditional theory of a natural and a revealed knowledge of God, in that it does not restrict what is meant by "knowledge of God" to know-ledge of the ratiocinative kind, such as comes by science and philosophy. It allows us to admit that, for example, the Buddha and Mohammed might have understood something of truth, although they were not scientists or philosophers and did not arrive at their truth primarily by ratiocinative methods. On the traditional view "natural knowledge" means, of course, *rational* knowledge; it might be admitted that Aristotle possessed a knowledge of God without making a like admission about Mohammed—a point which doubtless occurred to Aquinas in his controversy with Averroes. The theory of general and special revelation, however, does not restrict the general knowledge of God, to which all men have access, by limiting it to knowledge of one type only, namely, the knowledge which comes by rational reflection. It recognizes that there may be a knowledge of God through general religious experience, far outside the biblical and Christian frontiers. Furthermore—and this is a gain of the greatest importance for the Christian apologist—it helps us to see that there may be a genuine knowledge of God that comes through all forms of art and artistic experience—music, poetry, drama, architecture, sculpture, painting. Indeed, we must claim that the obligation which the artist acknowledges, his inner compulsion to create that which is beautiful and to destroy that which is ugly, is nothing other than the pressure of God upon his life, though beauty may be the only sacredness that he recognizes and though he may call himself an atheist.[1] It may or

[1] For an example of the type of modern mind which denies the Christian view of God yet finds in aesthetic experience "a revelation" of some kind, see A. L. Rowse, *A Cornish Childhood* (1942), p. 17: "I could not know then that it was an early taste of aesthetic sensation, a kind of revelation which has since become a secret touchstone of experience for me, an inner resource and con-solation. Later on, though still a schoolboy . . . when I read Wordsworth's *Tintern Abbey* and *Intimations of Immortality*, I realized that that was the experience

may not be true that all men at some time in their lives undergo some kind of religious experience; it would probably be more widely acknowledged that all men sooner or later enjoy aesthetic experience of some sort. In both these cases the apologist has a foundation upon which to build. In the sense of the "numinous" we may recognize one of the ways in which the fact of general revelation enters in an undeniable manner into the lives of many people; from the ordinary man's awareness of the "holy" to the mystical experiences of the Brahman or Sufi or Christian type, there exists a phenomenon which must not be explained away; and to such experiences we must add the witness of writers of our own scientific age of the Heard-Huxley variety. Similarly with regard to aesthetic experience, especially the creative impulse of the artist, there is that in human experience which provides an analogy by which the men and women of our generation may be led to understand the biblical teaching concerning the creativity of God. But it is no part of the purpose of this book to attempt to develop an argument which belongs rather to the sphere of general religious apologetic; we are concerned merely to point out the way in which the theory of general and special revelation makes room for the fuller understanding of these matters. Christian apologetics as such is not based upon an appeal to any Christian religious experience, which must inevitably be private to Christians and incommunicable until faith is aroused; it is based primarily upon the historical and contemporary evidence of Christian existence. The theory of general and special revelation releases us from the attempt to find (as many Christian thinkers in the nineteenth century sought to find) an alternative authority in Christian religious experience to the vanished authority of an infallible scriptural revelation, while at the same time it does not compel us to decry the apologetic value and genuinely theological significance of aesthetic and religious experience as such.

he was writing about. In time it became my creed—if that word can be used of a religion which has no dogma, no need of dogma; for with this ultimate aesthetic experience, this apprehension of the world and life as having value essentially in the moment of being apprehended *qua* beauty, I had no need of religion." Cf. also p. 154: "When I think of my life as a whole, I do not in the end think of myself, but of the sum of those moments of ecstasy which is my real inner life. They constitute my revealed religion—a revelation of the world as beauty."

It is, however, in the moral sphere that the chief evidence of general revelation is found. Even though some might hold that there are certain people who are totally devoid of religious experience, it is indubitable that all people have had moral experience —the experience of knowing that one *ought* to do this and *ought not* to do that. Every human being who is not clearly imbecile has a knowledge of right and wrong. It is, of course, possible that in some men the sense of right and wrong may be perverted, whether through bad upbringing, corrupting social influences or sheer personal wickedness. Nevertheless everyone knows that right is not the same thing as wrong, and the various brands of anarchists, nihilists, utilitarians and hedonists are all clearly aware that there is something to be explained away in the phenomenon of moral consciousness. Even though moral philosophers cannot agree upon the explanation of what the difference is, they all perceive that there is a difference between right and wrong. Nor must we allow ourselves to be misled by superficial talk about the relativity of moral standards. It is true that moral standards vary widely from age to age and from place to place; it is true that there is a vast difference between the content of the moral consciousness of, let us say, a City stock-broker and that of a Leningrad factory-worker or a Borneo head-hunter: yet they all acknowledge, according to their own standards, that there *is* a difference between right and wrong. It is true that education and social environment "condition" the content of an individual's moral consciousness; but it remains true also that all men—*qua* men and not beasts—have a knowledge that there is a distinction between right and wrong and feel an obligation to do the right, even though they may perhaps hardly ever do it. They may often be mistaken about *what* is right—the head-hunter is doubtless mistaken about the rightness of collecting heads—but the sense of obligation to do that which seems to one to be right is universal. Even dictators who are about to break a treaty or commit a flagrant aggression find it necessary to discover high-sounding moral reasons for their deeds. The phenomenon of conscience is universal. By conscience here is meant simply the knowledge that there is a difference between right and wrong actions.

According to the teaching of the Bible itself, knowledge of the right is the beginning of the knowledge of God; moreover, knowledge of God in this sense is universal, although apart from special revelation men do not recognize it for what it truly is. The sense of obligation to do that which is believed to be right is in fact the pressure of God upon every human life. God is made known to all men, even though they may not have learned to call Him God, as moral demand; and obedience to the behests of conscience is the essential condition of growth in the knowledge of God, just as disobedience to the known moral law is the degrading of the knowledge of God.[1] According to the Bible our knowledge of God is not like our knowledge of electrons or square roots: we know truth about God only by doing it, not by talking or reasoning about it, just as we know love only by loving. Truth in the biblical sense is something to be practised. By engaging actively in the task of setting up justice, of promoting useful ends in society, or of ordering the common life on the basis of one's knowledge of the right—this is the way in which the knowledge of God is attained,[2] rather than by reading books upon theology or by reasoning about the First Cause. Theology and reasoning are not in themselves sources of our knowledge of God; they are only the intellectual means by which the truth about God is formulated and its meaning more clearly seen. Hence it is that neither the Bible nor the classical Christian theologians (unlike some moderns) make a sharp distinction between pagan and Jewish-Christian knowledge of God; the New Testament itself is willing to draw upon Stoic codes of morals;[3] a Christian moralist, like St. Ambrose in his *De Officiis* is content to borrow his categories from Cicero, and the four cardinal virtues of traditional Christian morality are gratefully taken over from Plato. If we care to speak with the Catholic theologians about "natural law" there is nothing in the Bible to forbid us to do so; or if we prefer to use the language of some present-day continental Protestant

[1] Cf. Rom. i. 18–23.

[2] Jer. xxii. 15f.: "Did not thy father do judgment and justice? Then it was well with him. He judged the cause of the poor and needy; then it was well. *Was not this to know me? saith the Lord.*" Cf. also Matt. vii. 21; John vii. 17; James i. 27; 1 John v. 2f.

[3] See C. H. Dodd, art. "Natural Law in the Bible", *Theology*, Vol. XLIX. Nos. 311, 312, (May and June, 1946); also E. G. Selwyn, *The First Epistle of St. Peter* (London, 1946), pp. 101–9.

theologians and to speak about "orders of creation", we shall find that we are talking about the same thing.[1]

Thus, the knowledge of God which comes through moral experience is not limited to Christians; it is accessible to all men at all times and in all places, and it belongs to the sphere of general revelation. It is the basis upon which Christians may co-operate in all kinds of useful social and political enterprises with men of good will who do not call themselves Christians.[2] The recognition of a general revelation amongst men of all nations provides a valuable clarification of our thinking upon the Christian's participation in the affairs of "secular" life. It supplies us also with a reasonable explanation of the phenomenon of the existence of some kind of common standard of behaviour amongst nations and individuals, such as is necessarily pre-supposed by conceptions like those of "the United Nations", "one world", "collective security", or even "civilization".[3] The humanist's respect for personality and personal liberty, the statesman's idea of the "four freedoms", the democrat's ideal of "the rights of

[1] See further, *Natural Law, a Christian Reconsideration*, ed. A. R. Vidler and W. A. Whitehouse (London, 1946); and cf. E. Brunner, *Justice and the Social Order*, Eng. trans. (London, 1945), p. 49: "The law, the order of creation, is that primal order to which every man appeals, even though unwittingly, who thinks the thought of justice. What is dimly apprehended by the plain man's sense of justice—Everyman's sense of justice—is revealed in divine revelation as the order established by the Creator."

[2] In a B.B.C. broadcast on August 30th, 1942, M. André Philip described how French Catholic and Protestant groups within the Resistance movement worked in harmony with non-Christians of all kinds, including communists and freethinkers. But all, he said, believed in moral values that are independent of the will of rulers and the vicissitudes of national fortune, and to which even States are subject. Where there is belief in the objectivity of moral values, Christian co-operation with non-Christian groups is possible and desirable. M. Philip is, of course, an able theologian.

[3] There is much confusion of thought upon these topics to-day. For instance, during Hitler's war we were constantly told by statesmen and churchmen alike that we were fighting for "Christian principles". The Mohammedan subjects of King George or our Russian allies might perhaps have wondered what they were fighting for. Of course, Mohammedans, Russians and British (in so far as they were fighting for principles at all) were fighting, not for distinctively Christian principles, but for those fundamental human values of which mankind has knowledge through the grace of God in general revelation. Distinctively Christian truth cannot be either defended or propagated by the sword.

man"—all these things are from God, but they are not distinctively Christian; they are the result of His gracious disclosure of His nature and purpose in the general revelation of Himself given in the common life.

## § 5. *The Necessity of General Revelation—and of Something More*

As we have said that all revelation is from God, so we must now add that all revelation is *saving* revelation. The knowledge of God is always saving knowledge. We cannot for one moment entertain the view which, in the imagined interests of the Gospel, is ready to argue that only the biblical-Christian knowledge of God, or special revelation, is redemptive, and that general revelation falls outside the sphere of saving grace.[1] And here we are not appealing to sentiment but to facts. It is nothing but the respect for personality and the humane values which does in truth save man's life from becoming a nightmare of frightfulness, such as supervened recently under the totalitarianism which deliberately rejected those values. The recognition of obligation and of the values is the means whereby human life is preserved and enriched, and they are themselves the fruits of the saving activity of God's general revelation of Himself in the world. In

[1] It will be seen that we part company with both Barth and Brunner. Barth holds that there is no general revelation at all, and that we have no knowledge of God or saving grace apart from Christ. Brunner disagrees with Barth and holds that, though there is a general revelation, it is not the vehicle of saving grace, which comes by Christ alone. Barth rightly retorts that revelation which is not saving revelation is not revelation at all. Barth believes that the divine image in man has been totally obliterated by the Fall. Brunner holds that the *form* of the image remains but that the matter is entirely lost, that is to say, man remains formally a creature responsible to God, but materially he is incapable of making a right response at all. Barth again rightly points out that this distinction is meaningless. Brunner's half-hearted compromise is no truer to the facts of our human situation than is Barth's extremism. The hypothesis of general revelation and its correlate, that of the divine image in man, are necessary to explain actually observed phenomena, which need explanation. See Barth's essay in *Revelation* (ed. Baillie and Martin); Brunner's *Natur und Gnade* (1934) and Barth's reply, *Nein!* (1934). These pamphlets have been translated into English by Peter Fraenkel and published under the title *Natural Theology* (London, 1946). A clear summary and sound criticism of the views of Barth and Brunner will be found in John Baillie, *Our Knowledge of God* (1939), pp. 17–34.

the enlightened conscience and the high sense of moral responsibility of the humanist or communist, Jew or Mohammedan,
even though with his lips he may deny Christ and the God whom
He revealed, we must discern at work nothing other than the
saving grace of God.[1] It is the diffusion of this knowledge of God
throughout human society that makes social living possible and
wholesome; such knowledge is not "natural" or "unaided", and
it is therefore more appropriate to speak of general revelation
than of a natural knowledge of God.[2]

Thus, by means of the understanding of the knowledge of God
that is summed up in the formula of "general and special revelation" we may rejoice in the reality of the God-given humanist
values without fearing that by doing so we shall impugn the
unique value of the biblical revelation itself. We can thank God
for the vision and idealism of humanists and others and co-operate
with them wholeheartedly in all good works, while at the same
time we are not committed to sharing with them their illusions.
Our recognition of the necessity of a further or special revelation
implies that we know that humanism and its ideals are not enough.
Those who understand their real need of a special, in addition to
general, revelation will not fall into the error of imagining that
special revelation is only a kind of concrete illustration of the
truth that is already accessible to the human religious consciousness as such. For alas! it is not only the phenomenon of conscience
that is universal, but the phenomenon of the guilty conscience:

[1] Cf. J. Maritain, *True Humanism* (Eng. trans., 1938), pp. 56f. Even those
who imagine that they are atheists may really choose God as the true end of life.
"Under many names, names which are not that of God, in ways only known to
God, the interior act of a soul's thought can be directed towards a reality which
in fact truly may be God. . . . To every soul, even to one ignorant of the name
of God, even one reared in atheism, grace offers . . . that Reality of absolute
goodness, which merits all our love and is able to save our life."

[2] It may be worth while to point out that we are not objecting to the idea of
natural theology as such; the discussion of the traditional contents of natural
theology (the ontological, cosmological and teleological arguments for the
existence of God, and so on) falls outside the scope of this book and belongs to
general religious apologetic rather than to Christian apologetic. The arguments
for God's existence must be treated on their merits. It is, of course, possible to
believe (with Walter Marshall Horton; see his essay in *Revelation*, ed. Baillie and
Martin) in the existence of general revelation and the validity of natural
theology at the same time.

man's universal consciousness of his sin is God's means of recalling the sinners to Himself.[1] Men knowing the right everywhere do that which is wrong, and human idealism itself, by becoming the occasion of sinful pride in man's ability to save himself, so easily turns into the daemonic force which brings human life to the abyss of destruction. To save him from the Gadarene madness into which his pride impels him man needs more than a general revelation: God in His mercy has vouchsafed a special revelation of Himself that will accomplish the salvation which the general knowledge of God cannot achieve. Without the full Christian revelation all man's reason, science, ideals and hopes are powerless to redeem human life from destruction and indeed become the very forces which impel him towards it. The history of Europe in the twentieth century discourages the view of T. H. Huxley and other nineteenth-century agnostics that Christian ethical standards will be received and practised when the active belief in the Christian revelation of God has been generally discarded.

The problem, therefore, of the relationship between the gift of general and that of special revelation is more complicated than the relationship between the natural and revealed knowledge of God was thought to be in the traditional teaching; it is an oversimplification of the situation to say *tout court* that "grace fulfils nature". The special revelation in Christ both fulfils and at the same time judges and condemns the ideals and values of all non-Christian humanism. There is indeed a sense in which the noblest insights of the humanist are fulfilled in Christ, but there is also a sense in which they are judged and transcended by Him. Whereas the traditional theory suggested that the revealed knowledge of God was a kind of quantitative extension in a straight line of our natural knowledge of Him, we must regard special revelation as being dialectically both an affirmation and a negation of general revelation. The actual situation is that, until

[1] Cf. J. Baillie, *Our Knowledge of God*, p. 13: "This hidden canker of an uneasy conscience is in itself our greatest scathe and scourge, and for that only our own disobedience is to blame; yet it is but the reverse side of our most precious blessing, and for that we must thank God as for nothing else that has come to us. For it means that however much we try to keep to ourselves, yet He will not leave us to ourselves. . . . It means that His is a love that has claimed us from the beginning, and that to the end refuses to let us go."

we accept the truth of special revelation, the truth as it is in Christ, we do not clearly see any portion of the truth as it really is; we see things in the distorted perspective of our own egocentrism, which general revelation is not able to correct. Special revelation is not something which is added on quantitatively to general revelation, as Book II of Euclid is added on to Book I, thus increasing our geometrical knowledge by a measurable proportion; it alters our knowing of everything that we thought we had known before. This, again, is not mere sentiment or theorizing; it is the experience of thousands whose eyes have been "opened" to the truth of Christ. The process of conversion brings about a total change of view: "whereas I was blind, now I see." "What the 'natural man' knows apart from Christ is not half the truth but distorted truth": to this extent we may agree with Brunner.[1] The "natural man" sees men as trees walking, and this seeing is itself possible only through the operation of God in general revelation; before he sees all things clearly he must encounter the touch of God's Messiah. Although all that we have said about the necessity and value of general revelation is true, it is also true that apart from faith in Christ there is no undistorted knowledge of God or of truth at all. Thus, special revelation is not a concrete illustration of general revelation, but a correction and transvaluation of it. General revelation is not and can never be the consummation of man's knowledge of God; it is only God's "point of connection" with men, and this is its essential character and *raison d'être*. It is the condition of Christ's speaking with man's soul, the jumping-off ground for the leap of faith in Christ. It is a means to an end, a *praeparatio evangelica*, a possibility of salvation; it is on the human side what makes man capable of responding to the challenge and summons of Christ.

This teaching concerning general revelation receives perhaps its clearest biblical expression in St. Paul's Epistle to the Romans. The Apostle agrees that the Gentiles, though entirely beyond the reach of the biblical message and knowing nothing of the Law of Moses, nevertheless do by nature the things of God's law, thereby proving that they are their own law—"a law unto themselves"; that is, he explains, they prove that the knowledge of divine law, what God requires of man, is written on their hearts, because their

[1] Emil Brunner, *The Mediator* (Eng. trans., 1934), p. 33.

conscience is their own inner witness to God's law when it approves or condemns their actions.[1] But the Gentiles do not obey the law that is in their hearts any more than the Jews obey the Law of Moses: "all have sinned and fall short of the glory of God".[2] Neither Jew nor Gentile can claim justification in the light of the law which he knows. Indeed, the Gentiles who have not the fuller and more austere Law of Moses to correct their aberrations, turn their knowledge of God's power and divinity, perceived through the works of His creation, into gross superstition; and they worship not God but the creatures He has made, and this leads to all kinds of unnatural, cruel and obscene excesses.[3] In the twentieth century we have had spectacular lessons in what happens when men worship the creature instead of the Creator; we cannot plead ignorance of the results of the worship of state, dictator, emperor, race, class, wealth, power, science, or any other creature.[4] Indeed, all history is a commentary upon the teaching of St. Paul.

The truth about human nature is enshrined in the biblical myths of the Creation and the Fall of Man. Man is made in the image of God, but through his fall into sin the image of God in him is damaged but not obliterated. If our foregoing description of the nature of general revelation be held to be in any way sound, it follows that the image of God in man is not totally destroyed by the Fall; there is that in man to which God can appeal and through which His grace can work.[5] Such powers as man retains of recognizing truth, beauty and righteousness, though he always sees them through the distorting medium of his own self-interest, are nevertheless the "vestiges" of the divine image, which is marred but not lost. The myth of the Fall utilizes the tale of an event in time ("in the beginning") to

[1] Rom. ii. 14f.        [2] Rom. iii. 23.        [3] Rom. i. 18ff.

[4] "The wish to worship a man seems to be more widespread now than it has been for centuries. The decay of faith in traditional Christianity has let in a flood of idolatry uglier far than any excess of nominally Christian superstition. . . . Voltaire and Helvetius, Huxley and Haeckel, laboured to destroy men's faith in the divinity of One who was indubitably good. And they succeeded so far that men now have faith in the divinity of those who are indubitably bad." Raymond Mortimer in *The New Statesman and Nation*, May 16th, 1936.

[5] For the true meaning of "Total Corruption" or "Total Depravity" see J. S. Whale, *Christian Doctrine* (Cambridge, 1941), pp. 41ff.

represent a truth of man's condition that is independent of time and is ingredient in all human living. It is a mythological way of speaking of an observable fact, namely, the universal human propensity to rebel against God's sovereignty by setting the self at the centre of the universe, which is the place that God alone can rightfully occupy. Thus, the Fall signifies no mere loss of a *donum superadditum,* an endowment of grace which was forfeited through man's lapse, leaving man's natural virtues and capacities (such as reason) intact. If we take the biblical myth of the Fall seriously, it follows that the rationalism of Thomistic or eighteenth-century theories of a natural or rational knowledge of God is based upon an unduly optimistic view of human nature. As a matter of everyday experience we do in fact find that men's reason is "conditioned" by their social environment and selfish interests and that in all their reasonings there is an element of rationalization; man's thinking is never quite immune from the irrationality intruded by his self-centredness: we see all things from the viewpoint of our own position falsely conceived to be at the centre of things. Reason itself must be justified by faith. What is true of reason is also true of conscience; our knowledge of the right becomes itself an occasion of pride and gives rise to self-righteousness and intolerance. Yet it remains true that human reason and conscience are the disfigured remnants of God's image in man. They are his "original righteousness", which should be mentioned also every time we speak of his "original sin". If man comes into the world with a propensity for selfishness, he possesses also within himself the means of knowing that selfishness is wrong. The high achievements of many forms of non-Christian humanism and of non-Christian ethical and religious systems demonstrate the reality of man's original righteousness and the fact that it has not been altogether lost; the divine grace given in general revelation is manifestly at work through them. But if human life is to be thoroughly redeemed and cleansed from sin, so that the Sun of Truth and Righteousness may shine forth in its might, a further grace is needed beyond that which is available in general revelation; and it is to the Christian understanding of a special revelation that we must now turn our attention.

# CHAPTER SIX

# SPECIAL REVELATION

## § 1. *The Special Revelation through the Biblical History*

WE HAVE seen that general revelation, though it is indispensable in the lives of individuals and societies, does not satisfy man's deepest need. It serves rather to make him more acutely aware of the necessity of a further revelation. When the Christian observer studies the religious condition of the non-Christian world or enters into discussion with his non-Christian friends, he is forced to the conclusion that general revelation hardly provides the means by which its own nature and implications may be rightly understood, and that its true significance is clearly perceivable only in the fuller light of the Christian revelation. The proper nature of general revelation is understood only from the standpoint of special revelation. If we may employ an analogy, general is related to special revelation as consciousness is related to self-consciousness. The latter presupposes the former, but the former can exist without the latter. There is no simple, quantitative or unbroken line of development from the former to the latter, since the latter is an emergently new kind of existence; there is a *saltus*, a leap from the one to the other. That which is emergently new cannot be explained in terms of what has gone before; the new fact must be accepted, as in other realms of scientific enquiry, "with natural piety", if we may apply Alexander's famous phrase.[1] From the standpoint of scientific or rational explanation, whatever comes into existence as emergently new is entirely unaccountable; it is

[1] The words are, of course, borrowed by Alexander from Wordsworth (*My Heart Leaps Up*). The expression "emergent" was taken over by Alexander from Lloyd Morgan (see S. Alexander, *Space, Time and Deity*, 1920, Vol. II, p. 14) and the concept of "emergence" became a key-category of his philosophy. The idea of "emergence" and the philosophy of "emergent evolution" may perhaps best be studied in C. Lloyd Morgan, *Emergent Evolution* (1923) and *Life, Mind and Spirit* (1926). A useful but perhaps too sweeping criticism will be found in W. McDougall, *Modern Materialism and Emergent Evolution* (1929).

sheer miracle, and we need not be surprised to find that theologians have in fact always so regarded the reception and enjoyment of special revelation. The result of the operation of special revelation upon the minds or souls of individuals is Christian faith. Just as the result of the operation of God in general revelation is active belief in truth, beauty and goodness and the recognition of obligation in the matter of the values, so also the result of special revelation is belief in Christ and the acceptance of responsibility in His Church.

According to the understanding of revelation which we have reached, Christian faith, which is the effect of the operation of special revelation upon us, is not to be conceived of as an addition to the natural knowledge, which we already possess, of super-natural knowledge about matters that are beyond the reach of human reason; it is rather a new seeing, a restoration of man's lost power of perceiving higher truth, a correction of the distortions of his perverted natural vision. Special revelation is no mere addition to general revelation, as revealed knowledge was formerly thought to be an addition to natural knowledge; it is rather the means by which the truths given in general revelation can be adequately apprehended and known to be true. Christian faith is thus the means by which, through the operation of special revelation, the general revelation of God may be assimilated by minds which have been darkened through sin. Hence faith is not a last resort which credulous men adopt when natural reason can take them no farther; it is the condition of the operation of the natural reason itself. Anyone who has been brought up in the assumptions of rationalism will doubtless find this conception of the nature and function of faith somewhat difficult to understand; but if he will attend to the criticisms of the older rationalism which have been brought forward by modern philosophers and to the teachings of the psychologists about the part played by faith in the act of understanding itself, he will soon learn to recognize analogies in many non-Christian spheres to the workings of Christian faith in the formulation of the Christian view of the world and its purpose. When a man embraces or is converted to a new point of view, he at once begins to interpret all history and all experience in the light of it. Marxists, for example, write Marxist history and even produce Marxist chemistry and Marxist mathematics. Similarly, and more commonly in this country, scientific humanists find in their view-point a convincing method of interpreting all things from religion to economics or biology in terms of their "liberal" assumptions. To have *some* faith or other is the condition of understanding, since faith supplies the key-category by means of which access to a unified view of things is gained; or, in a metaphor widely used nowadays, it provides the spectacles without which the truth of things cannot be seen at all. Thus arises what is to-day often spoken of as "the problem of communication": the Marxist, the secular humanist and the Christian all wear their own spectacles and therefore cannot see the truth which the others see.[1] Each inhabits his own universe of discourse and cannot understand the others' language. Here for the Christian (as for the others) arises the supreme difficulty in the task of evangelization, that of making real contact with those for whom the very language which one uses has no meaning because their thought-forms have been shaped by such widely differing assumptions. It is a difficulty which is not always appreciated by those who speak and write about evangelism, and consequently they often talk as if the truth of Christianity has only to be proclaimed in a sufficiently arresting manner in order to secure its glad acceptance by all rational and moral persons. The problem is, however, much more serious than this. It is not true that "we must needs love the highest when we see it", since the "natural man", even though possessing the help of general revelation, has lost the natural power of perceiving truth as it is.

[1] Miss Emmet rightly calls attention to the inadequacy of the spectacles-metaphor. "It is frequently urged, in reaction to what is called *Historismus*, or historical positivism, that a form of faith gives us the spectacles through which we can see events, and that without spectacles we could not see at all. The analogy is not a very good one. The function of spectacles is to correct distortions or blurring due to our personal defects in vision, so that we can see objects in sharp focus as they appear in 'standard' vision" (*The Nature of Metaphysical Thinking*, p. 163). The Christian view, of course, is that faith does thus correct the distortions and blurring of our natural seeing, so that we see the truth "in standard vision", that is, as God sees it. The analogy of spectacles also suggests another aspect of the matter: if I borrow my friend's spectacles, I do not see what he sees; I see a confused blur. But is not this precisely what seems to happen when a Marxist or a liberal-humanist tries to borrow a Christian's categories, or *vice versa*? Like all metaphors, that of our pair of spectacles is not entirely adequate, but, if not pressed too far, it is useful in its way.

The Christian understanding of special revelation is that in Christ the truth which man cannot see for himself without divine aid is presented through the operation of the divine grace.

One of the ways in which a faith-principle (such as that of Marxism or that of Christianity) commends itself to such reflective men as it attracts is by its ability to make a rational understanding of the universe possible. It must help in explaining all the facts without explaining them away. But before it can do this it must first formulate a judgment of significance and declare which of the countless millions of "facts" in history and life are the truly suggestive ones, by means of which our whole experience may be interpreted. Now Christian faith is bound to regard the existence in history and to-day of the Christian Church as being a fact of the utmost significance, because it is in the Christian Church that the existence of Christian faith is found. But the Church itself exists only where a proclamation of certain historical facts that are recorded in the Bible has been made: it does not arise by a process of spontaneous generation out of the natural religiosity of mankind. The believing Church is thus called into existence by the proclamation of an historical Gospel, and in no other way; special revelation, if such there be, must operate within the sphere of the Church through the proclamation of a message concerning things which have actually happened in time past. The vitality of the believing and witnessing Church in the present age will therefore be the clearest testimony to the truth of the historical message of which it is the bearer; the quality of the Church's witness, worship and fellowship will be the principal evidence of its possession of an enduring special revelation which creates the faith that bears such fruit. When skeptics try to dismiss Christian faith as "wishful thinking", their argument carries little conviction to those who know something of the quality of the life of the Church in the twentieth century: its power to overcome the antagonisms of race, nation and class, its strength to resist the most terrible persecuting fanaticisms, its ability to raise up men and women of prophetic insight or of pastoral devotion, its steady growth and penetration to every corner of the world. Those who stand outside the Church understand little of these things and are out of touch with the facts; and one of the principal tasks of the Christian apologist in every age is to call the attention of the world to the facts of what the Church is and is doing.[1]

The supreme apologetic value of the Church's life and witness has been noticed ever since the days of the Christian apologists of the second century. The apologists of the ancient Church were concerned not merely to demonstrate the intellectual superiority of Christian belief over Greek philosophy and pagan superstition; they were quick to point out the fruits of Christian faith in the fellowship, charity, mutual aid, self-restraint and self-forgetfulness of the whole Christian community. Thus, Justin Martyr addressing his *Apology* to the Emperor Antoninus Pius about A.D. 150 declared:

"Since our persuasion by the Word, . . . we who once used magical arts dedicate ourselves to the good and unbegotten God; we who valued above all things the acquisition of wealth and possessions now bring what we have into a common stock and communicate to everyone in need; we who hated and destroyed one another, and on account of their different manners would not share the same hearth with men of another tribe, now since the coming of Christ live on intimate terms with them, and pray for our enemies and endeavour to persuade those who hate us to live according to the good precepts of Christ, so that they may become partakers with us of the same joyful hope. . . ."[2]

About the same date another Christian apologist addressed a person of distinction in Roman society, who may perhaps have been the tutor of Marcus Aurelius; he appealed effectively to the witness of the Christian community in its daily life:

[1] It cannot be too strongly stressed that the Church's own life and witness are the true apology for the Christian faith. The facts of contemporary Church history should therefore be made known as widely as possible. The story of the Church's expansion and activity during the last century and a half and in our own days constitutes as impressive a record of victorious living as anything which previous centuries can show. Amongst recent short books dealing with this theme we may mention: H. P. Van Dusen, *What is the Church Doing?* and *They Found the Church There*; John Foster, *Then and Now* and *World-Church*; K. S. Latourette, *The Unquenchable Light*; E. A. Payne, *The Church Awakes*; W. A. Visser 't Hooft, *The Wretchedness and Greatness of the Church*.

[2] *Apol.* i. 14.

"(The Christians) obey the established laws, and they surpass the laws in their own lives. They love all men, and they are persecuted by all. . . . They are put to death, and yet they are endued with life. They are in beggary, and yet they make many rich. . . . They are reviled, and they bless; they are insulted and they respect. Doing good they are punished as evil-doers; being punished they rejoice, as if they were thereby quickened by life. . . . (Dost thou not see) them thrown to the wild beasts so that they may deny the Lord, and yet not overcome? Dost thou not see that the more of them are punished, just so many others abound? These things do not look like the works of man; they are the power of God; they are proofs of His presence."[1]

To such witness Christian apologists have been able to appeal in every century of Christian history. Our own time, the century of totalitarian barbarism and total war, is not lacking in the power of its testimony, and the twentieth century has added many immortal names to the calendar of the noble army of martyrs and confessors. The unique phenomenon of Christian faith and life extending across the centuries is the significant fact which must be explained. The testimony of those who have in every age translated into deeds and life the faith of the Church is the primary apologetic evidence of a continuing special revelation of God. It is a testimony which points unanimously to the origin of this faith and life in the historical events recorded in the Bible and culminating in the person and work of Jesus Christ:

> *"I ask them whence their victory came;*
> *They, with united breath,*
> *Ascribe their conquest to the Lamb,*
> *Their triumph to His death."*

The Christian Church was historically the outcome of a long series of events in the life-story of a particular nation, and its birth marked the moment at which the developing purpose manifest in the life of that nation overflowed into a supra-national and world-embracing purpose which still in the twentieth century is in process of fulfilling itself. The Church was not

---

[1] *Ep. Diog.*, v and vii.

brought into being by a group of philosophers or religious teachers who had agreed to adopt and propagate a certain set of ideas about God and the world. Nor was it the result of the flowering of men's religious consciousness in the personalities of a few religious geniuses who happened to have come together. "The one incontestable historical result of the ministry, death and resurrection of Jesus Christ was the emergence of the Christian Church."[1] It is clear that the special revelation which the Church claims as the open secret of its life and power was and is mediated through historical happenings at certain moments of the world's history; it did not originate in philosophical speculation or in general mystical or religious experience.

## § 2. *The Particularity of Special Revelation: Objections Answered*

The special revelation which Christianity claims to possess was thus mediated through the long series of events of Jewish history which culminated in Christ and His Church, as these events were interpreted by the prophets and apostles through whose witness the Bible came to be written. At this point the Christian apologist will have to meet a serious difficulty which this conception of special revelation raises for the modern mind. To many people in our times the position of supreme importance thus given to a particular section of the world's history, that is, to the history of a particular nation, constitutes an occasion of stumbling. Can we believe that God is revealed in the vicissitudes of Jewish history more than in the histories of other races and peoples? Is God not revealed also in the history of Egypt and Babylon, of Greece and Rome, of Britain and America? To the modern mind, with its desire to reduce all particular events to the pattern of a general law, the selection of Jewish history as the source of a special revelation seems arbitrary and irrational. The only way of meeting this objection is to invite the objectors to look at the facts, to make a study of the historical evidence. The facts themselves compel the admission that there is indeed a unique element in Jewish history, an ingredient that is not present in the history of Egypt, Babylon, Greece and Rome. This element is Hebrew prophecy, which is responsible (humanly speaking) for

[1] C. H. Dodd, *History and the Gospel* (London, 1938), p. 149.

the existence of the biblical record and revelation. There is no parallel to it in the history and religion of any other nation. It is in the succession of the prophets that the distinctive element of Hebrew history consists, that which differentiates it from all other history. No believer in God is so stupid as to assert that God Himself works in the history of the Hebrews alone; indeed, the Hebrew prophets themselves insist that God is the Lord of all history, and that He works through other nations and uses them as the instruments of His universal and sovereign purpose.[1] There is, as we have maintained, a general revelation of God's nature and purpose amongst all nations; but the historical truth would certainly seem to be that it was only amongst the Hebrew people that the inner significance of this general knowledge of God was perceived amidst the concrete situations and events of the life of a particular nation, and that this general revelation became, as it were, conscious of itself here and here alone in all world-history. This understanding and interpretation of history was the work of the Hebrew prophets, and it is a unique phenomenon in world-religion. Taught by the prophets the Hebrew people of Old Testament times, when they were true to themselves, were unique amongst the nations of the world in regarding themselves as bound in a Covenant-relationship to the God who was discerned to be the Lord of history and they thus recognized themselves to be committed to the realization of the will and purpose of God in their national life. In the great crises of Israel's history there arose a succession of prophets who interpreted to those who would listen what God was doing in the various upheavals and reconstructions of their life as a nation. It is an indisputable fact that such a prophetic interpretation of history arose in Israel and nowhere else. God indeed worked through Egypt, Babylon, Greece and Rome; but these nations and empires produced no prophets of the biblical type to interpret to them what God was doing; they remained blind to the operations of the Lord of history, and hence no special revelation came forth from them. The events of history as such do not themselves constitute a revelation; it is the prophetic interpretation of historical events which is the vehicle of special revelation in the sense in which the biblical and Christian tradition understands

[1] E.g. Amos ix. 7; Isa. x. 5, xlv. 1; Hab. i. 6; etc.

that conception. Where there are no prophets, there can be no special revelation. And if the phenomenon of prophecy is found nowhere except in the Jewish-Christian tradition, then we must cease to complain about "the scandal of particularity" and resolve to accept facts as facts, refusing to explain them away in obedience to a quite unscientific predilection for a general theory which was conceived before the facts were examined. If we ask why this special revelation or special type of the knowledge of God as active in history should have arisen in Israel only, or why other nations did not give birth to prophets of the biblical type, we are in the presence of mystery; we do not know the answer to this question, which must inevitably remain concealed within the secret counsels of God; this is the mystery of "election", which is not, after all, an invention of theologians but an admission that there are facts that we cannot explain but must not try to explain away. That we cannot explain why God chose the Jewish people to be the special instrument of His purpose in history is no reason for denying the plentiful evidence that He did so choose them.

In view of the remarkable history of the Jewish people over a period of three thousand years it ought not to seem strange to us that they should have some unique destiny to fulfil in the providence of God. In the light of the demonstrable fact that the Jews are a peculiar people out of all the peoples of the earth, the only surprising thing about the biblical view that their destiny is intimately bound up with God's purpose in history is that the modern man should be surprised at it. The history of other nations provides not even a single remote parallel to the phenomenon of Jewish existence down the ages and to-day. What other nation of antiquity has preserved its identity and character as the Jews have done, though exiled from their homeland and dispersed throughout the world? To-day there are British Jews, German Jews, Polish Jews, Portuguese Jews, American Jews, Brazilian Jews, Chinese Jews—and many others—and yet they are all recognizably Jews. Through centuries of persecution the Jewish race has survived the catastrophes which have so often destroyed the national identity of other peoples. Deliberate attempts to assimilate themselves into the country of their sojourning, whenever these have been made, have failed to eradicate their national identity. Religious or secularized, the Jew remains a

Jew—*malgré lui* a voluntary or involuntary witness to the truth that is symbolized in the story of God's Covenant with Abraham.[1] This striking fact of the persistence of the Jewish race has long been recognized as important evidence of the truth of the biblical interpretation of history. Writing more than two hundred years ago Bishop Butler stated the argument in the following manner:

"(The Jews are) dispersed through the most distant countries; in which state of dispersion they have remained fifteen hundred years: and . . . they remain a numerous people, united amongst themselves, and distinguished from the rest of the world . . .; and everywhere looked upon in a manner, which one scarce knows how to express, but in the words of the prophetic account of it, given so many ages before it came to pass: *Thou shalt become an astonishment and a proverb and a byword, among all the nations whither the Lord shall lead thee.*"[2]

Butler goes on to speak of "the appearance of a standing miracle in the Jews remaining a distinct people in their dispersion, and the confirmation which the event appears to give to the truth of revelation".[3] Like the Christian Church itself, the New Israel, the strange phenomenon of world-Jewry, as a fact of our own times, requires explanation, and it is inconceivable that any considerations of ethnology or racial biology will be sufficient to provide it. When Disraeli was asked what he thought was the most convincing proof of the existence of God, he replied, "The Jews".[4] It would seem that the Jewish people cannot escape their appointed mission of calling the attention of the rest of the world

[1] Gen. xvii.

[2] *The Analogy of Religion* (1736), Part II, Chap. vii. (ed. Halifax, *Butler's Works*, Vol. I, pp. 284f.). The quotation is from Deut. xxviii. 37.

[3] Long before Butler's time "the Jewish problem" had been discussed by the Church's thinkers and apologists. Thus, St. Augustine wrote (*Ep.* CXXXVII, iv. 16): "The Jewish nation, itself rejected because of unbelief, being now rooted out from its own land, is dispersed to every region of the world, in order that it may carry elsewhere the Holy Scriptures, and that in this way our adversaries themselves may bring before mankind the testimony furnished by the prophecies concerning Christ and His Church, thus precluding the possibility of the supposition that these predictions were forged by us to suit the time; in which prophecies also the unbelief of these very Jews is foretold."

[4] Cited in Otto Piper, *God in History* (New York, 1939), p. 103. The whole of Chapter V on "The Jewish Problem" is valuable in this connection.

to the truth that God exists and has a purpose in history which must be carried out; they remain scattered through all the world as a question addressed to every nation concerning its responsibility before the Lord of history. It is probable that those who raise the objection of "the scandal of particularity" have never seriously considered the deeper implications of "the Jewish problem". For that problem is not primarily a political, economic or racial problem, but a religious one. The particularity or uniqueness of the Jewish people is not something which has been invented by theologians in the interests of their doctrine of revelation; it is a startling fact of world history, a very special fact, and one which is taken fully into account in the Christian doctrine of a special revelation.

Objection is sometimes made to the view that there has been a special revelation of God through biblical history on the grounds that this implies sheer favouritism on the part of God, the capricious selection of a particular nation for preferential treatment. This objection is based upon ignorance of the facts of Old Testament history. Israel's history is indeed there revealed as little more than the register of the crimes, follies and misfortunes of mankind, even though on its pages the light of the prophetic understanding shines. Save for the brief period of the glory of King David's empire, the Hebrews hardly ever enjoyed peace and prosperity; they rarely experienced good government, and their country was for centuries the battle-ground of mighty foreign powers. After the exile they tasted only once for a brief spell under the Maccabees "the first of earthly blessings, independence". The Jewish nation did not receive preferential treatment but rather that kind of harsh handling amongst the nations which makes a people bitterly xenophobe; and thus we find in New Testament times that Jewish nationalism had hardened into the hatred and pride which eventually prompted the disastrous and hopeless rebellion against the occupying Roman power. Only the prophets and their faithful remnant were able to resist the pressure of historical circumstances towards national pride and exclusiveness, and it was the prophetic remnant alone which made possible a special revelation of God through the events of their nation's history. Sometimes we hear the Hebrews spoken of as if they were a race of religious geniuses, endowed with a remarkable faculty for the knowledge of God. There is nothing in the Bible to suggest such a notion, and the prophets themselves would have been astonished to hear it propounded. Their constant complaint was that their people, though possessing the means of knowing the one true God, did not care about Him or do His will. God worked through the Hebrew people as He worked through the Assyrians or Babylonians, that is, in spite of and not because of their attitude and conduct, save only in so far as the prophetic remnant was now and then able to make its influence felt. The events of the Old Testament history do not disclose that God worked in them in any other way than He worked in the history of other nations. It was not through the events alone but through their prophetic interpretation that the revelation of God's purpose came. God's judgment upon Jerusalem in 585 B.C. or in A.D. 70 is not different in kind from His judgment upon Babylon in 539 B.C. or upon Rome in A.D. 410— or for that matter upon Berlin and Tokyo in A.D. 1945. But the inhabitants of Babylon did not understand the significance of their fate at the hands of Cyrus because they had no prophets who could interpret it to them; whereas St. Augustine was able to interpret the divine verdict upon Rome because he had learnt from the Bible the prophetic view of history. We (if we will learn wisdom) may understand in fear and trembling the lesson of the fate of Berlin and Tokyo, precisely because through special revelation the prophetic record of the Bible shows us how to discern the signs of the times when Jerusalem was destroyed by Nebuchadnezzar or Titus. The Bible does not allow us to suppose that the divine requirement of righteousness was relaxed or the divine laws of judgment suspended on behalf of the Chosen People; whatever the divine election of the Jewish people may mean, it certainly did not mean preferential treatment for them. Indeed, the prophets strongly condemn the assumption of their contemporaries that there was any "most favoured nation clause" in their Covenant with Jehovah.[1] The only privilege which the Jew possessed was that to him first was given through the prophets the special knowledge of God, but it was a knowledge that was destined also for the Gentiles; and this kind of privilege is one from which in such a world as ours even the boldest hearts will shrink.

[1] Cf. Amos iii. 2, etc.

## § 3. *Historical Events and their Interpretation as Biblical Revelation*

It is not, then, the historical events as such which are themselves the content of the special revelation through history, since without the prophetic interpretation of events no revelation would be given through them. It must be in some way the whole complex of the events together with their interpretation which constitutes the revelation of God in history. The late Archbishop William Temple has discussed this question in his Gifford Lectures[1] and elsewhere,[2] and it will be profitable for us to consider his view of the nature of historical revelation. Rejecting the view that revelation is given to us in the form of propositions written down in a verbally inspired book, Dr. Temple roundly declares that "there is no such thing as revealed truth". He continues: "There are truths of revelation, that is to say, propositions which express the results of correct thinking concerning revelation; but they are not themselves directly revealed."[3] The importance of the correct formulation of these truths of revelation, of course, he emphatically affirms. But the formulation of the truth, whether in creeds or in systems of dogmatic theology, comes only after the original revelation has been given.[4] In what, then, does the revelation itself consist? Dr. Temple answers that revelation is given in historical events when the prophetic mind is present and able to appreciate and interpret their significance. Two things are thus requisite before there can be special revelation—the significant event and the mind which is able to appreciate it. Revelation results from "the coincidence of event and appreciation". "Its essence is intercourse of mind and event, not the communication of doctrine distilled from that intercourse."[5] Or, as Dr. Temple succinctly puts it elsewhere, "the essential condition of effectual revelation is the coincidence of divinely controlled event and minds divinely illumined to read it aright".[6]

[1] *Nature, Man and God* (1934), Lecture XII.

[2] See especially Dr. Temple's essay in *Revelation* (ed. Baillie and Martin, 1937).

[3] *Nature, Man and God*, p. 317.

[4] *Ibid.*, p. 322.

[5] *Ibid.*, p. 316.

[6] *Revelation, op. cit.*, p. 107.

KCA

Revelation is thus due to the twofold form of the activity of God: God controls the historical events which constitute the *media* of revelation, and He also inspires the minds of the prophets and thus enables them to interpret the events aright. "He guides the process; He guides the minds of men; the interaction of the process and the minds which are alike guided by Him is the essence of revelation."[1]

The Archbishop's view has undoubted advantages over the older view which was based upon the assumption that the Bible contained a written revelation given in propositional form, and it also avoids the error of attempting to locate the revelation in the religious experience of the prophets and apostles. The revelation is firmly grounded in history; it is based on events which have actually happened. Dr. Temple considers that the historical event is the objective element in revelation, which is thus not merely a subjective matter of the visions and experiences of a number of religious geniuses. There must be an objective element (the historical event) and a subjective element (the prophetic appreciation and interpretation) in every specific instance of special revelation.[2] Thus Dr. Temple seeks to safeguard the objectivity of the Christian revelation. But in doing so he over-simplifies the problem; for when we say that the historical event guarantees the objectivity of the revelation we are concealing the ambiguity of the word "history", which means either the sequence of the events as they occurred or our knowledge of the events, written or remembered. Doubtless history in the former sense was the original object of the interpreted revelation, but our knowledge of the event cannot be simply described as objective. We know of what happened only through the written and interpreted (and therefore subjectivized) history of the biblical record. As we have previously seen, not only does the significance of the event for us depend upon our (or the prophets') admittedly subjective interpretation of it, but the very nature of the event, or even whether it occurred at all, is bound up (as far as our knowledge of it is concerned) with our (or the prophets') subjective appreciation of it. We cannot thus divide the content of revelation into history and interpretation, the

---

[1] *Nature, Man and God,* p. 312.
[2] *Ibid.,* p. 318; *Revelation, op. cit.,* pp. 103f.

objective and the subjective; whatever history in the former sense of the word may be, history in the second sense, written history, is never simply "objective". Any account of historical events is conditioned by the principle of interpretation that has been adopted in the presentation of them. If we do not accept the biblical or prophetic principle of interpretation, it is unlikely that we shall accept the biblical record as true or "objective" history. This does not mean that no historical account can be said to be more objectively true than another; it means that we must revise our notion of what objectivity in history-writing is. We must abandon a "correspondence theory" of truth in favour of a "coherence theory" of truth or objectivity. It is not that a true account will not be one that corresponds with the facts that happened, but that since we can never know directly the facts which happened, correspondence is for us no criterion of objectivity at all. The criterion of objectivity in history-writing will be rather coherence or rationality; a true history will be one which gives us the most coherently rational account of the facts, and it will do this because of the soundness of its principle of interpretation. The right principle of interpretation in history will be the one which gives us the most satisfactorily reasonable account of the events of history. It is the principle of interpretation which illuminates the past and makes sense of it; and of this our reason will judge by the test of coherence. We may therefore, if we wish, speak of the objectivity of the principle of interpretation in history, since it is this which gives objectivity to our knowledge of the events that have occurred in the past. Christians claim that the biblical principle of interpretation, as developed by the prophets and apostles, gives to us, when we accept it, the guarantee that the facts recorded in the Bible are broadly historical. It enables us to explain them coherently and rationally, without having to explain them away, and judged by the test of coherence it is more successful than any other interpretation.

Thus, we cannot assent to a dichotomy of event and interpretation, regarding the former as objective and the latter as subjective. The event and its interpretation are much too closely bound together, so far as our knowledge is concerned. Dr. Temple's view is, after all, only a variant of the Ritschlian theory of the distinction between "theoretical judgments" and "value judgments". Seeking to escape from the subjectivism of Schleier-macher, for whom theological truth was given in the religious consciousness, the followers of Ritschl found that the objectivity of revelation was guaranteed by the historical events through which it had been received. "Theoretical judgments" were ordinary judgments of fact, such as a secular historian might make (for example, "Jesus died on Calvary"), and were the scientific basis of theology; "value judgments" were the assessments of the religious meaning of such facts for the individual personally (for example, "Jesus died for me"), and can be made only through the illumination of our minds by divine revelation. Through revelation we know the meaning of the biblical events, and we know the nature of God and Christ only in their worth for us. Dogmatic theology is the clarification and formulation of these value judgments, or personal convictions (which, says Dr. H. R. Mackintosh,[1] is what the expression "value judgments" means in plain English). The consequences of this false distinction between judgments of fact and judgments of value have proved a veritable *hereditas damnosa* in subsequent theological discussion. From it springs directly the false contrast between the "simple Gospel" of Jesus and the "theology" of the apostolic Church. The true Gospel is regarded as consisting in the simple facts about and teachings of the historical Jesus, who can thus be objectively portrayed by modern historical research, while the interpretations of St. Paul and the other apostles may be discarded as representing values for them which are no longer values for us. Hence the Ritschlians present the history of Christian dogma as pronouncing its own condemnation in the eyes of all unprejudiced Christian people.[2] Harnack worked out this view with massive thoroughness in the learned volumes of his *History of Dogma*. The Creed of Nicea, the formulary of Chalcedon, the dogmatic writings of the Fathers, even the Epistles of St. Paul, represent "the work of the spirit of a decadent antiquity on the soil of the Gospel". The chief emphasis is placed upon the contrast between the original Gospel of Jesus and the theological interpretations of the Church, between the Sermon on the Mount and the Nicene Creed. "The one belongs to a world of Syrian peasants, the other to a world of

[1] *Types of Modern Theology* (London, 1937), p. 153.
[2] Cf. A. E. Garvie, *The Ritschlian Theology* (Edinburgh, 1899), p. 101.

Greek philosophers."[1] Thus, it was thought necessary to separate the kernel from the husk, to get back behind "the religion about Jesus" to "the religion of Jesus". The apostles ought to have been content to report the words and record the deeds of Jesus, instead of becoming, as they did, interpreters of the significance and value of His person.[2] So we come to the familiar antithesis, beloved still to-day of the rationalist press, between Jesus and Paul: Jesus taught a simple, ethical monotheism; Paul invented Christology and is the real founder of Christianity. Paul was the first on the basis of the death and resurrection of Jesus to develop a theology as a means of separation from the religion of the Old Testament.[3] Not dogmas but value-judgments were the fruits of revelation, and so Ritschl refused to discuss such doctrines as the pre-existence of Christ, or the Two Natures in Christ, or the relation of the Persons within the Trinity, as having no real bearing upon our experience and as therefore lying beyond our range;[4] we understand Christ's person and nature by understanding what He has done for men, by His worth for our own souls, by recognizing that He has done for us what only God can do.

Thus, according to the Ritschlian theology revelation is given in the formation of true judgments of value upon certain historical events or deeds. It is an error to suppose that the Ritschlians thought that judgments of fact were more important than judgments of value, or that judgments of value were false because they were subjective. They were trying to safeguard the objectivity of the facts themselves, as existing independently of the wishes of the believer. They thus placed great emphasis upon the historical character of the revelation, and they held that historical research, being scientific and independent of all value-judgments, could put an end to subjective speculation and free us from all the "accretions" of traditional dogma. Hence the importance of "the quest of the historical Jesus". Sometimes the followers of Ritschl go so far as to speak of the historical facts as

[1] Hatch's Hibbert Lectures (1888), p. 1.

[2] Garvie, *op. cit.*, p. 117.

[3] Cf. A. Harnack, *History of Dogma* (Eng. trans., 1894), Vol. I, p. 87.

[4] Of course, the Ritschlians as a school did not necessarily follow Ritschl in regarding all these doctrines as having little relevance or value.

being themselves the revelation, a view which, it should be noted, Dr. Temple carefully avoids, though he seems to come near it when he speaks of the Incarnation as "objective".[1] Dr. H. R. Mackintosh characterizes this aspect of the Ritschlian thesis thus: "The argument as actually unfolded often appears to rest on the assumption that the Person and life-work of Jesus confront us as a homogeneous piece of 'profane' history, the divine import of which is accessible to direct historical inspection, or can be made plain by sober rational deduction from obvious facts. The facts simply *qua* history are revelation."[2] But in fairness it should be pointed out that Ritschlians like Herrmann well knew that revelation cannot be understood as an historical event of the remote past, but only as a personal experience of the immediate present, and thus they emphasize the value-judgment as the product in the heart of the believer of the operation of the revealing Spirit of God. They are aware that many able and well-disposed minds have looked at the historical facts and have found no revelation in them; and they have insisted that the faith by which the historical facts become revelation for us is the result of the divine illumination of our eyes. When this admission is pressed to its logical conclusion, it is seen, as we have noted, that our very view of the facts themselves, or of recorded history, is altered; the distinction between judgments of fact regarded as objective and judgments of value regarded as subjective can no longer be maintained, and the illusion of "objective" or un-interpreted history is finally swept away. The facts of history cannot be disentangled from the principles of interpretation by which alone they can be presented to us *as history*, that is, as a coherent and connected series or order of events. Christian faith supplies the necessary principle of interpretation by which the facts of the biblical and Christian history can be rationally seen and understood. No other principle of interpretation can give us so reasonable a view of the facts which the prophetic and apostolic witnesses record. As we have noted in a previous chapter, the rejection of the apostolic interpretation of the Gospel facts led inevitably to skepticism about the possibility of our knowledge of the historical Jesus; and the view that after making a dis-interested study of the "objective facts" of the Gospel history

[1] *Revelation, op. cit.,* p. 104.          [2] *Types of Modern Theology,* p. 178.

we should then be able to make a re-interpretation or re-valuation of the real, historical Jesus led in the end of the day to the strange conclusion that the truth about Jesus can never be discovered by historical science but must come in a blinding and compelling flash of insight, like a bolt from the blue, and that Jesus the Word must stand proxy for the vanished Jesus of history.[1]

## § 4. *Biblical History as the Source of Christian Doctrine*

Thus, our view of special revelation is that it arises from the prophetic insight of men whose minds are illuminated by the Spirit of God as they wrestle with the problem of interpreting God's will in the midst of the concrete historical situation of their own day. It is in thus seeking the will of God that a new and deeper revelation of the character and purpose of God is given to them. Their faithful obedience is rewarded by clearer understanding. It was in the midst of the upheavals and crises of Israel's history that the prophets of the Old Testament, as they sought to find and to teach God's will in days of confusion and perplexity, first enunciated that biblical conception of God as righteous and merciful which the New Testament deepened and enlarged but did not outgrow. In the same way the apostolic bearers of the Christian Gospel, and those who were responsible for the formulation and writing down of the apostolic message in the New Testament, interpreted the crisis of Jewish history in the first century A.D., finding in the teaching and work of Jesus the clue not only to God's judgment upon the disobedient Jewish people—and therefore by implication upon the sin of the whole world—but also His purpose of restoration and forgiveness for mankind in the setting up of the New Israel, the Church of Jesus Christ. Special revelation is thus revelation in and through history, received in the first instance in the act of seeking and obeying the will and purpose of God, usually in times of change and crisis and bewilderment; it is received by those who are themselves wholly involved in the situation, not by detached philosophical minds coolly making rational inferences from or

[1] Cf. R. Bultmann, *Jesus* (Berlin, 1929); Eng. trans., *Jesus and the Word* (London, 1935). See the critical note on Bultmann's view in E. Brunner, *The Mediator* (Eng. trans., 1934), p. 157n.

passing "value-judgments" upon "objective" historical events. That is to say, the biblical revelation was originally received existentially, and it must be received in every subsequent age of the Church also existentially—by those who are themselves seeking to find and to teach the will of God in the actual historical situation which confronts them in their own day. It is in this way that the Christian knowledge of God comes into being—in the first or in the twentieth century.

Though it is given in history and provides for us an interpretation of historical events, special revelation gives us an insight into other kinds of truth than the truth of history. Because it gives us knowledge of the character and purpose of God, it is the source of Christian doctrine in its entirety. Dr. Leonard Hodgson's recent book on *The Doctrine of the Trinity* shows us very clearly how such a doctrine as that of the triune being of God is formulated upon the basis of the historical revelation given in and through the biblical events: "it could not have been discovered without the occurrence of those events which drove human reason to see that they required a trinitarian God for their cause".[1] Even doctrines like that of the creation of the world by God, which do not at first sight appear to be grounded upon any observed historical event, are nevertheless given in special revelation through history. This is one of those doctrines which Ritschl in his reaction from speculative rationalism would have considered beyond the range of our experience and value-judgments; and it would seem to be beyond the range of our knowledge in any sense, if we take literally Dr. Temple's statement that revelation occurs only when there is a coincidence of the significant event and the mind illumined to read it aright, since no prophet was present at the creation of the world. We might think that, having abandoned the literalist view of the scriptural revelation, there were no longer any grounds for regarding the doctrine of the creation of the world as given to us by revelation at all. St. Thomas Aquinas, indeed, thought that, were it not for the scriptural revelation, we could not have known the doctrine of creation to be true, since natural reason would lead us (as it led Aristotle and Averroes) to the opposite doctrine of the eternity of the world of matter. Reason, he held, could not disprove the Aristotelian doctrine of the

---

[1] L. Hodgson, *The Doctrine of the Trinity* (London, 1943), p. 25.

eternity of the world, though it did not absolutely necessitate it; but, at the behest of Scripture, St. Thomas loyally but reluctantly accepted the truth of the doctrine of creation *ex nihilo*. To-day, however, philosophy is not dominated by Aristotle interpreted in the direction of Averroistic materialism, and it is widely held that the conception of creation and creativity is a valuable contribution of Christian theology to philosophical understanding. But in what sense can we regard the idea of creation as a truth of revelation given in history? The answer, which can be stated only briefly here, will be found in a study of the Bible itself, beginning with the great prophets of the Old Testament, and especially the Second Isaiah. Jehovah had been encountered by the prophets as the Lord of history, the almighty ruler of the destinies of the nations; and it was inevitable that they should conclude that the world of nature, the theatre and stage of history, was also under the sovereign control of the same Lord. Moreover, in their understanding of the commanding and creative word of God, which spoke through them and which utterly accomplished the divine will in history, it was inevitable that they should recognize also the power which controlled the forces of nature as well as the rise and fall of nations, beside whom the fertility-baals and foreign deities were no gods at all. The doctrine of the God who creates the world by the word of His mouth is necessarily involved in the prophetic knowledge of the Lord of history. But, of course, the knowledge of God as the Creator of the world was possessed long before the times of the great prophets, since the J narratives of Genesis are some centuries older than these; how this knowledge was attained we can but infer by analogy from the writings of the later prophets by whom it was fully developed. As with the Old Testament prophets, so in the New Testament, the encounter with the creative word of God in history served to deepen for the apostolic Church the knowledge of God as Creator: the apostles had seen God by the power of His incarnate Word bringing into being a New Creation, the Church of those who knew themselves to be a new creation in Christ. In this kind of way the biblical doctrines of the Church are developed from the special revelation of God given in the prophetic and apostolic history which the Bible records.

# CHAPTER SEVEN

# THE ARGUMENT FROM MIRACLE

## § 1. *The Traditional Rôle of Miracle in Christian Apologetics*

UNTIL THE nineteenth century it was generally agreed by Christian theologians, Catholic and Protestant alike, that the divine revelation given in the Scriptures was divinely guaranteed by the supernatural evidences of miracle and prophecy. A supernatural revelation, it was held, required supernatural testimonies to demonstrate its authority to rational beings. In so far as Christians believed truths which were beyond the power of reason to establish, it was held to be reasonable to believe them because they had been attested by the divinely given signs of miracle and prophecy. Miracle and prophecy were thus regarded as the "external evidences" of revelation, and hence the argument from miracle and the argument from prophecy have played a very important part in traditional Christian apologetic down the centuries. We must ask what part they can play to-day in the task of Christian apologetics in the twentieth century, having regard to our altered views concerning the nature of the scriptural revelation.

It is essential that we should realize at the outset that in the traditional theological scheme miracles were thought to be necessary to safeguard the rationality of revelation. They were not irrational and inexplicable irruptions into the natural order; as St. Augustine is fond of repeating, miracles are not contrary to nature but only to what is known by us about nature.[1] Thus, a gramophone is a terrifying miracle from the standpoint of a savage; the cure of certain maladies by means of mental or spiritual agencies is still a miracle from ours. There is much in nature which in view of our limited knowledge in the field of

---

[1] E.g. *De Civ. Dei*, Bk. XXI, Chap. viii: "A miracle (*portentum*) is not contrary to nature, but to what is known of nature" (*fit non contra naturam, sed contra quam est nota natura*); *Con. Faust. Manich.*, xxvi. 3: "We do not say that God does something contrary to nature because He acts in a way that is contrary to our knowledge of nature."

empirical science must be deemed miraculous; from the stand-point of science certain things are miraculous to-day which may not appear miraculous to the scientists of to-morrow. The workings of the homing instincts of bees or pigeons, for example, will cease to be sheer miracle to us when scientists can give us a full account of them. In the nature of the case "science" as such can have no objection to the conception of miracle as it is under-stood in traditional theology, for miracle is merely that which occurs according to the operation of those laws of nature which are as yet unknown to us; every day scientists are enlarging our knowledge of the workings of nature. From the standpoint of God Himself, there can be no such thing as "miracle" in this sense, since if God is God, He must *ex hypothesi* know how all the laws of nature work; but from our standpoint, even though we make the fullest allowances for all the achievements of man's scientific discoveries, it is probable that the concept of miracle will be necessary yet for a long time to come.

There is, however, another sense in which the words "miracle" and "miraculous" may legitimately be used. The miraculous is that which arouses in us the feeling of wonder, of awe, and even of humility in its presence. This is the kind of emotion which, for example, the contemplation of the starry heavens aroused in the hearts of such diverse observers as the Hebrew Psalmist and Immanuel Kant.[1] It is also the kind of response which every new scientific discovery awakens in the hearts of thinking men and women; scientific knowledge does not remove but heightens our sense of wonder and increases our appreciation of the mystery of things. Science and poetry do not belong to two worlds but to one. A gramophone or a radio set is no less miraculous to a man of science than to a savage, if we use the word "miraculous" in this second sense. A Christian who is also a scientist can at this point contribute much to the argument of a general religious apologetic by developing the implications of this deep human insight, but the development of such an argument falls beyond the scope of our purpose in this place. But we must note that the traditional Christian theology, particularly in its Augustinian form, has always laid great stress upon the fact that the whole universe is

[1] Ps. viii. 3f.; *Critique of Practical Reason* (Conclusion) (T. K. Abbott, *Kant's Theory of Ethics*, 6th Ed., 1923, p. 260).

miraculous in this sense, becoming for us more and not less miraculous as our knowledge of its processes increases. All the miraculous things which happen in this world, said St. Augustine, are not so miraculous as the universe itself, our whole heaven and earth and all that is in them; and all the miraculous things which man by his skill and science can work are not so great a miracle as is man himself.[1] All the miraculous things in the world are themselves a part of the general revelation of the everlasting power and divinity of the Creator. Similarly within the sphere of special revelation, which is our proper concern in this chapter, it is Christ Himself, rather than any of the things which He did, who is the supreme miracle and the chief attestation of the truth of the biblical revelation.

Thus, so far from regarding the miraculous as being in any way opposed to reason or to nature, traditional Christian theology has always regarded the miracles as the rational grounds by means of which reasonable men may believe truths which go beyond the power of reason to establish. On this basis one of the principal arguments for the belief in the superiority of Christianity over Mohammedanism was developed in the Middle Ages. St. Thomas Aquinas pointed out that Mohammed had won men to his allegiance by promising carnal delights, whereas the greatest of all the Christian miracles was that Christianity effected the conversion on a vast scale of wise and simple alike, despite the fact that it promised not carnal but spiritual rewards—with persecutions. This "wondrous conversion of the world to the Christian faith" is proof that the miraculous signs did take place and were seen to guarantee the truth of the revelation in Christ. Mohammed had had to rely not merely on carnal promises but also on fables; "nor did he add any signs of supernatural agency, which alone are a fitting witness to divine inspiration, since a visible work that can be from God alone proves the teacher of truth to be invisibly inspired: but he [Mohammed] asserted that

[1] *De Civ. Dei*, Bk. X, Chap. xii: "Is not the universe itself a miracle, yet visible and of God's making? Nay, all the miracles done in this world are less than the world itself, the heaven and earth and all therein; yet God made them all, and after a manner that man cannot conceive or comprehend. For though these visible miracles of nature be now no more admired, yet ponder them wisely, and they are more astonishing than the strangest: for man is a greater miracle than all that he can work."

he was sent in the power of military arms—a sign that is not lacking even to robbers and tyrants."[1] So universally did it continue to be held amongst theologians that it is reasonable to expect supernatural evidences to authenticate a supra-rational revelation that in a later century we find Richard Hooker applying the principle as a test for the authority of a Reformer's teaching:

"When God Himself doth of Himself raise up any, whose labour He useth without requiring that men should authorize them; but then He doth ratify their calling by manifest signs and tokens Himself from heaven: and thus even such as believed not our Saviour's teaching, did yet acknowledge Him a lawful teacher sent from God: 'Thou art a teacher sent from God, otherwise none could do those things which Thou doest' (John iii. 2). Luther did but reasonably therefore, in declaring that the senate of Mulheuse should do well to ask of Muncer, from whence he received his power to teach, who it was that had called him; and if his answer were that God had given him his charge, then to require at his hands some evident sign thereof for men's satisfaction: because so is God wont, when He Himself is the author of any extraordinary calling."[2]

In the eighteenth century the deists held that it was not necessary to believe in miracles because they thought that it was not necessary to believe in a supernatural revelation at all: the natural reason could establish all the truth that men can know or need to know, without any help from a supernatural revelation. We may notice that the deistic rejection of miracles does not arise from any historical examination of the evidence but rather as a result of a philosophical consideration of our knowledge of God based upon the accepted principles of the thought of the day; the point is important, because there is here a close parallel to certain developments of the thought of our own age. It should furthermore be noted that the deistical movement of the eighteenth century was the first serious and sustained attempt in the

---

[1] *Contra Gentiles,* Bk. I, Chap. vi.
[2] *The Laws of Ecclesiastical Polity,* Bk. VII, Chap. xiv.

history of Christian thought to disavow belief in the biblical miracles. Both orthodox and heretic had previously agreed that the miracles as such had actually happened; even the enemies of Jesus in the flesh had not denied that He worked miracles.[1] Since the triumph of Christianity in the ancient world, only a few individual skeptics had within Christendom denied the historicity of the Gospel miracles. The disavowal of the miracles by those who generally styled themselves Christians occurred first as the consequence of a view of our knowledge of God which set aside the classical Christian conception of a supernatural revelation and was itself derived from the rationalism of the new philosophy of Descartes and his successors.[2] Supernatural revelation, if it had occurred at all, was merely a "republication of the religion of nature"[3] designed by a benevolent Deity for the benefit of those whose natural reason was too feeble or bemused to be able to think out the content of the religion of nature for themselves. Philosophers could get along without it and therefore also without the supernatural signs or miracles which were alleged to have accompanied it and were adduced to attest it. A religion of reason needs no miraculous attestation. Bishop Butler, although he went far towards the acceptance of deistical notions and to a marked degree shared the outlook of his opponents, could yet find a place for miracle in his world-view because he did not believe that natural reason could supply us with the whole of our knowledge of God. The width of the common ground which he shared with the deists, as well as his divergence from them, is amply illustrated by the following characteristic passage:

[1] Cf. Mark iii. 22.

[2] By "rationalism" is here meant the view which considers truth to be discoverable, or the limits of understanding to be ascertainable, by means of the operation of or the examination of the human reason alone, apart from "faith", "grace", etc. In this sense the term may be applied to the views of Locke and Hume as well as to those of Descartes and Spinoza. Locke himself did not find miracles incredible; the "external evidences of religion"—miracle and prophecy —convinced his reason of the authority of the Scriptural revelation. Cf. his *Reasonableness of Christianity* (1695). For Hume's view see p. 161 (*infra*), footnote.

[3] This famous phrase is taken over from Matthew Tindal, whose volume *Christianity as Old as the Creation; or the Gospel a Republication of the Religion of Nature* (1730) is probably the work that Butler had in mind more than any other when he wrote his *Analogy* (1736).

"Though natural Religion is the foundation and principal part of Christianity, it is not in any sense the whole of it. Christianity is a republication of natural Religion. It instructs mankind in the moral system of the world: that it is the work of an infinitely perfect Being . . .; that virtue is His law. . . . And, which is very material, it teaches natural Religion in its genuine simplicity; free from those superstitions, with which it was totally corrupted, and under which it was in a manner lost. Revelation is farther, an authoritative publication of natural Religion, and so affords the evidence of testimony for the truth of it. Indeed the miracles and prophecies recorded in Scripture, were intended to prove a particular dispensation of Providence, the redemption of the world by the Messiah. . . . The Law of Moses then, and the Gospel of Christ, are author-itative publications of the religion of nature; they afford a proof of God's general providence, as moral Governor of the world, as well as his particular dispensations of providence towards sinful creatures, revealed in the Law and the Gospel. As they are the only evidence of the latter, so they are additional evidence of the former."[1]

Butler, it is apparent, was prepared to go a long way with the deists in their high estimate of the place of reason in religion, but he comes down decisively on the side of the classical Christian conception of revelation as attested by miracle. To twentieth-century ears it sounds strange that any Christian should consider it irrational to accept the "mere word" of Jesus Christ unless His authority were demonstrated by miraculous signs; yet Butler, like St. Thomas, urges that the scale of the conversion wrought by the original preaching of Christianity shows that it must have been accompanied by compelling evidences—"approving itself to the reason of mankind and carrying its own evidences with it . . . and being in no way contrary to reason in those parts of it which require to be believed upon the mere authority of its Author".[2] Where reason cannot prove, miracle must. And we may note that, though he holds that we have "strong historical evidence" that

[1] *The Analogy of Religion*, Part II, Chap. i (ed. S. Halifax, 1874, Vol. I, pp. 154f.).
[2] *Analogy*, Part II, Chap. vii (*op. cit.*, p. 284).

the miracles really happened, Butler no more than his adversaries bases his argument upon historical investigations but like them upon philosophical considerations. At least there is this to be said in favour of the eighteenth-century approach to the subject: theology had not yet fallen into the delusion which became so prevalent in the nineteenth century, namely, that the question whether the miracles really happened could be settled by the objective and dispassionate methods of historical research.

Bishop Butler's view in the end triumphed over the deists, and we find that the traditional conception of a supra-rational revelation, guaranteed by supernatural signs, survived until well into the nineteenth century as the dominant view among English theologians. As recently as 1865 it was possible for a Bampton Lecturer to maintain before the University of Oxford the view that Christianity was superior to Mohammedanism because it could appeal to the witness of the miracles, whereas the latter could adduce no such testimony. This view, as we saw, had been put forward in the Middle Ages, when Mohammedanism presented a serious menace and a living challenge to Christian theologians. In the days of Aquinas, Islam, with its missionary fervour and military potential, aroused a nervous apprehensiveness amongst the conservatives and a revolutionary fascination amongst intellectuals comparable to the emotional and intellectual disturbance which Marxist Russia created in Western Europe in the years after the October Revolution; the latter period was, like the thirteenth century, a time of rapid social and economic evolution and of new modes of thought which necessitated (as many supposed) the "reconstruction" of Christian theology. Although the special circumstances which made Christian apologetic against the Mohammedans an urgent matter in the Middle Ages had along ago passed away, we find Dr. Mozley repeating—whether consciously or unconsciously does not appear —the argument of Aquinas as though it were an obvious and established truth of Christian apologetic and using it to demonstrate the inevitability and rationality of the Christian belief in the historicity of the biblical miracles. Mohammedanism, he says, is inferior to Christianity as a rational belief, because the former expects its supernatural revelation to be accepted on the mere word of Mohammed alone, which, says Dr. Mozley, "shews an utterly barbarous idea of evidence and a total miscalculation of the claims of reason which unfits his religion for the acceptance of an enlightened age and people; whereas the Gospel is adapted to perpetuity for this cause especially, with others, that it was founded upon a true calculation, and a foresight of the permanent need of evidence; our Lord admitting the inadequacy of His own mere word, and the necessity of a rational guarantee to His revelation of His own nature and commission (John xv. 24 and v. 36)."[1]

## § 2. *The Inadequacy of the Modern Alternative*

As Archdeacon A. L. Lilley pointed out in his Paddock Lectures,[2] the mere statement of Dr. Mozley's view amply demonstrates the immense distance traversed by English theology during the last two or three generations; but we must add that there is a truth behind Dr. Mozley's contention which has not been so completely disposed of as perhaps the Archdeacon supposed. Moreover, Dr. Mozley's argument is in general a faithful summary of the views of Christian apologists and theologians from the early Fathers to the leaders of the Oxford Movement and their contemporaries.[3] There would thus seem to be a considerable

[1] J. B. Mozley, *Eight Lectures on Miracles* (Bampton Lectures, 1865), pp. 31f.

[2] *Religion and Revelation* (London, 1932), p. 7.

[3] Some illustrative quotations may be added. "In what way can a revelation be made but by miracles? In none which we are able to conceive. Consequently in whatever degree it is possible, or not very improbable, that a revelation should be communicated to mankind at all, in the same degree it is probable or not very improbable, that miracles should be wrought" (Archdeacon Wm. Paley, *Evidences of Christianity*, Preparatory Considerations). "No religion could claim authority over the conscience which had no higher evidence to offer than the probabilities of human reasoning" (R. Payne-Smith, Regius Professor of Divinity, Oxford, *Prophecy a Preparation for Christ*, Bampton Lectures, 1869, p. viii). It is amusing to note the impeccable orthodoxy of the concluding sentences of Hume's skeptical essay *Of Miracles*: "Upon the whole we may conclude that the Christian religion not only was at first attended with miracles, but even at this day cannot be believed by any reasonable person without one. Mere reason is insufficient to convince us of its veracity. And whoever is moved by faith to assent to it, is conscious of a continued miracle in his own person, which subverts all the principles of his understanding, and gives him a determination to believe what is most contrary to custom and experience."

LCA

discrepancy between the attitude of many modern writers and that of traditional Christian thought upon the subject of miracle. To-day we frequently hear it said that we do not believe in the Christian revelation because it was attested by miracles in the giving of it, but that we believe in miracles (in so far as we believe in them at all) because we are convinced "on other grounds" of the fact that a revelation took place. We believe in the Incarnation of the Son of God not because of His alleged miraculous birth or the wonders that He is reported to have worked, but rather we believe in the Virgin Birth or the miracles (if we believe in them at all) because of our prior conviction concerning the truth of the Incarnation.[1] The "other grounds" usually mentioned for our belief in the Christian revelation or in such doctrines as that of the Incarnation generally appear to be the powerful appeal which Jesus makes to the spiritual, rational and moral consciousness of mankind. This modern view is, of course, the precise opposite of the traditional view.[2] St. Thomas, Bishop Butler and Dr. Mozley, as we have seen, agree in holding it to be irrational, even superstitious, to believe in the Christian revelation upon the "mere word" of Jesus alone. Hooker had agreed with Luther in thinking it preposterous that Muncer should have expected to be believed unless he could produce a sign that his revelation was authentic, just as St. Thomas and Dr. Mozley concur in holding that Mohammed's claim to have set forth a supernatural revelation must be disallowed because of his failure to produce supernatural evidence of its truth. The "mere word" of a prophet was not sufficient to establish theological truth. Rational men will ask for rational signs for the truth of all propositions that go beyond

---

[1] "It must be recognized that as regards the abnormal events recorded in the Gospels, a belief as to the Person of our Lord, which must mainly be reached on other grounds, constitutes a part of the ground for belief in their miraculous character. A similar principle must be applied in consideration of other events alleged to be miraculous" (*Doctrine in the Church of England*, Report of the Archbishops' Commission, 1938, p. 52).

[2] Cf. Bishop Butler: "There are also invisible miracles, the Incarnation of Christ, for instance, which being secret, cannot be alleged as a proof of such a (Divine) mission, but require themselves to be proved by visible miracles. Revelation itself is miraculous, and miracles are the proof of it" (*Analogy*, Part II, Chap. ii; *op. cit.*, p. 174).

the limits of natural reason, and the deists were able to dispense with miracle only because they held that the truths of the Christian religion did not thus go beyond the limits of the natural reason. The classical position in Christian theology was that a supra-rational revelation must be attested by supernatural proof. Reason, it was admitted by all but the deists and their precursors, cannot of itself discover or demonstrate the truths of the Christian revelation; the most that reason can do is to show that the truths of revelation are not inconsistent with reason. Therefore we must have supernatural evidence before we can, as rational beings, believe in the Christian or the Mohammedan revelation. The reply of the classical Christian theologians to the holders of the modern view would have been that, in accepting such doctrines as that of the Incarnation without being convinced that the miracles really happened, they were going beyond the evidence and credulously accepting what was from their own point of view a quite irrational speculation.

Nevertheless, we may note, this charge would leave unwrung the withers of the exponents of the modern point of view. For the modern view, if we may so refer to it, has in fact abandoned the classical belief in a supernatural revelation, at least in its traditional form. The belief in the Incarnation and in the other doctrines of the Christian faith does not, according to the modern view, rest upon any supra-rational divine revelation, but upon the very appeal which Jesus makes to the rational, spiritual and moral consciousness of mankind. It therefore requires no supernatural attestation, and consequently its upholders may remain agnostic or even skeptical about whether the miracles ever happened. At first sight this view seems attractive, but a closer examination of it shows, as we must again point out, that it does not account for the observable facts. In particular, it does not account for the phenomenon of "election", for the fact that Jesus does *not* appeal to a large number of eminently spiritual, rational and moral people in such a way as to lead them to believe in Him as Son of God. If the truths of the Christian faith were directly accessible to the perception of the spiritual, rational and moral consciousness of mankind, then it would be impossible that men who are at least as gifted as most of us Christians in such consciousness should not be able to perceive the truth of such doctrines as that of the Incarnation. Mr. Aldous Huxley, Lord Russell and Mr. Gandhi are doubtless more rational, more spiritual and more ethically perceptive than are many Christians, but yet they do not perceive the truth about Jesus as Christians see it. In other words, the modern view does not really account for the existence of the Christian Church and its understanding of itself, which is the very fact that any theory of revelation must seek to explain. No real advantage can be derived from the view that the Christian revelation is not after all supernatural and is only a normal or "natural" process of human spiritual, rational and moral appreciation. The facts of the case themselves compel us to insist that there is a special revelation which is not accessible to the organs of perception of men who have not been brought into contact with Christ and His Church. Our minds are not able of themselves to perceive the truth unless they are first illumined by the shining of the truth itself. It is only because of the gift of the divine grace in revelation (whether general or special) that we are able to perceive truth at all, and any theory which endows our minds with a natural faculty for discerning truth (whether the truth in Jesus or elsewhere) does not account for the observable facts. It is shipwrecked upon the hard fact of "election", the fact that some rational beings see the truth and others do not. A greater capacity for reason (or any other human endowment) is not what distinguishes those who see from those who do not; those who can see would themselves describe it as a gift of faith. The traditional view of supra-rational revelation attested by miracle conserves a truth which the modern view explains away, namely, the truth that (in Bishop Butler's words) "revelation itself is miraculous"; it cannot be explained in terms of the ordinary modes and processes of human knowing.

## § 3. *Revelation as Itself Essentially Miraculous*

The traditional view is fundamentally right, and can stand the test of criticism better than the modern view; but, of course, the traditional view requires re-statement in the light of the application of the scientific method by means of biblical research, so that we no longer need to think of revelation as consisting in truths delivered in propositional form. Our re-statement of the

Christian doctrine of revelation along the lines of the theory of general and special revelation, as we have outlined it in the preceding chapters, conserves the ancient and fundamental truth that revelation in all its forms is itself miraculous. It is miraculous in both senses of the word: it cannot be explained in terms of any known "natural" processes of human perceiving and apprehending, and it arouses in us in the highest degree the sense of wonder, awe and humility. Revelation, whether general or special, results from the unconditioned grace or self-giving of God, without which we could know nothing about Him or His truth; it is a miracle of grace, not a triumph of human discovery. The distinctively biblical (or special) revelation is the outcome of the wholly wonderful movement of God's love towards man, manifested in the long series of events which the Bible records, and culminating in the coming of Jesus Christ. All the events of this long process are the result of the miraculous guidance of the Hebrew people by the divine purpose; but supremely, the events of the marvellous life and triumphant death of Jesus, when they are properly understood and received by us according to the prophetic and apostolic witness of the Bible, are the culminating revelation of God's purpose, because they are the direct outcome of the embodiment of that purpose in human history. Hence amongst the stories of all the nations of the world the story of the Hebrew people is utterly and uniquely miraculous, in both senses of the word, and hence, too, amongst the lives of all the men who have ever lived, the life of Jesus is utterly and uniquely miraculous. Conversely, the miraculous quality of the biblical history and of the person of Jesus is the adequate and (for Christians) convincing reason for believing that in them a special revelation has taken place.

Revelation is itself miraculous: it is often said, and rightly, that Jesus Himself is the supreme miracle—what He was, as well as what He did and what He is doing. The very appearance of such a figure amongst the sinful race of men is wholly miraculous; the continuing life of His Church is miraculous, and His saving work amongst the souls of men is miraculous. That is to say, these things cannot be accounted for by the ordinary psychological and historical modes of explanation by which we attempt to account for other things. They are each of them in a class of one, and therefore they are not susceptible of treatment by the ordinary methods of scientific generalization and classification. There is nothing else in the world with which we can co-ordinate them; as we have noted, all the attempts made by students of the comparative study of religions to assimilate the Christian facts to those of the non-Christian religions have failed to account for those essential features which distinguish the Church from every other form of human organization. The traditional view is right in insisting that a miraculous revelation must find its attestation in the miraculous. If we were to acknowledge belief in a miraculous revelation which could be received and understood by the ordinary processes of human discovery and reasoning, our logic would clearly be at fault; if the thing revealed be miraculous, the act of revealing, by which it is made known to us, must be miraculous also. That is to say, revelation must be miraculous in both meanings of that ambiguous word: both the *revelatum* and the *revelatio* must be miraculous, and if they are not miraculous, it would be better to abandon the word "revelation" altogether and speak of "discovery" or "perceiving". The modern view, which tried to establish Christian truth on a kind of everyday basis of discovery and reasoning, ended, as we saw, by abolishing the distinctively Christian conception of revelation altogether. Revelation is miraculous and comes by miraculous means—by the gift of prophetic inspiration, by the divine opening of our eyes to the truth, by the mysterious awakening of faith. It is not a gift of knowledge, but a gift of seeing, by which knowledge comes; it is not the communication of ready-made truth, but the illumination of the eyes, so that they may behold truth. Revelation is thus not the rational deduction of truth (the *revelatum*) from certain given premises (assured to us by *revelatio*), nor yet is it a scientific induction which results in the framing of a "most probable hypothesis": faith is not the same thing as the acceptance of a philosophy known as Christian theism. Men do not arrive at faith through being convinced on rational grounds of the validity of a theistic philosophy; they arrive at Christian theism because they first had some gift of faith. Revelation, then, is primarily an opening of the eyes to see the truth, and the acceptance of truth thus seen through the act of revelation is made possible on its human side by the response of faith. The divine act of revealing (*revelatio*) is miraculous; it cannot be explained by the ordinary categories of psychology: the thing revealed(*revelatum*) is miraculous, for the whole content of Christian faith, as given in the apostolic preaching, cannot be known to be true without the grace of special revelation. Faith therefore comes to us by a miracle, the miracle of the divine revelation; but on its human side, *qua* our response, faith is not miraculous, since it is God (and not we) who works miracles. The traditional Christian theology was right in holding that to ask a man to believe in a divine revelation and to show him no signs of its miraculous character would be to treat him as something less than a rational being. Aquinas, Luther, Hooker, Butler and Mozley were right in their fundamental contention: supernatural revelation must be attested by miracle. The opening of his own blind eyes is a miracle of grace to which every Christian can testify.

General revelation is, of course, miraculous, in the sense that all our knowledge of God and truth is not "unaided" but comes to us through the operation of the divine grace. But those who do not possess the insights of special revelation do not understand it as it truly is, and thus they are often led to attribute what is in reality the work of God to their own power and cleverness. Special revelation itself, however, clearly needs miraculous attestation, since without such attestation we have no powers in ourselves by which we might know it to be true. We are incapable of finding out for ourselves the truth which comes to us through special revelation; our spiritual, rational and moral perceptions are inadequate to establish truth without divine attestation. Now the Church has never tried to commend its special revelation without adducing the evidence of the divine miracle which alone makes it credible to rational beings. The supreme miracle to which the Church has pointed since the earliest days is, of course, the miracle of the resurrection of Jesus from the dead. The development of modern New Testament research has left no room for doubt that Christianity originated with the preaching that the Lord was risen. Whether the original disciples were right or wrong about the fact, it cannot be gainsaid that their conviction that Jesus had risen from the dead was the starting-point of the Christian faith. They did not in the first place go out into the world with "the simple Gospel" that God is love, and they did

not regard the Sermon on the Mount as the basis of the Good
News. They proclaimed Jesus and the resurrection: the rest
followed later. The revelation in Jesus Christ was attested by the
miracle of His resurrection. Without the miracle of the resurrection the remembered life and the recorded teaching of Jesus might
have been nothing more than a beautiful dream, a vision and a
hope which might have been supposed to have been buried with
Jesus in the stone-sealed tomb: reason and spirituality could not
have proved it to be other than this. But the divine attestation by
the miracle of raising Jesus from the dead set the seal of God's
approval upon the revelation in Him, and thus made it possible
for rational beings to believe in the revelation in Christ.

## § 4. *Historical Attestation within an Historical Community*

This helps us to perceive an essential truth about the character
of the Christian revelation. It comes to us by attestation, by the
witness of the apostles to the things which they had seen and
heard and handled. It does not come by the insights of religious
geniuses, like the "spiritual" conceptions of "ethical religion";
nor does it come by mystical communication or esoteric divulga-
tion, like the "revelations" of the mystery religions; nor yet does
it come by philosophical speculations, like the "higher knowledge" of the gnostic sects. It spreads by proclamation, and it is
historical in the sense that it depends upon the attestation of the
historical witnesses who actually saw and heard what they
declared. The Church is the living community within which this
historical witness has been passed on from generation to generation: every Christian congregation, every local church, is bound
together into this continuing chain of witness down the ages and
across the world. Every church building, every great cathedral or
wayside Bethel, is a standing symbol and witness to the fact that
Jesus is risen. Witness within an historical community of men and
women is not the mere repetition of a truth from place to place
and from generation to generation; it is not the mere continued
teaching of a philosophical truth or outlook, though it includes
this: it is a living, self-communicating attestation of what has
actually happened in and to the community itself, a part of its
own inner life and meaning, a bearing within itself of its own past,

which gives vitality and significance to its present and future. This is, of course, true of other historical communities, such as nations, which can be understood only from inside their own life and standpoint: their history lives within them, making them what they are now—different from all other nations with other histories. Thus, a man who stands outside the Church, when he hears that Jesus was raised from the dead, might say that the matter might or might not be true, but in any case it is irrelevant to him: what does it matter if a man who lived nearly two thousand years ago was raised from the dead? Even if one could produce certain evidence of the fact, what of it? This is the attitude of many modern people towards the resurrection of Jesus; the world is a place where strange things happen, and if this strange thing happened, what does it matter to folk who live in the twentieth century? But within the community of the Church, this strange thing is a part of its own history, an ingredient of its own life, the essence of its own meaning. The apostolic testimony is not a dead voice from the past but a living witness to something which was and is a fact; the apostolic witness did not die when the last of the apostles died, for witness within an historical community does not die like the contents of yesterday's newspapers: it continues as long as the historical community itself, and thus the Church remains an apostolic community because, like the apostles themselves, it is a witness of the resurrection of Jesus from the dead.

Thus, the witness of an historical community to its own past is something other than the record which is written down in historical text-books, however useful and necessary these may be in the preservation of accurate knowledge and in the education of on-coming generations. The New Testament is for the Christian community the historical text-book, containing the first-hand testimony of the generation of the first apostles themselves. And as such its importance cannot be overestimated. Biblical criticism has, as we have noted, destroyed the notion of the New Testament as a source of inerrant revealed knowledge written down in propositional form, but it has not destroyed its value as an historical witness to the fact of the resurrection of Jesus. On the contrary, modern biblical scholarship has confirmed the general reliability of the books of our New Testament as the genuine records of what the people who came into contact with and were instructed by the very disciples of the historical Jesus believed about Him. This at the least we can say with confidence. The New Testament is a first-hand and authentic account of what those who knew Jesus best in the days of His ministry believed concerning His person and work. It gives us a coherent and rational account of the historical Jesus and His Church in its earliest days; and, it should be noted, it gives us all the history that we have upon the subject. But its history is interpreted history (as all history must be), and it depends for its coherence and rationality upon those categories of interpretation which the apostolic witnesses themselves gave to the history which they handed down. This consideration is of the greatest importance when we come to discuss the miraculous elements of the Gospel story.

It is indisputable that all the *historical* evidence that we have goes to show that Jesus worked miracles of the kind described in the Gospels. There is no historical evidence to show that Jesus did not work miracles. It cannot be disputed upon historical grounds that all the people who came into contact with Jesus during His ministry in Galilee believed that He worked miracles; even His enemies believed it. If our judgment were to be decided by strictly historical considerations and by nothing else, we could not avoid the conclusion that Jesus worked miracles. The evidence that Jesus worked miracles is just as strong, and is of precisely the same quality and texture, as that He taught that God is Father and that His disciples should forgive one another. We cannot *on historical grounds alone* accept the evidence for the one and reject that for the other. The evidence that Jesus healed a dropsical man on the Sabbath day is just as good as the evidence that He told the story of the Good Samaritan or the Prodigal Son. The type of modern interpretation which tried to select the teaching of Jesus as historical while rejecting the record of His wonderful deeds as unhistorical, as we have already noted, led eventually to a complete skepticism of the possibility of our knowledge of the historical Jesus at all. If the Gospels do not give us a reliable picture of the Jesus of history, we can have no genuinely historical knowledge about Him. The alternative to the Gospel portrait of the Jesus who showed His power in mighty acts of mercy, who caused the blind to see and the deaf to hear, who fed the hungry multitudes in the wilderness and calmed the storm with His word, is not—as the liberal Protestants supposed—a picture of Jesus as the good man who taught a lofty ethical ideal and died for it, the greatest perhaps of the prophets and a sublime religious genius: the alternative is historical skepticism about Him. The only *historical* evidence that we possess is that of a Jesus whose deeds as well as His words led His disciples to perceive that He was the Christ, the Son of God.[1] The logical working out of the liberal interpretation of the Jesus of history led inexorably to skepticism, and the failure of that interpretation serves to underline the truth that we possess no historical evidence whatever for the existence of a Jesus who did not work miracles and who was not raised from the dead. Such a Jesus is the product only of the historical imagination. The sole evidence for the existence of Jesus is, after all, that of the apostolic testimony, and the historical Jesus to whom the apostles bore their witness is the Christ of Christian faith.

But we must note the limitations of this conclusion and not try to make it carry a greater weight than it can bear. It indeed disposes of the nonsense of the assumption that historical criticism has made it impossible for us to believe in the historicity of the Gospel miracles, but it does not enable us to go to non-Christians and confront them with a piece of "objective" history which must necessarily compel their assent to the statement that the miracles really happened. They will be able to see "what happened" only when they see through the apostles' eyes, when they accept the categories of interpretation which the apostles themselves used, or, in other words, when they see Jesus as the

---

[1] It may be noted how near to and yet how far from the position of Reinhold Niebuhr is the viewpoint which we are advocating here. There is surely something unsound in the view that history confronts us with a "liberal" Jesus, but that the truth of history is seen only in the (presumably non-historical) Christ of Christian faith. Cf. the following striking sentences: "The message of the Son of God who dies upon the cross, of a God who transcends history and is yet in history, who condemns and judges sin and yet suffers with and for the sinner, this message is the truth about life. It cannot be stated without deceptions; but the truths which seek to avoid the deceptions are immeasurably less profound. Compared to this Christ who died for men's sins upon the cross, Jesus, the good man who tells all men to be good, is more solidly historical. But He is the bearer of no more than a pale truism" (*Beyond Tragedy*, London, 1938, pp. 20f.).

Christ of the Church's faith. We cannot by argument cause them
to see in this way; all that we can do is to show that the apostolic
interpretation of Jesus gives a rational and coherent understanding
of the history of a vital moment in the world's life, and that the
alternative to this interpretation is a *lacuna* in history, an admission
of ignorance about "what happened" at precisely that historical
moment at which the Christian Church and its faith were born.
Belief in the historicity of the Gospel miracles does not come by
means of any "scientific" and "objective" examination of the
evidence: it comes when we decide to accept the testimony of the
apostles concerning the things which they saw with their eyes
and which they heard and handled concerning the Word of Life.
The principle of interpretation which we use in our study of the
Gospel history will be that which the apostolic historians themselves supplied. Non-believers in the Christian revelation may,
of course, accept the historicity of the Gospel miracles, if they
make use of categories of a certain kind—for example, the belief
in the power of mind over matter; but this kind of theory has
nothing at all to do with distinctively Christian faith. For the
apostolic Church the significance of the miracles of Jesus was
that they were the signs of His divine mission, foretold by the
prophets of old; they were the tokens of the power of God Himself and of His loving purpose. To the New Testament writers
the miracles of Jesus were, for those who had eyes to see, signs
that enabled them to penetrate the mystery of His person.[1]
Though they were mere empty portents to those who had not that
gift of sight, and though they were not intended and were not
used to compel unwilling belief, they were none the less for
those whose eyes had been opened the veritable authentication of
the divine revelation in Christ. This is supremely true of the
greatest of all the Gospel miracles, that of the resurrection.
Jesus appeared after His resurrection to believers only, never
to unbelievers; and this is entirely consistent with His use of
His miraculous powers during His earthly ministry to demonstrate the truth of His revelation to those who had eyes to see—
and to those alone. In this sense the New Testament considers
the miracles to be supernatural evidences of the revelation given

[1] For the vindication and elaboration of this statement see the author's *The
Miracle-Stories of the Gospels* (London, 1941).

to the apostles. The traditional Christian view of miracle as necessary to authenticate a supernatural revelation is entirely in harmony with the outlook of the New Testament. Aquinas, Butler and Mozley did not suppose that the miracles were given to compel unbelievers—whether Mohammedans, or deists or skeptical undergraduates—to accept the truth of Christianity, but to enable believers to believe rationally and upon evidence. The apostolic witness testifies to the miraculous authentication of the divine mission of Jesus, which enables those who accept it by faith to have a rational belief in the revelation through Him.

## § 5. *Miracles and the Interpretation of Historical Evidence*

It must not be thought that any disadvantage attaches to the Christian's belief in the historicity of the Gospel miracles because that belief involves what we have called a principle of interpretation in history. Disbelief equally is based upon some principle of interpretation, which cannot be derived from a "scientific" or "impartial" study of the records. Our interpretation of those records must ultimately be derived from our total outlook upon life, our philosophical standpoint in general, whatever it may be, whether we think of the miracles of Jesus as manifestations of the power and love of God, or as illustrations of the power of mind over nature, or as instances of sympathetic magic (whatever that may be), or as unscrupulous trickery, or as pure fiction. The part played by what some critics would call "subjective factors" is equally important, whether we are believers or unbelievers. The Christian is well aware that he cannot get behind the testimony of the apostles and that Christian faith is always a matter of accepting the apostolic witness; Christian faith, that is to say, *is* faith, and it is not proof. It is not communicable to outsiders by any process of reasoning, deductive or inductive, because in such matters the categories by which reason operates must be present before the processes of reason can begin. Nevertheless faith in the apostolic testimony is not a "blind" act of believing apart from any evidence; it is a characteristic of faith that it carries its own evidence with it, as it comes to us by the miracle of God's grace; and when it comes, it receives fresh attestation in the coherence and rationality of the view of the historical facts which it enables us to see. And it possesses the supreme advantage of thus making sense of such historical evidence as exists, since all the historical sources of our knowledge of Jesus represent Him as miraculous in His person and in His deeds. The Christian therefore will welcome the fullest and most searching examination of all the historical evidence at our disposal, with the help of all the critical apparatus which modern scholarship can provide. But he well knows that the question of the historicity of the miracles or of the Gospel record in general is not settled in the field of historical and critical research: just as the deists did not base their objection to miracles upon historical considerations but upon the philosophical assumptions of their theory of revelation, so to-day and in every age the denial of the historicity of miracles, though often claiming to be based upon strictly historical enquiry, is in reality founded upon a philosophical attitude, an outlook upon the world and life, such as that of scientific humanism. The skepticism of the modern mind concerning the Gospel miracles actually arises not from any historical understanding but from a garbled view of the "conclusions" of "science", and physical science at that. This means that for the unreflective mind of to-day historical questions can be answered by means of the study of physics and chemistry, since one of the conclusions established by research in those subjects is held to be that miracles do not and cannot happen. A few moments' reflection, however, should suffice to show that the complicated questions of history cannot be settled in such a manner, and that whether or not the miracles of the Gospels really happened is not a question which can be even discussed with propriety from the standpoint of the physical sciences. If the Gospel miracles occurred, it is clear that they were not the result of the operation of any force which the physical sciences can measure or describe. The view that physical science can solve the problem of the miracles can be justified only by the assumption that the only forces in the universe are those which physical science can measure and describe, but that is a philosophical and not a scientific assumption.

It may be worth while to counter in advance one or two objections to the view which we have advanced in this chapter that our acceptance or rejection of the biblical miracles will depend upon our prior acceptance or rejection of the prophetic and apostolic testimony of the Bible concerning God's revelation in Christ. Some will doubtless object that this conclusion is obscurantist, and that it lifts the discussion of miracle out of the sphere of scientific and historical enquiry and transfers it to the regions of make-believe and mystery. It will be said that we might as well accept the view that Joshua made the sun stand still and that Elisha made the axe-head float, since all the historical evidence in our possession assures us that these things happened and there is no evidence that they did not happen. Such arguments are frivolous, and they merely parody the view which they are designed to refute. The question which should be asked is whether Christian faith, or the biblical principle of interpretation in history, requires us, if we accept it, to believe that Joshua made the sun stand still or that Elisha's axe-head floated. An affirmative answer is not likely to be given by Christians who have abandoned the older theory of an infallibly inspired written revelation. On the other hand, if we ask whether Christian faith, or the biblical principle of historical interpretation, if accepted, requires belief in the historical resurrection of Christ or of His wonderful accomplishment of the Messianic signs, it will be seen that an affirmative answer must be returned. Any other answer would make nonsense of the biblical principle of interpretation itself. Moreover, the biblical principle of historical interpretation, which it is the task of biblical theology to elucidate, will be the criterion for determining our view of the historicity of any particular Gospel or biblical miracle. Herein lies the answer to the objection that our view of miracle is cunningly devised to enable us to pick and choose amongst the biblical miracles and narratives those which we subjectively prefer to think are historical while leaving us at liberty to reject what we do not like. A sensible person will not expect to find agreement in detail amongst all theologians, since there are various permissible differences of opinion concerning the precise definition of the biblical principle of historical interpretation itself. For instance, Christian theologians will differ (as they do differ) upon the question of the actual mode in which the resurrection of Jesus took place, or upon the question of the manner of His birth, or whether He destroyed a fig-tree or a herd of swine. These are not questions which can be settled by direct appeals to historical evidence alone, still less by appeals to physical science; they are questions of the interpretation of evidence; they involve the careful exposition of the biblical principle of interpretation itself. They are questions of biblical theology. It is probable that many theologians will wish to suspend judgment concerning the precise historical details of many of the biblical and even of the Gospel miracles, and a large measure of agnosticism upon such points is not incompatible with a full and whole-hearted Christian faith. They will hold that many opinions are permissible and that upon such matters none of them should be asserted to be *de fide*. Believing that the biblical miracles occurred does not involve the necessity of explaining in detail how any particular miracle occurred. Finally, it is merely an unhelpful parody of the position here advocated to say that it inculcates belief in all the miracles in general and in none of them in particular. Briefly stated our contention is that the biblical principle of historical interpretation necessitates the belief that Jesus was raised from the dead and that He worked the works of the Messiah, but it allows a wide variety of view concerning the details of particular incidents. The great saying commonly but wrongly attributed to St. Augustine is applicable here: *In necessariis unitas, in non necessariis libertas, in utrisque caritas.*

# CHAPTER EIGHT

# THE ARGUMENT FROM PROPHECY

## § 1. *The Breakdown of Literalism in the Interpretation of Prophecy*

IN THE traditional scheme of Christian apologetics the argument from prophecy has from the earliest days taken a leading place. In the words of Harnack, "a glance at the early Christian writers, and especially at the apologists, reveals the prominent and indeed the commanding rôle played by the argument from prophecy".[1] We may perhaps characterize this argument as the demonstration of the validity of the witness of the Old Testament to the truth of Christ. The question is one which should receive our attention before we go on to consider the wider question of the nature of the inspiration and authority of the Bible as such. It is clear that our changed views of divine inspiration, which result from the progress of biblical criticism during the last hundred years, have rendered necessary a re-stating of the argument from prophecy; but, as we shall see, this does not imply that the argument itself has lost any of its traditional force, when it is thus re-stated in the light of the wider knowledge of biblical origins which we now possess.

Before the rise of modern biblical criticism the argument from prophecy was always regarded as complementary to the argument from miracle, or indeed as part of it. As Dr. J. B. Mozley said, "Prophecy is one department of the miraculous".[2] It was held to be one of the chief evidences of a miraculous divine revelation. The argument from prophecy in its traditional form laid great stress upon the literal fulfilment of detailed prediction; prophecy was conceived primarily as the predicting of events which came

---

[1] *Mission and Expansion of Christianity*, Eng. trans., Vol. I, p. 282.

[2] Bampton Lectures, 1865, p. 21. Cf. also David Hume, *Of Miracles (ad fin.)*: "What we have said of miracles may be applied, without any variation, to prophecies; and indeed, all prophecies are real miracles; and, as such only, can be admitted as proofs of any revelation. If it did not exceed the capacity of human nature to foretell future events, it would be absurd to employ any prophecy as an argument for a divine mission or authority from heaven."

to pass years or centuries after the prophetic utterance had been given: no other explanation was possible than that of miraculous divine disclosure. Thus, Bishop Butler argued that, even if we were to consider the birth of Jesus as being in the mode of its occurrence a natural event, nevertheless "the concurrence of our Saviour's being born at Bethlehem with a long foregoing series of prophecy and other coincidences, is doubtless miraculous".[1] Calvin confidently urges the fulfilment of scriptural prophecies as a proof, wholly acceptable to our natural reason, of the divine inspiration of the Bible; he brings forward as an instance Isaiah's prediction of the release by Cyrus the Persian of the Jewish captives in Babylon more than a hundred years before Cyrus was born, and he asks: "Does not this simple, unadorned narrative plainly demonstrate that what Isaiah spoke was not the conjecture of man but the undoubted oracle of God?"[2] What Calvin would have said about the discovery by modern critics of a "Second Isaiah", who was a contemporary of Cyrus, it is easy to guess: he would have dismissed the critics as "miscreants" inspired by "the father of lies". But the work of the biblical critics has clearly made this kind of reliance upon the fulfilment of prediction no longer possible in the twentieth century. The uselessness of the argument from prophecy in its traditional form is clearly seen by a glance at Calvin's "proof" from Daniel:

> "What shall I say of Daniel? Did he not deliver prophecies embracing a future period of almost six hundred years, as if he had been writing of past events generally known? (Dan. ix. etc.) If the pious will duly meditate upon these things, they will be sufficiently instructed to silence the cavils of the ungodly. The demonstration is too clear to be gainsaid."[3]

But since there are to-day few people who have studied the Book of Daniel in the light of modern methods of historical and literary research who are able to believe that the author of Daniel was not in fact "writing of past events generally known", this

---

[1] *Analogy of Religion*, Part II, Chap. vii; ed. *op. cit.*, p. 285.
[2] *Institutes of the Christian Religion*, Bk. I, Chap. viii, par. 8.
[3] *Ibid.*

kind of argument from prophecy can no longer be used in the service of the Lord of truth.

It is clear that we cannot nowadays look for exact fulfilments of particular verses in the Old Testament and regard them as "proofs from prophecy" of the truth of the Christian revelation, even though this kind of argument goes back to the New Testament itself. Those who acknowledge (as we are forced to do) the validity of the categories of modern scientific biblical criticism in the interpretation of the scriptural records are thereby compelled to admit that some at least of our categories of biblical interpretation are derived from non-biblical insights, such as those of the Renaissance, of the Enlightenment of the eighteenth century, and of modern scientific method. For those who see in reason no "point of connection" between God and man such an admission would doubtless be a stumbling-block; but for those of us who regard every insight into truth as a gift and revelation from God Himself, whencesoever it may be derived, there is no real difficulty here. The Lord of truth does not desire us to remain for ever content with the limited historical understanding of the ancients, even that of the apostles themselves. Hosea's "Out of Egypt have I called my son", or Jeremiah's "A voice was heard in Ramah . . . Rachel weeping for her children", will not appear to us to indicate a wonderful divine foreknowledge on the part of Hosea and Jeremiah of the circumstances of the Saviour's birth, as it seemed to do to St. Matthew[1]—or to Bishop Butler: we have to-day, as we cannot but think, too clear a notion of what was actually in the minds of Hosea and Jeremiah when they uttered these "prophecies". As it would seem to us, there is nothing here which requires the hypothesis of a miraculous divine revelation. We may, of course, rightly discern that there are deep spiritual analogies in the pattern of Israel's history with that of Israel's Messiah, and that these analogies of events are truly discovered by St. Matthew and the other New Testament writers; but, important though this truth assuredly is, it does not imply that there was any fulfilment of a miraculous written oracle in the sense in which the matter has been traditionally understood. An argument which had proved to be of inestimable apologetic value since the days of the New Testament writers was

[1] Matt. ii. 15, 17f.; Hos. xi. 1; Jer. xxxi. 15.

beginning to show signs of vulnerability when a Bampton lecturer
tried to revive it in the second half of the nineteenth century.[1]
Perhaps Bishop Butler was the last great apologist who could
*ex animo* make full use of the notion of a long foregoing series of
prophecies of the Saviour's birth at Bethlehem. So long as it was
possible to think of the Bible as a divinely dictated written record
of revelation, it was possible to understand prophecy as a matter
of the detailed fulfilment of predictions contained in particular
verses or passages of the Old Testament; but with the abandonment of such a theory of biblical inspiration a different view of
the nature of the fulfilment of prophecy is required.

## § 2. *Allegorical Interpretation and the "Analogy of Faith"*

Along with literalism in the interpretation of the Scriptures
we must also discard allegorism, since (as we shall notice in the
next paragraph) allegorism and literalism go hand in hand and are
necessary to each other. By allegorism is meant the reading into a
biblical passage of a meaning which its author did not intend and
could not have understood. This method of interpreting the
Scriptures had been developed before New Testament times by
the Jews themselves, notably in Alexandria, and by its means the
philosophy of Plato and the Stoics had been discovered in
Moses; it was thus possible for philosophically minded Jews to
invest Platonism and Stoicism with something of the authority
of divine revelation. The New Testament, however, is unin-
fluenced by the more luxuriant kind of Alexandrian allegorizing,
although in one book—the Epistle to the Hebrews—there are
marked tendencies towards it. St. Paul gives us a few examples of
the more pedestrian Palestinian or rabbinic variety of allegorizing,
but this is practical rather than philosophical in its object.[2] From
St. Paul's use of it one might conclude that it is legitimate to
employ allegory as a method of teaching or exhortation; but it is
hardly possible to find in his example a biblical sanction for

[1] R. Payne-Smith, *Prophecy a Preparation for Christ*, 1869.

[2] For example, in 1 Cor. ix. 9f. (the muzzled ox); 1 Cor. x. 4 ("the rock was
Christ"); 2 Cor. iii. 13–15 (Moses' veil), and uniquely in Gal. iv. 21–31, where
he explicitly asserts that Hagar and Sarah allegorically represent the Old and the
New Covenants; this is the only use of the word "allegory" or "allegorize" in
the LXX and N.T.

allegorism as a means of reaching a truth that lies beneath the letter of Scripture. The surprising thing is indeed that, though the New Testament writers are entirely literalist in their attitude towards the Old Testament, they are driven so rarely to resort to allegorism. This is doubtless because they were not philosophers and were not interested in metaphysical speculations. It was only after the close of the New Testament period that the allegorical method of scriptural interpretation became for the Christian Church an accepted method of biblical exegesis and criticism. In some periods and places—notably in the Alexandrian Church in the time of Clement and Origen—allegorism luxuriated into what was almost a riot of fanciful interpretation; but, generally speaking, the doctors of the Church were well aware of the dangers of subjectivism, and they insisted that all allegorical interpretations of any given passage of Holy Scripture must be controlled by the Church's understanding of the teaching of the Bible as a whole. Thus, St. Augustine, who in his work on *Christian Doctrine* carefully examines the principles that govern the figurative interpretation of Scripture, lays it down that obscure passages and figurative interpretations must always be checked by other passages of Scripture where the truth is clearly and literally stated;[1] and likewise St. Thomas Aquinas insists that no allegorical interpretation is to be believed unless its truth is demonstrable from other passages of Scripture in which it is literally stated: no Christian dogma can be built upon a "spiritual" or figurative interpretation unsupported by the plain letter of other passages.[2] Allegory might be used in the illustration of the truth of the scriptural meaning, but not in the establishment of it.

Sometimes we are inclined to forget that allegorism is a veritable necessity for those who, knowing nothing of our modern critical method of approach to the Bible, believe that they are committed to its literalist interpretation, if they are at all philosophically or

[1] *De Doct. Christ.*, Bk. III, Chaps. xxvi–xxviii. Cp. *Ep.* XCIII, 24: "What else is it but superlative impudence for anyone to interpret in his own favour any allegorical statements, unless he has also plain testimonies by the light of which the obscure meaning of the former may be made manifest?"

[2] *Summa Theol.*, I, i, 10 ad 1; cf. A. L. Lilley, *Religion and Revelation*, p. 67: "There is no principle of interpretation on which Aquinas is more insistent than that no theological argument can legitimately proceed from any spiritual meaning. Every spiritual meaning is a conclusion, never a premiss."

critically minded. Allegorism was not opposed to literalism, but
was a necessary complement of it.[1] There was much in the Old
Testament which was repugnant to the reason and the conscience
of Christians who, whether before or after their conversion, had
received the illumination of the lofty teachings of the Platonists
and Stoics. Allegorism presented an acceptable method of dealing
with the scandals created by the literalist theory of biblical
inspiration. As St. Augustine remarked, since all or nearly all of
the transactions of the Old Testament are to be taken not merely
literally but figuratively as well, even the sins of the patriarchs
contain figures of "things to come", and are thus given to teach
us spiritual truth, not as examples for us to imitate.[2] Thus, even
though he could not travel the whole length of the Alexandrian
way and hold that the *only* meaning of unethical passages was the
figurative one, and that such passages were never meant to be
taken literally, at least he could appease his reason and conscience
by believing that these immoral doings were divinely permitted
for the sake of the wider education of the elect people of God
through the spiritual truth which they conveyed. This seems an
odd theory to us, but that is because we are blessed by being able
to look through the categories of modern biblical scholarship, as
they have been shaped for us by men who stood on Augustine's
shoulders. The sense of relief brought by the employment of the
allegorical method to the minds and consciences of those who
lived long before the discovery of modern critical methods,
and their joyful liberation from bondage to the letter of the
Scriptures, can be compared to the parallel sense of relief and

[1] Cf. Harnack, *Mission and Expansion of Christianity*, Eng. trans., Vol. I,
p. 286, footnote: "It may not be superfluous to recall that any authoritative
text, especially one which was explained as of divine authority, *demanded* the
allegorical interpretation, since those who recognized or maintained its authority
usually connected the text with ideas which were quite different from the
interpretation sanctioned by the historical interpretation. Nay, more. Authority
was desired and devised for such ideas themselves. For example, to treat the
Song of Solomon as a love-song and then to vindicate the authority of its sacred
text, is the acme of absurdity; it became an intolerable burden for the Church
to do so. But the same difficulty arose in connection with a book like Genesis.
Those who admitted the book to the canon had no desire to canonize a wretched
Jacob, etc.; but they were prepared for all such contingencies, and employed the
allegorical method to remove any stumbling-blocks."

[2] *De Doct. Christ.*, Bk. III, Chaps. xxii and xxiii.

liberation which has been bestowed upon many in our own or in recent times through the acceptance of the critical standpoint. Thus, St. Augustine in a well-known passage in the *Confessions* describes his experience of relief on first coming across the use of the allegorical method in the preaching of St. Ambrose:

> "I rejoiced because I was enabled to read with other eyes those ancient Scriptures of the Law and the Prophets which used to seem so absurd. . . . Gladly did I hear Ambrose in his sermons to the people insisting upon the words, 'The letter killeth but the spirit giveth life', as a rule to be most carefully observed, taking off the mystic veil and opening the spiritual sense of those passages which in their literal acceptation seemed to teach folly, never saying anything that could offend me."[1]

A little further on he describes the stage in his development at which he himself had learnt how to employ the allegorical method:

> "By this time I could find an explanation for the contradictions that used to repel me, an explanation in the depths of its mysteries, having heard many of them reasonably explained; and the authority of Scripture appeared to me all the more august, and all the more worthy of reverential faith, because, while all might read it, it shrouded the grandeur of its inmost thought within the deeper meaning."[2]

The Reformation did not change in its essentials the traditional methods of scriptural interpretation; indeed, in some respects it strengthened and re-affirmed them. It re-emphasized the Patristic and Thomistic teaching that Scripture was the exclusive authority in matters of faith. Luther, it is true, rejected the allegorical method as a seductive and "beautiful harlot", doubtless because of its frequent employment as a means of deriving non-biblical or "popish" meanings from the biblical text; yet no doctor of the Church in any century could outdo Luther as a discoverer of spiritual meanings beneath the letter of the Old Testament.

[1] *Conf.*, Bk. VI, Chap. iv.     [2] Bk. VI, Chap. v.

It is not that Luther objects to spiritual interpretations as such; his intention is rather to insist that all spiritual interpretations must be controlled by the meaning of the Bible as a whole, and that meaning for him is Christ. "When I was a monk," he wrote in his *Table-Talk*, "I was an adept in allegory. I allegorized everything. But after lecturing on the Epistle to the Romans I came to have some knowledge of Christ. For therein I saw that Christ is no allegory, and came to know what Christ actually was." He castigates the Fathers for their obscuring of the literal or historical meaning of the sacred text; even Augustine is blamed, while of Origen Luther says with characteristic exaggeration that in the whole of him there is not a single word about Christ.[1] But Luther, while he strives to understand the historical meaning of the biblical text, rightly realizes that something more than historical exegesis is required if the Old Testament is to be regarded as Christian Scripture. Scripture must be interpreted by Scripture, the part by the clear intention of the whole, the obscure passages by the plain, and therefore the Old Testament by the New. In all this, of course, Luther is re-affirming principles that had been laid down by Augustine and Aquinas. But, instead of allegorical interpretation in its traditional sense Luther substitutes his principle of "the analogy of faith", that is, the interpretation of the whole Bible, including the Old Testament, by the analogy of saving faith in Christ. This principle is in reality a device for the control of allegory, not for its complete rejection; since the purpose of the whole biblical record is to reveal Christ, any allegorical interpretation which is Christological is permissible, while all other allegorical interpretations are based upon mere conjecture. Thus, Luther doubtless held that, by providing a fully Christian and biblical category of interpretation for the elucidation of spiritual meanings in the historical record, he was doing away with all subjectivity and wishful-thinking in the theological exegesis of the Bible. We have here a nice illustration of the paradoxical nature of all categories of interpretation, which, while they appear to provide an utterly valid or objective way of looking at things from the standpoint of those who see through them, nevertheless appear to other men, who make use

[1] See J. Mackinnon, *Luther and the Reformation* (1930), Vol. IV, pp. 290f., where plentiful references to Luther's various writings will be found.

of other categories, to be quite subjective and arbitrary. Thus, it is often objected that Luther's method of biblical interpretation and exegesis is wholly subjective, being based upon his own intense experience of salvation and justification by faith; and indeed much of his writing is subjective in this sense. "Here stand I; I can no other": such a declaration, however impressively and emphatically asserted, seems nothing more than a personal and subjective idiosyncrasy to those who cannot see through Luther's spectacles. The "problem of communication" remains as intransigent as ever, but perhaps Luther, had he not disdained to do so, might have shown to others the rationality of his categories and the coherence of the view of truth which they were able to commend. Luther nevertheless points our attention to an important principle, which must be safeguarded in any attempt to formulate a Christian doctrine of Holy Scripture. For he sees clearly that, even if the Bible were a collection of divinely dictated oracles, it would have no intelligible meaning and therefore no religious or saving value, unless it contained within itself a principle of interpretation or key to its mysteries; and for Luther this key-principle is Christ. The elucidation and the formulation of the key-principle of biblical interpretation is the primary task of biblical theology.

By means of his "analogy of faith" Luther is able to discover allusions to Christ and prophecies concerning him in almost every part of the Old Testament. This is unquestionably allegorism of the most thorough-going kind, but with the important quali-fication that every figurative interpretation must be Christological in character.[1] The problem which calls for solution here is whether

[1] This kind of biblical interpretation to-day appears to be enjoying again a certain vogue upon the Continent. See, for example, W. Vischer, *Das Christus-zeugnis des Alten Testaments* (Zürich, Band I, 1934; Band II, 1942). Here we have a kind of Christological allegorism, which rapidly passes from the historical sense of a passage to its alleged fulfilment in the New Testament. For example, we pass in a few pages from the discussion of Gressmann's views of the his-toricity of the narrative of Solomon's Judgment (1 Kings iii. 16–28) to the judgment given by Christ about who belongs to the True Israel; this is the judgment of the Son of David; the True Israel is the mother of the living child; she represents the Church over against the Synagogue (*Band* II, *Die früheren Propheten*, pp. 290–8). Vischer's principle of allegorical interpretation is unquestionably Christological, but is it for that reason any less subjective and fanciful?

allegorical interpretation is a legitimate method of scriptural exegesis, provided that the allegory is itself controlled by means of a category of interpretation that has been scientifically formulated (without the use of allegory) by biblical theologians working with the apparatus of the modern critical method. Our answer will doubtless be that such a use of allegory, or of the analogy of faith, may be useful for pedagogic and hortatory purposes, but that it is useless for the establishment either of the historical meaning of particular biblical passages or of theological truth. But this does not mean that those who were searching for the true meaning of the Old Testament by means of allegorical interpretation or of the analogy of faith were not feeling after a truth about the Bible which is still true and still important. Luther himself believed firmly in the classical Christian view that what is patent in the New Testament is latent in the Old,[1] and it is this conviction that led him to look for and to find many references in the Old Testament to the doctrine of justification by faith; and in this matter he is but following in the footsteps of St. Paul. The whole of the Old Testament is for Luther "an evangelical book", since from start to finish it is a book about Christ, and here we must agree that Luther's insight was not wrong. The witness of the Old Testament to Christ is hardly less clear than that of the New Testament: the Scriptures of the Jewish Church were the swaddling-clothes in which the Christ was laid. The Old Testament is revelation because it bears testimony to Christ: what does not speak about Christ is not revelation. In Luther's view, after the application of the exegetical method of the analogy of faith, there is little in the Old Testament which does not speak about Christ, and such secondary material is of small importance. Luther did not hold that all parts of the Bible were equally significant as vehicles of the Word of God; he sought for the Word of God in the Bible but he did not identify it with the words of the Bible: he taught that there was a Bible within the Bible. The books which pre-eminently show forth Christ and impart to us saving knowledge of Him are the Gospel and First Epistle of St. John, St. Paul's Epistles,

[1] Cf. St. Augustine's famous epigrams: *Novum Testamentum in Vetere latet, Vetus Testamentum in Novo patet* (*Quaest. in Heptateuch*, ii. 73); *Novum Testamentum in Vetere velabatur, Vetus Testamentum in Novo revelatur* (*Serm.* clx. 6).

especially Romans, Galatians and Ephesians, and the First Epistle of St. Peter. As everyone knows, Luther thought that, compared with these books, the Epistle of St. James is "a right strawy epistle", because it has nothing in it of a saving kind.[1] He denies the apostolic authority of Hebrews, questions that of the Apocalypse and rejects Jude; his treatment of the Old Testament is equally independent. Luther was certainly no bibliolater,[2] but equally he was very far from being a biblical critic in the modern sense;[3] it was indeed his lack of any knowledge of the principles of historical and literary criticsm, as these have been formulated in the nineteenth and twentieth centuries, which prevented him from arriving at a Christian doctrine of Holy Scripture which can satisfy our minds to-day. But he points us along the right way by his insistence upon truths which any Christian doctrine of Holy Scripture must embody, such as that Scripture itself must be the primary interpreter of Scripture, and that the interpretation of Scripture must depend upon the consistent employment of some master-key, which for Christians can only be Christ. By his bold selection of a single principle of interpretation which springs out of his own experience of salvation through the Word of God in the Bible, he gives us a living demonstration of the way in which faith in Christ becomes the vital principle of scriptural interpretation. As the result of his own deep understanding of faith, he finds in the Epistle to

[1] *Werke*, Erlangen Ed., lxiii. 115.

[2] Cf. A. L. Lilley, *Religion and Revelation*, p. 79; "Strange as it may sound, no Christian doctor of the front rank ever disparaged the revelational rôle of Scripture more consistently than the great Reformer [Luther]. It was he who had the daring to say, 'It is for Christ's sake that we believe in the Scriptures, not for the Scriptures' sake that we believe in Christ'."

[3] Cf. J. Mackinnon, *Luther and the Reformation*, Vol. IV, pp. 303f.: "He [Luther] is not . . . the father of modern biblical criticism, though his principle of critical discrimination might ultimately lead this way. He is, in fact, the sworn foe of the application of a purely rational historic criticism to the Bible. His unfortunate antagonism to reason, as applied in the religious sphere, led him, in contrast to Erasmus and Zwingli, for instance, to blaze the trail for the more unenlightened Biblicism of a later time, even if his own startling application of the critical reason was in the direction of the modern critical movement. His distinctive conviction is that reason, applied to Scripture in any other way than that which commended itself to him, can only lead to error and spiritual ruin."

the Romans a light so clear that it is sufficient to illuminate the whole Scripture, and he thus becomes a classic witness to the truth that personal faith is the condition and source of all truly Christian biblical interpretation and exegesis.

## § 3. *The Typological Fulfilment of the Scriptures*

Between Luther's day and our own there has taken place the rise of the modern critical method of biblical research, one of the results of which has been to transfer interest from the question of interpreting a written book, supposed to contain infallible (though sometimes inscrutable) oracles of God, to the problem of interpreting the events which that book records. Attention is nowadays fixed upon the events of the biblical history, and the Bible is seen to be itself an interpretation of those events; our task is no longer that of interpreting oracles but that of interpreting history. The fulfilment of prophecy is thus seen to involve more than the fulfilment of words and predictions; it involves the fulfilment of history, the validation of the prophetic understanding of history in the events which the New Testament records and interprets for us. Though the critical approach to biblical studies thus places a new stress upon the idea of the fulfilment of history in this sense, the conception itself is not a novel one, since the classical Christian attitude has always been that history itself is prophetic: the course of historical events, and not merely the words uttered by the prophets,[1] contains an anticipation or fore-shadowing of that which is to come. In the traditional language of Christian theology, the earlier is a "type" of the later, or the events of the New Testament history may be described as the fulfilment of the Old Testament "types". Thus, the deliverance of Israel from the Egyptian bondage by the miracle of the Red Sea is understood in the New Testament and the Church to be but the "type" of that greater Deliverance of the New Israel from bondage to sin and death through the miracle of the Resurrection of Christ from the dead; and the Jewish Passover becomes the "type" of the Christian Eucharist.[2] Or again, the destruction of Jerusalem

[1] Cf. St. Augustine, *De Civ. Dei*, Bk. VII, Chap. xxxii.

[2] It should be noted that the liturgical use of the Bible in the Church is based upon the typological rather than the allegorical interpretation of the Bible.

by the Babylonians in 586 B.C., an event which had been clearly predicted by the prophets of Israel and explained by them in the light of their understanding of the righteousness of Jehovah, became for the Church not merely a fore-shadowing of the judgment pronounced by Jesus Himself upon Jerusalem and Judaism, the barren fig-tree, and fulfilled in a literal sense in A.D. 70, in the destruction of the Holy City by the armies of Titus: it became also the "type" of that universal judgment of the world as *civitas terrena* by the God of Righteousness; and the prophetic Saved and Saving Remnant of the Old Testament became the "type" of the Christian Church, which had been raised up in the midst of the judgment by the mercy of God, a light to lighten the Gentiles and to be the glory—the fulfilment—of Israel's true vocation and history. Typological interpretation of the biblical history is thus based upon the actual course of that history, as recorded and interpreted by the prophetic and apostolic witness; it grows, as it were, out of the history itself, and is not imposed upon history by the reading into it of fanciful meanings of our own. It is the work, not of imaginative mediaeval or modern historians and theologians, intent upon finding clues and patterns in history which are not there, but of men who actually took part in the history which they record and interpret, as actors and not as spectators, as participants in the events which provided them with their master-key of interpretation. Such typological interpretation is, according to the New Testament writers themselves, the real meaning of the history both of the Old and of the New Israel, as well as the explanation of the dialectical relationship of fulfilment and transcendence which exists between the

Cf. the deep symbolism of the reading of Exod. xii. 1–14 as the First Lesson on Easter Sunday morning, or the symbolism of many of the Easter hymns, e.g. St. John of Damascus's Ἄισωμεν πάντες λαοί (*c.* A.D. 750):

> "*Come, ye faithful, raise the strain*
> *Of triumphant gladness;*
> *God hath brought His Israel*
> *Into joy from sadness;*
> *Loosed from Pharaoh's bitter yoke*
> *Jacob's sons and daughters;*
> *Led them with unmoistened foot*
> *Through the Red Sea waters.*"

(Trans., J. M. Neale.)

two. According to the biblical and Christian interpretation of history, this typological fulfilment of the earlier in the later exhibits the true meaning of history, and without such typological interpretation the true historical development of the events themselves cannot be understood. That is to say, the biblical history itself falls into a pattern, a pattern which is there to be discovered, not one which is imposed upon history from outside or beyond it; this pattern is not indeed discerned, as if it were part of the structure of profane historical development, by eyes without faith, but is visible only to those who see history through the category of biblical faith. Hence typological interpretation of the Bible differs from allegorical interpretation in that it detects a real and necessary correspondence in the structure and meaning of the original or "typical" event or complex of events to the new application or fulfilment of it. Accordingly the idea of the fulfilment of the Scriptures will mean for us the fulfilment of history, the making explicit of what was implicit in the pattern of the earlier historical events by the *dénouement* of the later events, the deepening of the meaning of history itself as this meaning is revealed to the prophetic insight of those whose eyes are illumined by the light of truth, that is to say, by the Lord who Himself not only controls history but also reveals its secrets to His servants the prophets.

This is essentially the way in which the New Testament writers understand the Old Testament. There is, as we have seen, little allegorizing as such in the New Testament writings, and what there is is chiefly didactic and hortatory in character; but there is, on the other hand, the pervading realization in all the New Testament books that the events of Israel's history are no mere past happenings, gone and done with, but are of an eternal significance which can be discerned only in the light of Christ's life and death and resurrection.[1] The Old Testament as a whole

[1] On this theme see R. V. G. Tasker's valuable study, *The Old Testament in the New Testament* (London, 1946). "To them (the N.T. writers) the whole story of the people of Israel, their divine call, their redemption from Egypt, the giving of the Law on Mount Sinai, the triumphant establishment of the worship of Jehovah in the Holy Land, the building of the temple, the tragedy of the exile, and the subsequent resurrection and return of the remnant to Zion—are all foreshadowings of the greater and final salvation given in the life, death and resurrection of Jesus, apart from which they have in themselves no abiding

displays the pattern of the divine salvation, a pattern which typologically anticipates the salvation which was accomplished through the coming of God's Messiah, of whom the prophets had spoken. Thus, the Old Testament is for the New Testament writers, no less than for Luther, "an evangelical book", and hence the apostolic Church boldly claimed the Jewish Scriptures as a Christian book. Thus, too, it came about that what we now call the Old Testament should have been the only sacred Scripture that was known in the apostolic Church; and when at last at a later date the Church had collected the *corpus* of apostolic writings, they were added to the Hebrew Scriptures as a kind of appendix —but an important appendix, which gave the clue to their true meaning and interpretation. In this way the Christian Bible became a book of two Covenants, not of one. "Ye search the Scriptures", says Jesus to the Jews in the Fourth Gospel, "because in them ye think that ye have eternal life; and these are they which testify of Me".[1]

If, then, we follow the teaching of the New Testament and interpret the biblical history in the light of it, we shall realize that the fulfilment of prophecy does not primarily mean the detailed accomplishment of precise predictions, made centuries beforehand, of the events which came to pass in the days of the Herods; it means rather that the prophets were able to discern the inner significance of the events of their own days in such a manner that they apprehended, however dimly, the very pattern of the process of salvation in history. The meaning which they detected in the events of the historical crisis of Judea in, say, the eighth or the sixth century B.C. is seen to be fulfilled and universalized in the world-crisis of the first century A.D., when "the Prince of this world" was judged. We sometimes hear it said that the

significance and are not fully comprehensible. And the same may be said with reference to the attitude of Jesus Himself" (p. 12). The classical Christian position down the centuries may be summed up in the following words of Richard Hooker: "The general end both of the Old and the New (Testaments) is one; the difference between them consisting in this, that the Old did make wise by teaching salvation through Christ that should come, the New by teaching that Christ the Saviour is come, and that Jesus whom the Jews did crucify, and whom God did raise again from the dead, is He" (*Laws of Ecclesiastical Polity* Bk. I, Chap. xiv).

[1] John v. 39.

prophet is not one who foretells the future but one who "forth tells" the truth about the events of his own day. Indeed, this attitude towards Old Testament prophecy was characteristic of the period which followed upon the first triumphs of the modern critical method, which undoubtedly succeeded in bringing to life for us the great prophets of Israel and setting them forth as real men faced by real problems in the actual concrete historical situation of their own days. It tended to be assumed that, when the meaning of the prophetic utterances was made clear in relation to the historical situation of the days in which they were originally spoken, there was nothing further to be said and that the task of biblical scholarship had been successfully brought to an end. The contrast between the traditional Christian understanding of the nature of prophecy and this kind of "modern" outlook is so great that, if the modern view were held to be correct, most of the Christian value of the Old Testament would be lost and the argument from prophecy would have to be discarded.[1] Prophecy in the Old Testament would have no apologetic value beyond that of the "relevance" of the social and ethical teaching of the prophets to our modern problems; and this indeed has apparently been all that many intending apologists for the Christian faith have been able to say of the Old Testament in recent decades. Such an attitude overlooks the fact that what is at issue is not merely the question of the fulfilment of oracles or predictions about the future but the larger question of the fulfilment of history itself, the question of the realization of a purpose in history

[1] Cf. J. E. C. Welldon, *Augustine's De Civitate Dei*, 1924, Vol. II. p. 683: "There is, perhaps, no point upon which ancient and modern apologetics for Christianity more widely differ than the estimate of the Jewish prophetical literature, if by 'modern apologetics' are understood the writings which have expounded and defended the evidence of the Christian Faith since the birth of the Higher Criticism . . . in the nineteenth century. For the evidential value set upon the fulfilment of the prophecies, which the Old Testament contains or was supposed to contain, was scarcely higher in the opinion of the early Fathers than in that of the Christian scholars who represented the newborn learning of the Reformation and the Renaissance. . . . Modern criticism is apt to assume that the argument once derived from prophecy is now wholly invalid, as the prophets were not 'fore-tellers' but 'forth-tellers', or men whose peculiar strength lay not in the correct anticipation of events lying in the distant future, but in the severely moral interpretation of events occurring in their own time. . . ."

that is both disclosed and achieved in the process of history. Is there in the Bible a pattern of sacred history, clearly revealed in the New Testament, but adumbrated and partially revealed in the Old Testament history?

## § 4. *The Fulfilment of History*

What is meant by "the fulfilment of history"? The phrase at least involves the assertion that in the earlier stages of history there is a partial disclosure of the purpose and goal of the historical process as a whole, and that at a later stage there is a final disclosure that completes and brings to its consummation all that had been implicated in and adumbrated by the earlier and partial stages. The pattern that the earlier historical events, when rightly interpreted, begin to exhibit is finally made explicit and visible in the "end" of history, the realization of its purpose. Now the Bible gives us the account of Israel's history as it was interpreted by the prophetic writers of the Old Testament and later by the apostolic witness of the New. The biblical history, like all history, is written from a definite standpoint, and the Old Testament history is written throughout from the standpoint of the prophets' faith in God as the Lord of history. The whole of the Old Testament is dependent upon the insight and work of the prophets, and the whole of the Old Testament history is history seen through the prophets' eyes. Even the Pentateuch itself, the Law of Israel, is prophetic, since it represents the conversion of the priests and lawyers of Israel to the ideals of the prophets.[1] The Decalogue and each of the legislative codes represent the crystallization or codification of the prophetic insights of one or other of the various prophetic groups that arose in Hebrew history; what, for instance, is the code of Deuteronomy but the systematization in legal and social forms of the lofty ethical teaching of the Deuteronomic prophetic school, with all its characteristic prophetic insights into the nature and purpose of God and His requirements from the people that would serve Him? Of course, within the general prophetic outlook of the Old

---

[1] For the expansion of this point see art. by F. C. Burkitt, "A Corpus of Sacred Writings", in the *Modern Churchman*, Vol. XIX, Nos. 6–8 (Conference Number, 1929), pp. 395–408, especially pp. 397f.

Testament considered as a whole there are several distinguishable schools of thought or points of view, and each of these is represented in the different codes which we now find "scrambled" together in the Pentateuch; there were stages of development, and there were wider and narrower points of view. Nor should it be inferred that the deepest insights of any prophet or group of prophets was ever or could ever be wholly embodied in any system of law that we find in the Pentateuch, since there is a tension inherent in the contrast between the absolute demands of God made known to the prophetic consciousness and the inevitable relativities and practical accommodations and compromises inherent in even the best and most elaborate system of law—a tension which increases rather than decreases with every improvement in the actual formulation of positive law and with every deepening prophetic insight into the nature of the divine demand upon man's obedience. It was the discovery of this irresolvable tension between his own consciousness of the ideal requirements of the divine law of obedience and the actual possibilities of its realization in history which led Jeremiah to his despairing hope of the divine miracle of sanctification, the gift of the New Covenant and of the writing of the New Law in the hearts of men.[1] But the fact remains that the prophetic understanding of Israel's destiny underlies the whole of the Jewish Law, as it underlies the whole of the Old Testament—the Law and the Writings as well as the Former and the Latter Prophets themselves. The biblical tradition itself shows a right recognition of this truth when it insists that Moses the Lawgiver is also a prophet.[2] It is also highly significant that the works which we call "the historical books" were known to the Jews as "the Former Prophets". Thus, the Old Testament as a whole was created and is informed by the insights of the prophets into the character of God and His purpose for Israel and for the world; all its history and all its law are written from the point of view of one or other of the prophetic schools; all its high teaching about God as Creator and Lord of the whole earth springs from the encounter of the prophets with the living and active God in the historical events and crises of their own days. All this is a part of the meaning of the assertion that the biblical history is prophetic history.

[1] Jer. xxxi. 31ff.    [2] Deut. xviii. 15, 18.

Because the biblical history (both *qua* events themselves and *qua* the written record of them) is prophetic, it can therefore have a fulfilment. The insights of the prophets into the character and purpose of God, coming to them through divine revelation amidst the critical situations in which they were involved, penetrated to the inner meaning of the events of contemporary history, and therefore carried with them profound implications concerning the purpose of God in all history and concerning the goal of history itself. For if history has a meaning or purpose, it must therefore have a goal. Now the goal of history cannot itself be historical, that is, realizable within history; it must lie beyond history, since the very conception of a goal of history implies that history has come to an end or is realized. Here we reach a limit of human understanding, since we can be aware of the "end" of history, or of that which lies beyond history, just as we can be aware of eternity or infinity, but we cannot comprehend it and reason about it in the same way that we can comprehend and reason about the historical, the temporal and the finite. This "end" of history, which represents an "end-stop" in our thinking, is indicated in the general usage of biblical theology by the term "eschatological", which has reference to the summing up of the whole of world-process in the ultimate realization of the divine purpose at the "end of history". An eschatological *motif* runs through the writings of all the prophets, and indeed it underlies the whole of the Bible and biblical history. The Bible and the biblical history are consistently forward-looking; they look towards a goal, a coming future climax, in which history shall be consummated and its purpose realized. This goal or end of history is variously described as the Day of the Lord, the Kingdom (Reign) of God, the Times of the Messiah, or simply as "that Day". In this sense biblical history is Messianic and the prophetic writings are Messianic, whether or not they make explicit reference to the specific figure of a Messiah.[1] The apocalyptic writings of the Bible clothe the prophetic looking-forward of all biblical

---

[1] On this whole topic see Reinhold Niebuhr, *Nature and Destiny of Man*, Vol. II (London, 1943), Chaps. I and II. Cf. especially p. 5: "A Christ is expected whenever history is thought of as a realm of fragmentary revelations of purpose and power transcending history, pointing to a fuller disclosure of that purpose and power."

religion in strange imagery, but they are nevertheless in general faithful to the biblical-prophetic outlook;[1] their distinctive characteristic is the manner of their looking forward to a *dénouement*, to a revelation of the hidden Messiah or Messianic Kingdom, which shall finally make manifest "at the end of the times" the Lordship of God and the triumph of His purpose, which have been temporarily obscured by the transient success of human sinfulness or rebellion against God's sovereign will. They are assertions of faith in the ultimate triumph of God's purpose, despite all appearances to the contrary.

The biblical history, then, is prophetic history, since it is the record of events interpreted in the light of the faith of the Hebrew prophets in the justice and mercy of God; the whole of the Old Testament—Law, Prophets and Writings—is inspired by this insight of the prophets, and this is what gives to it its unique character amongst all the religious literature of the world. The prophets were divinely inspired men who penetrated to the inner meaning of the events of the times of crisis through which they were living, and, by shewing the key-significance of those events for the understanding of God's purpose in history, they were able to adumbrate the "end" of history because they had discerned its direction and necessary outcome. Therefore what they say of the coming events which they actually predict—for example, in Amos's prediction of the doom of Samaria or the Deutero-Isaiah's prediction of the restoration of Jerusalem—bears an analogical relation to the goal or end of history beyond history; and the utterances of the prophets, though their literal and historical sense relates to present or foreseeable coming events of their own times, thus inevitably take on an eschatological character, because the events of their own day, as interpreted by the prophets, bear a genuine analogical relation, or real correspondence, to the end (*eschaton*) of history itself. There is nothing fanciful or allegorical about this correspondence: it is given in the very fabric of biblical history. The insights of the prophets of the

---

[1] Cf. Niebuhr, *op. cit.*, p. 33n.: "The idea that Hebraic apocalypse is a corruption rather than a logical culmination of the Messianic hope has gained currency in secularized schools of criticism which do not understand the basic significance of the problem of time and eternity, of history and super-history, with which the apocalyptic writings are concerned."

Old Testament and of the apostles (taught by the Lord Himself) in the New Testament lay bare to our believing eyes the actual correspondence between the pattern of historical events and the "end" of history, which cannot be conceived by our minds except analogically or mythologically. Our revealed knowledge, that is to say, of the nature of the *eschaton* or end of history is analogical, and the biblical method of conveying analogical knowledge in this sense is through myth—in this case the myths of "the Day of the Lord", the "Second Coming", "the Judgment", and so on. As in other spheres, poetry and pictures can convey truth which can be grasped by our minds only analogically, where prose and scientific description fail; when we thus come to the limits of human understanding, as we do in the notion of the end of history, such knowledge as we can possess is necessarily analogical and is best communicated by myths which use historical events to symbolize things which strictly lie beyond history. Such myths are spoilt if they are taken literally. Thus, we find that in the New Testament the destruction of Jerusalem in A.D. 70, prophesied by Jesus, is regarded as the "type" of God's judgment upon the whole rebellious *civitas terrena*, the secular world-order, and it is difficult in some passages (as in Mark xiii) to know at all points whether the reference is primarily historical (that is, to the impending destruction of Jerusalem) or eschatological (that is, to the destruction of "this age"—which is also impending, but in a different yet analogous sense). Behind the biblical typology there is real analogy, and this is, as we have said, what distinguishes typology from allegory.

That the prophets were in some sense aware, at least at certain solemn moments of their life and work, of the eschatological reference of their utterances there can hardly be any doubt, although classical Christian theology has rightly insisted that it matters little whether the prophets themselves were aware of the full implications of their prophecies for the future;[1] one cannot read the predictions of Amos or Jeremiah concerning the fate of Samaria or Jerusalem, or the promises of Ezekiel or the Deutero-Isaiah concerning the resurrection and restoration of Israel, without being convinced that in the prophets' minds there was a deep awareness of an eschatological reality which would transcend

[1] E.g. St. Augustine, *De Civ. Dei*, Bk. VII, Chap. xxxii.

any merely historical fulfilment of their oracles. However that may be, it is clear that we can believe in and understand a fulfilment of prophecy which takes place on the eschatological plane, a fulfilment that is none the less significant because we no longer suppose that, for example, the authors of Psalm xxii or Isaiah liii were given either a miraculous "pre-view" of the events of the Passion of our Lord or a pre-dictated account of those events, which they did not understand. Nor shall we be disconcerted to find that there are in the Old Testament many prophecies or prophetic interpretations which have not in fact been fulfilled at all, and which indeed could not have been fulfilled, because they were false clues; as modern biblical research has shown us, the prophets were real men struggling with real problems, often puzzled, sometimes mistaken. False clues, such as those suggested by Jewish nationalistic pride, frequently and sometimes all-too-successfully gain the ascendancy, and lead to utterances which the pattern of history does not and cannot fulfil. If we think of prophecy as primarily the discernment of the underlying purpose of contemporary events, which carries with it an insight into the pattern and goal of history, we shall understand that the fulfilment of prophecy means the corroboration by later historical happenings of the prophetic foreshadowings of the truth, the typological fulfilment, that is to say, of patterns that have been given in the earlier stages of Israel's history. It is this fulfilment of Israel's history, and therefore of the insights of the prophets, which the New Testament claims to have been accomplished in the coming of Jesus and His Church.[1]

---

[1] W. Sanday in his *Inspiration* (Bampton Lectures, 1893), pp. 404f., has thus finely expressed the idea of Christ's fulfilment of the varied expectations of the prophets: "What they (the prophets) saw was something arising out of, suggested by, the circumstances of their own time, an ideal figure, projected into the future, and, as probably they may have thought, the immediate future. No one of the figures thus imagined adequately corresponds to the real Birth and Life and Death of Christ. They need to be combined, and a key by which to combine them has to be sought. How are we to bring together those two parallel lines of prophecy, which exist side by side in the Old Testament but nowhere meet, the ideal King, the descendant of David, and the ideal Prophet, the suffering Servant of Jehovah? What have two such different conceptions in common with each other? They seem to move in different planes, with nothing even to suggest the coalescence. We turn the page which separates the New Testament from the Old. We look at the figure which is delineated there, and we find in it a

## § 5. *The Re-statement of the Argument from Prophecy*

The biblical prophets, then, are "forth-tellers" and also "fore-tellers". Underlying all the prophetic writings, and also in a sense the whole Old Testament, there is an atmosphere of expectation, a looking-forward to a climax of history or a fulfilment of God's sovereign purpose; this sense of expectation includes both a glad and eager anticipation and also an element of fearful foreboding, according as the prophet's mind is concentrated upon God's mercy or His judgment, upon God's faithfulness or man's rebellion. These two *motifs*, the expectation of deliverance and the apprehension of judgment, are intertwined with one another in all Old Testament prophecy in a well-balanced counterpoint. Throughout there is the conviction that God's salvation and God's judgment must from sheer divine necessity—because God is God—work themselves out in the sphere of history. God is the Lord of history and His will must be ultimately and wholly expressed in it. In the light of this knowledge of God's purpose in history the prophets scan the political and international horizon of their day with clearer eyes than those of the contemporary statesmen and politicians; they see what will be the inevitable outcome of the situation in which they live, and they tell it forth. But because of their faith in the ultimate realization of God's purpose they perceive, however dimly, the real analogical relation between God's action in the crises of their own days and the final end of world history, when God's purpose shall at last be completely accomplished. It is impossible to distinguish precisely between all the elements of literal historical prediction and those of analogical and eschatological insight in their prophecies; but it is not difficult to see how and why the apostolic Church came

marvellous meeting of traits derived from the most different and distant sources, from Nathan, from Amos, from First Isaiah, from Second Isaiah, from Zechariah, from Daniel, from the Second Psalm, from the Twenty Second, from the Sixty-ninth, from the Hundred-and-tenth. And these traits do not meet, as we might expect them to do, in some laboured and artificial compound, but in the sweet and gracious figure of Jesus of Nazareth—King, but not as men count kingship; crowned, but with the crown of thorns; suffering for our redemption, but suffering only that He may reign."

to believe that those analogical and eschatological elements of prophecy had received their true historical realization and fulfilment in the coming of Jesus and the Church. The *eschaton* or "end" of history had manifested itself as fully realized and fulfilled in an historical person, the Lord Jesus Christ, and life within the Church which was His Body was an eschatological life, within history yet paradoxically standing on the other side of the "end" of history, beyond the Judgment and beyond the final great act of God's salvation.

The Church did not fail to see how the deepest insights of the prophets had been fulfilled in her Lord.[1] Jesus Christ was the fulfilment of the whole long prophetic history of the ancient people of God. Liberated from a bondage more terrible than Egypt's by the mighty deliverance He had wrought, the Messiah had led His flock, the Faithful Remnant of Israel, into the Promised Land of that Kingdom or Reign of God which the prophets had foretold; the New Covenant in the blood of Jesus was the fulfilment both of the Old Covenant of Moses and of Jeremiah's explicit prophecy of its renewal; the Messianic Judgment which He brought, though He had come not to judge but to save the world, was more searching than Amos had conceived: Jerusalem had fallen, the Prince of this world had been judged; yet the Faithful Remnant of the true Israel had been restored, the New Temple, not made with hands, had been built; the New Law had been given and was now lived by faith within the Resurrected Israel; the Age of Spiritual Vision foretold by Joel had arrived; the signs of the Messiah had been given in the mighty works of Jesus and His apostles; the New Community had become the universal priesthood and the Spirit-sealed people; the Light had lightened the Gentiles, and the Babel confusion of nations and races had been done away in the one new humanity of the Second Adam. Every significant insight of the Hebrew Scriptures had indeed been fulfilled in Christ and the Church. The argument from prophecy has lost none of its traditional apologetic power. It is an argument of which the real strength is known only by means of the careful and scholarly study of the Bible, and it is in proportion as our minds are steeped in the words and thoughts

[1] For a brilliant summary of the argument from prophecy as it was developed in the ancient Church see St. Augustine, *Ep.* CXXXVII, 15, 16.

of the Bible that its analogies make their full impression upon us and we come to discern in them real correspondences within the whole pattern of the biblical history, which in whole and in part becomes effective testimony to the truth of Christ.

# CHAPTER NINE

# THE INSPIRATION AND AUTHORITY
# OF THE BIBLE

## § 1. *The Nineteenth-century Revolution in Biblical Studies*

FOR MANY people who have grown up in the twentieth century it is difficult to appreciate the magnitude of the revolution which took place in the nineteenth century, when biblical scholars formulated the critical method and made it impossible any longer to accept the traditional theory of biblical revelation, which identified inspiration with infallibility and the written record with the *revelatum*.[1] To-day the original shock and pain created amongst thoughtful Christian people by this revolution is now but a memory of "old, unhappy, far-off things, and battles long ago"—except amongst the unfortunate few who have been brought up in old-fashioned ways. By the beginning of the twentieth century the revolution had been accomplished and the critical position accepted by the leading scholars and teachers of most of the principal Churches of the Reformation; and it was possible for an historian of the new movement in biblical studies to write that "the Regius Professor of Hebrew at the University of Oxford tranquilly expounds, as scientifically assured, results which his predecessor would have laid down his life to avert."[2]

The old view, now discarded, had had a very long history. The belief in the plenary inspiration of the Scriptures had been inherited from Judaism by the apostolic Church along with the

---

[1] As recently as 1861 it was possible for an Oxford theologian to speak these words from the University pulpit: "The Bible is none other than the voice of Him that sitteth upon the throne. Every book of it, every chapter of it, every word of it, every syllable of it (where are we to stop?), every letter of it, is the direct utterance of the Most High. The Bible is none other than the Word of God, not some part of it more, some part of it less, but all alike the utterance of Him who sitteth upon the throne, faultless, unerring, supreme" (Burgon, *Inspiration and Interpretation*, 1861, p. 89; cited by J. Estlin Carpenter, *The Bible in the Nineteenth Century*, 1903, p. 7).

[2] J. Estlin Carpenter, *op. cit.*, p. 38.

Scriptures themselves. By New Testament times the Jews both in Palestine and generally throughout the Diaspora had come to invest the Prophets and the Writings with the same kind of unconditional authority as at an earlier date had been ascribed to the Law alone. No distinction was drawn between the giving of the revelation and the writing of it. The legend of the miraculous making of the Septuagint translation by the seventy translators, however it originated, provides us with a good illustration of the Jewish view of the nature of the inspiration of the Scriptures at the beginning of the Christian era. The New Testament writers share the common Jewish outlook in the matter of the authority of the Scriptures; they quote the Greek Bible or Septuagint as inspired Scripture: God spoke by His prophets in the Holy Scriptures,[1] and Scripture is cited as the direct utterance of God Himself.[2] But there is little trace in the New Testament of any kind of theory about the method of inspiration; indeed, the word "inspiration" is hardly a biblical word at all. In the New Testament it occurs only in 2 Tim. iii. 16: "All Scripture is given by inspiration of God and is profitable for doctrine" (A.V.); "every Scripture inspired (θεόπνευστος) of God is also profitable" (R.V.).[3] The word is doubtless intended to suggest that the Scriptures possess life-giving truth because God has breathed it into them, just as man became a living soul when God breathed into his nostrils the breath of life;[4] this is indeed a valuable and fruitful insight into the true nature of the Scriptures, and one which for Christians must remain permanently illuminating and authoritative. In this Hebrew and thoroughly biblical sense the metaphor of the breath or the spirit of God does not suggest any particular theory of the operation of the divine Spirit upon the minds or souls of the writers of the scriptural books; but the use of such a metaphor, when uprooted from its Jewish background and transplanted into a soil fertilized by Hellenic religious ideas,

---

[1] E.g. Paul in Rom. i. 2.

[2] E.g. Eph. iv. 8 ("He saith"), and frequently in Hebrews (cf. Heb. iii. 7, where Ps. xcv is cited as the utterance of the Spirit: "Even as the Holy Spirit saith, To-day if ye shall hear His voice . . .").

[3] Cf. also Job xxxii. 8, A.V., Wisdom xv. 11; but there is no reference in these passages to a written record.

[4] Gen. ii. 7; cf. Wisdom xv. 11.

makes it easy to pass over into Greek and unbiblical conceptions of inspiration as a kind of divine *afflatus* which takes possession of the whole mind and body of the writers of the sacred books. Already by New Testament times Alexandrian Judaism had begun to conceive of biblical inspiration after the heathen manner and to hold that in the giving of it the rational and critical faculties of the human writers were temporarily in abeyance. The way was thus prepared for those who approached Christianity from a Greek environment to think of the inspiration of the prophets in the fashion of the prophetic frenzy of Vergil's Sibyl.[1] Thus, Justin Martyr, whose conversion, like that of Tatian, illustrates the power of the Old Testament as a means of bringing thoughtful Greeks to acknowledge the truth of Christ,[2] regards the prophets as the lyre upon which the divine Spirit plays such music as He will, and Athenagoras represents the Spirit as a flute-player who uses the prophet as His instrument. The use of the metaphor of the scriptural writer as the pen in the hand of the Holy Spirit becomes frequent, and it comes to be regarded as of little importance whether or not the human writer understood the words which he wrote down. The true Author of the Scriptures was the Holy Spirit, and differences of style amongst the writers of the various biblical books were explained as the gracious and condescending accommodation of the Spirit to the individuality of the particular men by whose instrumentality He delivered His divine message. This kind of view became the accepted standpoint of Christian theology for many centuries; it was never precisely formulated, because it was never seriously challenged by any school of thought or heresy. If at the Reformation some of Luther's suggestions had been developed by his followers, a modification of the traditional position might have been effected; but in the seventeenth century Protestant theology hardened into the most rigid biblical literalism, chiefly through the exigencies of the controversial developments of the times. Throughout the eighteenth century, in England at any rate, "the doctrine of unerring literal inspiration was almost everywhere held in its strictest form";[3]

[1] *Aeneid*, Bk. VI.

[2] Cf. Harnack, *Mission and Expansion of Christianity*, Vol. I, p. 281.

[3] Abbey and Overton, *The English Church in the Eighteenth Century*, Vol. I, p. 560.

and so matters continued until biblical criticism in the nineteenth century opened the whole question of the inspiration and authority of the biblical revelation.

One of the most prominent and valuable results of the literary and historical criticism of the Bible has been to show us how as a matter of fact the various biblical books were written and to call attention to the actual motives and thoughts, insights and limitations, of the men who were engaged in writing them. As a result of the successes of the critical method we now know a great deal about the historical situation in which most of the books of the Bible were written, the general outlook of the times, the kind of persons who wrote them, their manner of life and "social conditioning", and the literary devices and conventions which were extant in their days. Of course, as in every field of scientific investigation, we do not know as much as we should like to know, and there are many problems still unsolved; but the outline of the solution of the main literary and historical problems both of the Old and of the New Testaments is now reasonably clear to us.[1] All this has meant a great and valuable enrichment of our understanding of the biblical material not only from the scientific point of view but also from the religious. Some indeed have thought that there is a danger that our scientific knowledge will outstrip our spiritual understanding of the Bible; but such fears must be proved groundless, for the servants of the Lord of truth cannot but believe that every gain in our scientific knowledge will make possible a fuller understanding of the revelation that He has vouchsafed to His Church. We must strive to attain a view of the nature of the inspiration and authority of the Bible which is at once in harmony with the findings of modern biblical science and capable of making real to us and enlarging the religious truth about the biblical revelation which the traditional view sought to conserve and to express.

[1] Perhaps the best introduction to the results of the modern study of the Bible as these may be summed up in a single volume is to be found in *A Companion to the Bible*, ed. T. W. Manson (Edinburgh, 1939).

## § 2. *Biblical Inspiration in the Light of Modern Knowledge*

What, then, are we taught by modern critical investigation to regard as the way in which the revelation came to the authors of the various biblical books? Does the modern scientific study of the Bible support the theory that it came by way of visions and voices, or that the rational and critical faculties of the writers were in abeyance while they received the communications of the divine Spirit? There can be no doubt that, in the light of our scientific understanding of the composition of the particular biblical writings and of the compilation of the Bible as a whole, all such theories are untenable. Though it is doubtless true that some of the biblical writers—especially the apocalyptists—experienced "visions" and heard "voices" and believed that they had received mystical communications transcending all normal and rational understanding,[1] it is clear to us that most of the writers of the scriptural books lay claim to no such experiences and do not regard them as being a necessary concomitant or authentication of their message. Though Isaiah experiences his vision in the Temple or St. Paul is upon occasion transported into the "third heaven", neither the prophets nor the apostolic writers give us the impression that their message has been reached by the passive acceptance of words dictated while their rational and critical faculties were asleep. Writers like Jeremiah or St. Paul, who at times are unselfconsciously autobiographical, reveal themselves as struggling for expression, wrestling with problems that perplex their intellect, striving to form a rational judgment and to persuade others of its validity. A study of St. Paul with this question in mind is probably the most helpful and suggestive means of reaching a sound understanding of the nature of scriptural inspiration upon its psychological or human side. St. Paul has no consciousness that he is engaged upon the task of writing sacred Scripture; he accepts the transmitted words of the Lord as authoritative and carefully distinguishes from them the authority of his own opinions; and yet, even while he does this, he claims in effect to be writing under the inspiration of the Holy

---

[1] E.g. Ezek. i. 1ff.; Zech. i. 8ff.; Rev. i. 10ff.

Spirit.[1] We may thus discover valuable and definite first-hand evidence concerning the mode of the reception of the biblical revelation. St. Paul's experience was clearly not that of being a mere pen in the fingers of the Holy Spirit; he was not a passive instrument but a man actually engaged in thinking out the given problems of a concrete situation in the light of certain historical happenings and experiences which had brought to him a new understanding of man's nature and destiny. We may deduce from his own writings that his experience is that of being guided to make decisions in accordance with the mind of Christ through the inward illumination of the Spirit of God. Non-Christians certainly may, if they wish, hold that the actual experience which St. Paul had was falsely interpreted by him and that some other and naturalistic interpretation is more plausible; but at least this was how the experience appeared to the man who underwent it, and who, after all, was in a better position to estimate its significance than those who have never had it. Moreover, it is an experience which has been shared, at least to some degree, by many Christian men and women in every century since St. Paul's day. The experience of the biblical writers does not seem to have been different in kind from that of Christian prophets and teachers in subsequent ages, including that of many Christians in our own times. That is to say, our twentieth-century view of the nature of biblical inspiration does not require us to assume that the scriptural writers possessed any mysterious faculty of knowing divine truth which Christians of post-biblical times do not possess, or that in general they enjoyed experiences different in kind from those of Christians in later ages, or indeed that the Holy Spirit "used" or "inspired" them in any way that is *formally* different from His employment and inspiration of Christian men and women to-day. The inspiration of the books of the Bible does not imply for us the view that they were produced or written in any manner generically different from that of the writing of other great Christian books, such as, for example, *The Imitation of Christ* or *The Pilgrim's Progress*. The inspiration of the Holy Spirit, in the sense in which St. Paul claimed to possess the

---

[1] Cf. 1 Cor. vii. 10, 12, 25, 40. See also W. Sanday's collection of early patristic comments upon these verses in his *Inspiration* (Bampton Lectures, 1893), pp. 387ff.

Spirit's guidance, did not cease when the New Testament books were all written, or when the canon of the New Testament was finally drawn up; there is a wide range of Christian literature from the second to the twentieth century which can with propriety be described as inspired by the Holy Spirit in precisely the same formal sense as were the books of the Bible.

Thus, the Christian view has never been and could not be that the biblical books are to be placed in a class apart from all other (including Christian) writings and labelled "Holy Scripture" on the grounds that they are "more inspired" than other literature. Does "more inspired", as the expression has been used by some moderns, mean "more inspiring"? If so, who is to judge whether the Epistle of St. Jude or the Book of Esther is more inspired than *The Pilgrim's Progress*? Discussion of "degrees of inspiration" is subjective and unprofitable. Yet the biblical books *are* placed by Christians in a class apart from all other writings and are treated as Holy Scripture, given by divine inspiration and profitable for doctrine. This is not because of any subjective effects they produce in their readers, but because they are the primary witnesses to and interpreters of the sequence of historical events, culminating in the coming of Jesus and His Church, in which Christians believe that God was working His purpose out and achieving the salvation of mankind. The books of the Old Testament contain the witness of the prophets of Israel to God's activity in the events of their own days, which, as the prophets discerned, foreshadowed the coming consummation when God's Messiah should bring the process to its appointed "end"; the books of the New Testament contain the historical witness of the apostles to the fulfilment of this prophetic expectation in the life, death and resurrection of Jesus the Messiah, and the gathering of redeemed humanity into His Body, the Church. Luther's judgment was sound in principle when he said that the right of a particular book to stand in the Church's Bible was the clearness of its testimony to the historical Christ. This in fact was the standard by which the canon of the New Testament was drawn up by the ancient Church in the second and third centuries of our era. The New Testament is the written testimony of the apostolic community. Though not all, perhaps not even a majority, of the twenty-seven writings which eventually secured admission into the Church's canon of New Testament Scriptures were actually written by the original apostles themselves, all the New Testament books are nevertheless the bearers of the apostolic testimony. Even if, as many critics suppose, none of the original Twelve Apostles of the Lord—indeed no apostle at all except St. Paul—is the author of a New Testament book, it is still true that the writings of the New Testament contain the witness of the apostles to the historical facts concerning Jesus Christ, as this witness was recorded by and in the Church of the apostles themselves. The course of modern biblical research has shown us good reason for supposing that the tradition of the Church concerning her Lord and her own origin came to be fixed within the days of the apostles of Jesus themselves, and that this tradition is in its original formulation the work of the apostles and of those who were from the beginning in the closest fellowship with them.

Sometimes we hear the question asked why the canon of the New Testament should have been limited to works written (approximately) in the first century: why should not the Christian Bible contain the testimony of every succeeding generation of Christians to the power of the Risen Christ in His Church? This question is tantamount to asking why the Church should have a canon of sacred scriptures at all. The answer, as will already be apparent, is that the Church and her faith are founded upon the historical redemption which God wrought at a definite time and place in the world's history—"under Pontius Pilate"—and that testimony to the historical reality of those events in which, *sub specie temporis*, that redemption was accomplished is of greater importance than any other kind of testimony; and this is the testimony of the apostles who from the beginning were eye-witnesses and ministers of the message. This testimony, the apostolic witness, is found in the New Testament—and nowhere else. The New Testament documents are the only first-hand historical attestations concerning those events which provide the key to the Christian understanding of God and His dealings with our world. All later re-writings of the Gospel-story, and all subsequent re-interpretations of it, are dependent for their historicity and validity upon the witness of the New Testament;

Oₐ

and, in general, the only first-hand historical evidence concerning the revelation that came through Israel and Israel's Messiah is contained in the books of the Old and New Testaments. The necessity of the Bible arises from the fact that Christianity is an historical religion. It is only those who have lost sight of the centrality of the historical element in the Christian religion who are heard to ask why the canon of the Christian Scriptures should have been closed when it was.

The fact that the Church determined the canon of her Scriptures does not mean that the Church created or is lord of the Gospel of Christ: the Church is the keeper and guardian of a historical testimony which she can neither alter nor augment. She is the bearer of the apostolic witness because she is the custodian and preacher of the Scriptures. In the days when the recognition of inspiration and authority in religion was held to involve infallibility, the question of Bible or Church was debated as though one could take priority over the other. The Church, it was said on the one hand, wrote the Bible: therefore the Bible possessed an authority which was merely derivative from that of the Church. The Bible, it was replied, was dictated by the Spirit of God: therefore the Church had no authority to teach anything but what was in the Bible—and the individual could read the Bible for himself. The controversy has no great or living interest for those who have discarded infallibilist theories about Church or Bible. The Church and the Bible belong together, and either is meaningless without the other. The same Spirit which enlightened the eyes of the apostles to perceive the significance of those matters which had been fulfilled among them also guided the "inspired Fathers" who drew up the canon of the New Testament, not without much anxious thought and eager debate. A survey of the rejected "apocryphal" writings convinces us that they were indeed guided by the Spirit of Wisdom in their choice. In fixing the canon of the Scriptures the Church acknowledged that she was the servant, not the creator, of the Gospel, and thereby bound herself to be loyal to the apostolic witness as it had been committed to her faithful keeping by the apostles themselves. That the Church is the rightful interpreter of the Scriptures must be axiomatic for Christians, since the Church as the Spirit-bearing community can alone rightly understand the testimony of the prophets and apostles who in the biblical record have left to us their enduring witness to the truth of Christ.[1]

Thus, the Church authorizes the canon of Scripture, the interpretation of Scripture, the formulations of scriptural doctrine, and the translations of Scripture into the vernacular tongues. But authorization is not to be confused with authority; the Church does not confer their authority upon the Scriptures. She recognizes their intrinsic authority, which she can neither create nor confer, just as the positive laws of the State may recognize but cannot create the authority of the moral law. The Church authorizes those books as canonical in which she finds the witness of the prophets and apostles who, through the inspiration of the Holy Spirit, foretell and tell forth the truth concerning Christ. In thus recognizing the authority of the biblical witness to Christ the Church believes that she herself is inspired and guided by that same Spirit who spoke by the prophets and gave bold utterance to the apostles. Without the presence of the Spirit within her the Church could not recognize the authority of the Scriptures, for it is only through the inspiration of the Holy Spirit that men can recognize and confess that Jesus is Lord.[2] Men must receive the illumination of the Spirit of God before they can recognize the authority of the Bible.

## § 3. *The Inner Witness of the Holy Spirit*

Calvin is the doctor of the Church who has given to this universal insight of Christendom its clearest formulation. The authority of the Scriptures is sealed upon the hearts of believers by the "secret testimony of the Holy Spirit". Of course, Calvin

[1] Cf. F. C. Synge, art. "The Gospel in and through the Church" in *The Presbyter*, October, 1943: "The Church authorized the New Testament; but the moment this was done, in the moment of doing it, the Church surrendered its own claim to be the arbiter of orthodoxy and transferred that title to the Scriptures. The Church no doubt preceded the New Testament in time, but the Gospel preceded both; and the Church gave the New Testament precedence over itself in order that it might itself remain under the lordship of the Gospel. Had the Church supposed itself to be the Lord of the Gospel, there would have been no need of Scriptures. The Church, then, must always be listening to the Word of God, proclaiming the Gospel to itself, expounding the Scriptures to itself, expounding its own nature and origin to itself."

[2] 1 Cor. xii. 3.

believed that ultimately the authority of the Bible was based upon the fact that it was dictated *verbatim* by God Himself to the human writers; and here we cannot follow him. But his teaching that the Christian's recognition of the authority of the Bible is due to the working of the Holy Spirit in his heart gives classical expression to a doctrine which has been believed by Christians in every century. Indeed, if ever there was a doctrine of the Church to which the Vincentian canon was strictly applicable, it is the Church's doctrine of the quickening work of the Holy Spirit through the hearing or reading of the words of the Bible. According to Calvin's statement of the doctrine, our conviction of the Bible's authority for our faith and life is due to the *testimonium Spiritus Sancti internum*, that is, to the inner witness of the Holy Spirit in our hearts. Calvin's own statement cannot be bettered:

> "For as God alone can properly bear witness to His own words, so these words will not obtain full credit in the hearts of men until they are sealed by the inward testimony of the Spirit (*testimonium Spiritus intus*). The same Spirit, therefore, who spoke by the mouth of the prophets, must penetrate our hearts in order to convince us that they faithfully delivered the message with which they were divinely entrusted."[1]

Calvin holds that the testimony of the Spirit is a higher authority than reason itself, though he does not desire to disparage reason as such; he believes, in common with the classical tradition of Christian thought, that a divine revelation must be supra-rational, possessing a supernatural guarantee. The external evidence of this guarantee was contained in the miraculous signs which accompanied the giving of the revelation in the first place; the inward evidence is contained in the witness of the Spirit to the truth of the biblical revelation, which thus supplies the inner, subjective guarantee and brings to the individual believer the personal conviction known as saving faith. Calvin says:

> "Let it therefore be held as fixed that those who are inwardly taught by the Holy Spirit acquiesce implicitly in Scripture; that Scripture, carrying its own evidence along with it, deigns

[1] *Institutes of the Christian Religion*, Bk. I, Chap. vii, par. 4.

not to submit to proofs and arguments, but owes the full conviction with which we ought to receive it to the testimony of the Spirit."[1]

In a word, the Bible is authoritative to the Christian believer because the Spirit of God commends to him the message in his heart; the authority of the Bible is the authority not of men, or of churches, or of councils, but of God. This teaching is strongly re-affirmed in the opening article of the *Westminster Confession* (1643):

> "The authority of the Holy Scripture dependeth not on the testimony of any man or Church, but wholly upon God (who is truth itself) the Author thereof. . . . Our full persuasion and assurance of the infallible truth and divine authority thereof is from the inward work of the Holy Spirit, bearing witness by and with the Word in our hearts. . . ."[2]

God speaks through the Bible His word to the Church and to the heart of the individual believer. This is an empirical fact, and one which has been known to Christians in every century since the days of the apostles.

Although it is Calvin and his followers who give this doctrine of the authority of the Scriptures its clearest expression, we must not suppose that the doctrine itself is a distinctively Protestant one. It is a doctrine of the whole Church. The mediaeval view did full justice to the self-evidencing character of Holy Scripture as revealed truth.[3] In the Augustinian teaching the dearest of all miracles was the illumination of the human mind, by which both the book of Nature and the books of Scripture were to be understood in their true meaning. St. Augustine's own intense personal experience of conversion and of the opening of his eyes to behold the truth, as it was made clear by the bright shining of the Sun of Righteousness, left him and the whole Augustinian tradition after him in no uncertainty about the necessity of the Spirit's

---

[1] *Institutes*, Bk. I. Chap. vii, par. 5.

[2] H. Bettenson, *Documents of the Christian Church*, Oxford, 1943, p. 344.

[3] Cf. A. L. Lilley, *Religion and Revelation*, p. 73.

aid in the matter of the understanding either of the world of
nature or of the Holy Scriptures.[1] The whole mediaeval Church
believed not only that the authority of the Scriptures was derived
from God Himself but also that our assurance of that authority
is the result of the operation of divine grace in our souls. St.
Thomas Aquinas teaches that the believer is induced to accept the
truth of the scriptural revelation not merely by means of the
evidence of the miracles, amazing though these are, but also by
the inward prompting of God who invites him to believe. What
excites even more wonder than the kind of miracles which the
Gospels recount is "the inspiration of human minds, so that
unlettered and simple persons are filled with the Holy Spirit"
and are enabled to assent to the truths of revealed religion. "That

[1] St. Augustine does not distinguish between our need of the divine illumination in the understanding of any sphere of truth—whether of mundane things
or of the biblical revelation. The passages in which he refers to the interior
illumination of the divine light are so numerous in his writings that it is
difficult to make a selection. He speaks of "the eyes of a believing mind"
(*In Ps.* XXXVI, *Serm.* ii. 2); or of "the truth, that is, the interior light by which
we understand Him" (*De Vera Relig.* lv. 113); he says that "no creature, however rational or intellectual, is lighted of itself, but is lighted by partaking of
the eternal truth" (*In Ps.* CXIX, *Serm.* xxiii. 1). Commenting on the Dominical
Commandments he says, "Logic is here, since God alone is the truth and light
of the rational soul" (*Ep.* CXXXVII, v. 17). The fact that Augustine does not
believe that we can understand the book of Nature ("natural philosophy")
apart from the illumination of God's Spirit merely serves to emphasize the
truth that we could never even begin to understand the books of Scripture
without that divine enlightenment. He can use similar words about the world
of nature and the truths of revelation: "The mysteries and secrets of the Kingdom of God first seek out believing men, that they may make them understand.
For faith is understanding's step and understanding is faith's reward. . . . God
hath given thee eyes in the body, reason in the heart. Arouse the reason of the
heart, awaken the interior inhabitant of thine interior eyes, let it take to its
windows, let it examine God's creation. . . . Believe on Him whom thou seest
not because of the things which thou seest" (*Serm. de Script. Nov. Test.* CXXVI,
i. 1; ii. 3). As a preacher Augustine well knows that the Spirit must quicken
the words which he implants; "What is done by men who bring tidings
from outside? What am I doing at this moment while I speak? I do but
pour into your ears a noise of words. So unless He that is within reveal it, what
is it that I say, or what do I speak? He that tendeth the tree is outside it, its
Creator is within it"; and he goes on to quote 1 Cor. iii. 7 (*In Joan. Evang.*,
XXVI, 7). Cf. Fr. Hugh Pope, O.P., *St. Augustine of Hippo*, London, 1937,
p. 160. For the last of the great mediaeval Augustinians see E. Gilson, *The
Philosophy of St. Bonaventure*, Eng. trans., London, 1938, especially pp. 364, 458.

the minds of mortal beings should assent to such things," he adds, "is both the greatest of miracles and the evident work of divine inspiration."[1] Faith for St. Thomas is an act of the intellect at the bidding of the will, but the will itself is moved by divine grace. Hence faith is always a supernatural virtue, which we attain only through the assistance of the Holy Spirit. There is therefore in the heart of the believer an interior and anterior divine persuasion of the truth of the scriptural revelation.[2] St. Thomas sees no less clearly than does Calvin that what is revealed, since it transcends the possibilities of our natural knowledge, must be supernaturally authenticated before it can be believed by us or be properly understood. Both Aquinas and Calvin are expressing, each in his own style, what Christians in all ages and places have known to be true: that, in the words of Archbishop Trench, Holy Scripture is not a book which can be interpreted apart from the Holy Spirit by whom it came.[3] Trench quotes a passage from Henry More, the Cambridge Platonist, to the effect that Holy Scripture is not like an artificial garden, with all its fruit and flowers ripe and ready to be plucked; it is rather "like an uncultivated field, where indeed we have the ground and hidden seeds of all precious things, but nothing can be brought to any great beauty, order, fulness or maturity without our industry, nor indeed with it, unless the dew of God's grace descend upon it, without whose blessing this spiritual culture will thrive as little as the labour of the husbandman without showers of rain."[4] The doctrine that the authority of the Bible must be made known to the believer by the operation of the Spirit in his heart is one for which support could be found in the writings of

---

[1] *Contra Gentiles*, Bk. I, Chap. vi.

[2] Cf. P. H. Wicksteed, *Reactions between Dogma and Philosophy Illustrated from the Works of S. Thomas Aquinas* (Hibbert Lectures, 1916), p. 194: "And so, after all, at the end of the chapter, the great Catholic theologian joins the Reformers, with their ultimate appeal to the *testimonium Spiritus Sancti*"; also John Baillie, *Our Knowledge of God*, pp. 113f.: "There is also by the grace of God a direct persuasion of its truth in the heart of the believer; and here St. Thomas approaches very near to the Reformation doctrine of the *testimonium internum spiritus sancti*."

[3] Hulsean Lectures, 1845, p. 100.

[4] Henry More, *The Grande Mystery of Godlinesse* (1660), i, 2.

practically every leading theologian of the Church in every age.[1]
It is, after all, but reasonable to assert that God, and no one
except God, can adequately attest the truth of divine revelation.
Or, as Archbishop Trench expressed the same contention,
"revelation, like the sun, must be seen by its own light; being
itself the highest, the ultimate appeal with regard to it cannot lie
with any (thing) lower than itself".[2]

From the earliest days of the Christian Church it would appear
that the illumination of the believer's mind in the reading of the
Scriptures has always been ascribed to the "interior persuasion"
of the Holy Spirit of God or the Spirit of the Risen Christ. The
Scriptures came at once to be regarded as peculiarly the meeting-
place of God with the souls of men, the means by which God
willed to make Himself known and to declare His will to the
Church which gathered to listen to His Word. God's Word was
not so much a series of written oracles divinely dictated and
delivered once for all in the past—such a view would be a kind
of hermeneutical deism: it was rather the living message which
God speaks in the *here and now* to His expectant disciples. This is
why the Bible should always be read by Christians, whether in
public or in private, in an attitude of prayerful waiting upon
God. The daily food of the Church was given in "the breaking of
the Word" no less than in the breaking of the bread.[3] Christ
Himself is both the Host at the feast and the Food that is
partaken of by the faithful through the Ministry of the Word
and through the Ministry of the Sacraments. This insight of the
ancient Church is found within the New Testament itself. We
may consider it as it is given expression in St. Luke's story of the
Walk to Emmaus.[4] This story gives us a clear example of the
apostolic understanding of the place and value of the Scriptures—
our Old Testament, of course—in the Christian Church.

[1] The classical Anglican divines, of course, accepted whole-heartedly the
doctrine of the inner witness of the Spirit in the Scriptures, but they demurred
against the exaggeration of this doctrine as a means of denigrating the natural
reason on the one hand and the Church and her tradition on the other; see the
quotations from Hooker and Laud cited below (p. 218, footnote 2).

[2] *Op. cit.*, p. 8.

[3] Cf. H. J. Carpenter's art., "The Bible in the Early Church", in *The
Interpretation of the Bible*, ed. C. W. Dugmore (London, 1944), p. 21.

[4] Luke xxiv. 13–35.

The Church existed to be a witness to the resurrection of Christ, and the Church was the place where the Risen Presence of Christ was known. To say that the Church is founded upon the resurrection of Christ implies much more than a mere statement concerning historical origins: it reveals the inner meaning of the Church, its life and worship. The Risen Christ was known in His Church in two ways: in the Ministry of the Word and in the breaking of the bread. Both were corporate activities of the whole Church, and both took place when the Church gathered for worship upon the first day of the week—the weekly Easter festival. The rich symbolism of St. Luke's Emmaus story brings out in a remarkable way the twofold knowledge of the Risen Lord as the deep experience at the heart of the Church's life. In the first place, Christ is present to His disciples at the exposition of the Scriptures: the inward illumination which reveals their Christian meaning and true interpretation is due to the presence of the living Christ in our hearts as we read the Bible or hear it read or preached. It is none other than the Spirit of the Risen Christ who expounds to us in all the Scriptures the things concerning Himself. And our hearts burn within us, while He is in the way with us, while He opens to us the Scriptures. Is not this the experience of Christians in every age, whenever the message of the Bible has been brought home to them? What is this but Calvin's "witness of the Spirit"? The Risen Christ was made known to the apostolic Church through the opening of the Scriptures; and it is worth recalling that, when St. Luke wrote this paradigm for our learning, the Church possessed no other Scriptures than those which we call the Old Testament. The apostolic view was that the Jewish Scriptures are able to make us wise unto salvation through faith which is in Christ Jesus.[1] But we must notice also that in St. Luke's teaching the expounding of the Scriptures is not the only or the final means of revelation: Jesus was not fully known to the wondering disciples until He took the bread and broke it. It was not until then that their eyes were opened, so that they knew Him. In other words, the whole act of revelation, the knowledge of God through Christ crucified and risen, is not completed until the Eucharist is celebrated after the expounding of the Scriptures. It is in the Ministry of the Word

[1] 2 Tim. iii. 15.

*and* the Ministry of the Sacraments that Christ is truly present and known within His Church.[1]

Sometimes it is objected to the doctrine of the witness of the Spirit through the Scriptures in the heart of the believer that it opens the way for all kinds of subjectivism and individualism; the supreme authority in the Church, it is said, becomes the individual Christian with the Bible in his hand: "every man his own pope". But such conclusions are a denial rather than a consequence of the true doctrine of the authority of the Spirit in the biblical revelation. Doubtless any Christian doctrine can be isolated from other doctrines, and, being thus exaggerated and distorted, become a source of error.[2] The doctrine of the supreme

[1] The historic Christian view of the visible Church is expressed in the *Thirty-Nine Articles of Religion* (Art. XIX): "The visible Church of Christ is a congregation of faithful men, in which the pure Word of God is preached and the Sacraments be duly administered. . . ." The attempt to exalt either the Ministry of the Word or that of the Sacraments at the expense of the other must falsify the New Testament and classical Christian teaching. The Anglican Reformers attempted to restore the primitive teaching by giving to each its full and proper place in the whole ministry of the Church. The complete and highest act of Christian worship contains a ministering both of the Word and of the Sacrament: the Eucharist is preceded by the reading and exposition of the Word. There is a deep significance in the giving of the Bible to the priest at his ordination. The Bible is the emblem of both Word and Sacraments. "Be thou a faithful dispenser of the Word of God and of His holy Sacraments", says the Bishop at the imposition of hands; and at the moment of the delivery of the Bible he says: "Take thou authority to preach the Word of God and to minister the Holy Sacraments. . . ." The giving of the Bible symbolizes the underlying unity of the ministries of the Word and the Sacraments: the ministry of the Word proclaims and expounds the great act of God by which the redeemed were gathered into the New Israel, the Eucharist shows forth and represents this act; both preaching and sacraments set forth the great and saving truth of the Bible.

[2] Hooker accepts without question the doctrine of the witness of the Spirit, but he does not enlarge upon it, as indeed he had little need to do so in the days when the Puritans were so strongly emphasizing it. He is anxious to guard against exaggerated notions, such as the view that the Spirit operates independently of man's rational faculty. It is "bootless", he urges, to present scriptural truth to unbelievers as attested by the Spirit in the hearts of believers, without showing them any *reason* why they should accept it; and he wisely adds that "even to ourselves it needeth caution and explication how the testimony of the Spirit may be discerned, by what means it may be known; lest men think that the Spirit of God doth testify those things which the spirit of error suggesteth. . . . Wherefore albeit the Spirit lead us into all truth and direct us in all good-

authority of the Spirit as the interpreter of Scripture was not thus understood by Augustine or Aquinas, by Hooker or Laud—or, for that matter, by Calvin. It has nothing in common with theories of an "inner light" ("guidance") which operates independently of Scripture. Nor can it in any way imply that the arbiter of Church-dogma is the private judgment of the individual rather than the mind of the Church as a whole, or that due weight should not be given to tradition, which represents the mind of the Church in the past, or that the work of the interpreting Spirit in the heart is in any way at variance with reason or operates irrationally. The doctrine implies the contrary of individualism, for it is the Spirit of God alone which makes men to be of one mind in a house: the Spirit in the Church is a corporate possession and is the bond of unity, and it brings individual Christians to a common mind, binding them in one fellowship of the Spirit, and leading them to think with the Church, not by themselves, that is, as "heretics".[1] The general position all down Christian history has been that the Holy Spirit is given to individuals as members of the Spirit-bearing and Spirit-guided community. The conclusion which we have reached is none other than the classical Christian view since the days of the apostles, namely, that the authority of the Bible is in the last resort the authority

ness, yet because these workings of the Spirit in us are so privy and secret; we therefore stand on a plainer ground, when we gather by reason from the quality of things believed or done, that the Spirit of God hath directed us in both, than if we settle ourselves to believe or to do any certain particular thing, as being moved thereto by the Spirit" (*Ecclesiastical Polity*, Bk. III, Chap. viii). Laud sums up a lengthy argument by saying that "the credit of Scripture to be Divine" rests on three main grounds: "The first is, the tradition of the Church. . . . The second is, the light of Nature. . . . The third is, the light of the Text itself, in conversing wherewith, we meet with the Spirit of God inwardly inclining our hearts, and sealing the full assurance of the sufficiency of all three unto us. And then, and not before, we are certain that the Scripture is the Word of God, both by Divine and by infallible proof" (*A Relation of the Conference between William Laud, Then Lord Bishop of St. David's, Now Lord Archbishop of Canterbury, and Mr. Fisher the Jesuit . . .*; issued by Laud in 1639, Sect. xvi; *Works of William Laud*, Vol. II, Library of Anglo-Catholic Theology, 1849, p. 130).

[1] For some suggestive reflections upon the corporate nature of the inspiration of the Holy Spirit see Theodore O. Wedel's *The Coming Great Church*, New York, 1945, pp. 56–66; London, 1947, pp. 56–65.

of the Holy Spirit in the Church. But, as Calvin so clearly saw, the individual does not and cannot truly recognize the divine authority of the Bible as the vehicle of God's word or message for himself or for the Church, until the words of the Bible are "sealed by the inward testimony of the Spirit" in his own heart and he comes to know that in his reading of the Bible or in the Church's Ministry of the Word God is addressing him personally. The final act of conversion, of the opening of the blind eyes, is God's work; the evangelist or preacher sows the seed of the Word by his proclamation and exposition of the biblical words; the apologist may assist by clearing the ground of weeds and preparing it for the seed; the pastor may protect and water the tender shoots; but it is God who gives the increase, who quickens the seed and brings forth the full corn in the ear.

## § 4. *The Divine Authority of the Bible*

Thus, for Christians the authority of the Bible is the authority of God Himself. There is nothing in the methods or conclusions of modern biblical science which contradicts this traditional Christian doctrine of Holy Scripture. It was the divine enlightenment of the eyes of the prophets and apostles which enabled them to understand and to interpret the events of the biblical history, and it is still this divine enlightenment which enables Christians to-day to believe and understand the message of the prophets and apostles, their testimony to Christ which the Bible contains. To-day the belief of Christians concerning the inspiration and authority of the Bible is based upon an induction[1] from the

[1] W. Sanday in his *Inspiration* (Bampton Lectures, 1893) called his view of inspiration "the inductive theory": "we call the theory 'inductive' because it starts by examining the consciousness of the biblical writers . . ." (p. 402). He proceeds to argue convincingly that the evidence of the continuing line of individual biblical writers, when carefully studied and weighed, leads inevitably to the hypothesis of "the operation of a larger Mind, that central Intelligence which directs and gives unity. . . ." But he fails to deal adequately with the contemporary evidence of the witness of the Spirit through the Bible to-day, though occasionally he mentions the Spirit's speaking through the printed page to-day (p. 430) or of "the Voice of God" still speaking through it to man "the same eternal truths in more intelligible and living tones" (p. 413). He does not mention Calvin or refer explicitly to the doctrine of the *testimonium Spiritus internum*.

empirical facts, both historical and contemporary. The divine inspiration and authority of the Bible are categories justified by the inductive study of the uniquely wonderful phenomena of the long series of prophetic insights, extending over a thousand years of Israel's history and culminating in the coming of the Messiah and His New Israel, the Church; they are attested also as valid by the personal experience of countless thousands of Christian men and women in every age of the Church, including our own. No other categories of explanation are adequate to account for such phenomena. To ascribe to the writers of the biblical books an authority which is merely that of religious geniuses does not account for the undeniable fact that the Bible comes to Christians in the Church not merely as possessing the highest human authority but as the unconditional demand and gracious invitation of God Himself; nor does it in the least help us to understand why such a remarkable succession of "religious geniuses" should have "happened" in Israel and nowhere else. Any theory which begins with the definition of religion as man's quest for God is proved false by the biblical and Christian facts. Such a definition might be excusable if advanced by someone who knew only the non-Christian religions, but even then it would still be untrue. The Christian evidence shows that religion—and not only Christian religion—is not man's search for God but God's search for man. Man could not begin to search for God unless he had already found Him, or, rather, been found by Him; and man could not desire to know God unless he already knew Him.[1] Without God we could not desire truth or goodness: it is God who works in us, to make us desire and do His will.[2] It is not we who with great skill find out God after a long and eager quest: we flee from God, who as a Good Shepherd goes out to seek and find us again. The Gospels do not represent Jesus as the supreme religious genius who found the way to the far-off and inaccessible God: on the contrary, they speak of God sending the prophets to

[1] Cf. Pascal's famous words, which he puts into the mouth of his Lord: "*Console-toi, tu ne me chercherais pas si tu ne m'avais trouvé—tu ne me chercherais pas si tu ne me possédais*" (*Pensées*, Sect. vii, 553). There is a fine passage on religion as God's search for man rather than as man's quest for God in John Baillie, *Invitation to Pilgrimage*, Oxford, 1942, pp. 84–86.

[2] Phil. ii. 13.

reason and plead with men, and finally sending His only Son. The whole biblical message is thus God's address, or Word, to mankind; it is His authentic Word, and herein lies its authority.

The fact that the Bible possesses a divine authority does not mean that it must be looked upon as "blind authority" which bludgeons the reason of men into unquestioning acquiescence or which asks of men a "blind faith". God is not "authoritarian" in the exercise of His authority, for authoritarianism is but the *ersatz* robe assumed by tyrants and dictators who possess no real authority. Christian theology is a theology of the Word, and a word is essentially the address of one rational being to another. A theory of revelation which takes seriously the theology of the Word cannot remain satisfied with a view of inspiration which teaches that at any stage of the receiving of divine truth there is a moment when men's rational and critical faculties are in abeyance. God addresses man as a rational and moral being; our reason, conscience and aesthetic sense are God's "point of connection" with us; and it is to us as fully rational and moral beings that the Spirit of God bears His testimony in our hearts. In short, we must use our reason and common sense when we seek to find God's message for us in the Bible. The judicious Hooker has summed up the matter with his usual insight and clarity: "Our words, when we extol the complete sufficiency of the whole entire body of Scripture, must . . . be understood with this caution, that the benefit of nature's light must not be thought excluded as unnecessary, because the necessity of a diviner light is magnified."[1] We are surely justified in thinking that if Hooker

[1] *Ecclesiastical Polity*, Bk. I, Chap. xiv. As against much present-day continental thought upon the subject of biblical hermeneutics, it is most necessary to maintain Hooker's insistence upon reason and conscience as valid principles of biblical interpretation. The insights of the Renaissance, of the Enlightenment, and even of the "scientific attitude" of the nineteenth and twentieth centuries do in fact (and rightly so) affect our interpretation of the authority and relevance of the biblical text. In the seventeenth century, for example, theologians generally thought that the command, "Thou shalt not suffer a witch to live" (Exod. xxii. 18), was as binding as (say) the command, "Thou shalt not commit adultery" (Exod. xx. 14). To-day we do not think so. The rationalism of the eighteenth century supplied a certain civilizing virtue which was lacking in all the zealous divinity of the seventeenth. Toleration is hardly a virtue which the Bible as a whole or in any place explicitly inculcates; and seventeen centuries of Christian theology did not effectively discover it to be

had lived in the nineteenth instead of the sixteenth century, he would have welcomed the benefit of nature's light in the attempt to understand the Bible by means of the application of scientific common sense, which we have spoken of as the critical method.

At the same time, however absorbed we may become in the fascinating critical study of the Bible, we must remember that its message for us can be understood only by means of a "diviner light". Biblical faith offers to us categories by which we may interpret and understand the world and its history and our lives in their relation to God, and it is uncompromisingly opposed to all forms of rationalism—the view that the human reason is, in virtue of its own inherent perfection, a competent and impartial judge of truth and falsehood in all matters, whether secular or religious. In the popular mind to-day, and in a good deal of popular Christianity, this type of rationalism still persists, a hang-over from the eighteenth century, and the very essence of "the liberal illusion"; even those "advanced" thinkers who boast of their acquaintance with Marx and Freud still trust in themselves that they are rational and despise others.[1] The idea of an impartial abstract reason is a mirage, a notable illustration of man's perennial temptation to exalt himself among the gods, knowing good and evil. Our reason is, as we have noted in previous contexts, "conditioned" by many things, such as education, environment, class position, and so on. In fact, unless it is thus

a virtue at all. Yet who to-day would deny its Christian significance or imagine that it could long exist in a non-Christian society? Those who hold that there is no such thing as "unaided reason" (or unaided conscience) and that all insight into truth and value is due to the revealing activity of God's Spirit will welcome the insights of the Renaissance, the Enlightenment, the Marxists and the scientific humanists, and they will apply new insights, whencesoever they come, to the task of interpreting the Bible and setting forth its authority and relevance for our own age.

[1] Cf. Reinhold Niebuhr, *Beyond Tragedy*, London, 1938, p. 265: "It is one of the curious ironies of modern culture that in the very moment when a rationalistic type of Christianity tended to consider the possibilities of human perfection in terms of its purely conscious activity, a secular science in the form of psychology on the one hand, and of social economics on the other, revealed the labyrinthian depths of the unconscious and of the endless possibilities of evil which were hidden there. Both Marx and Freud have, each in his own way, discovered the unconscious dishonesties which dog human actions and corrupt human ideals, even though the conscious mind is intent upon virtue."

conditioned, that is, supplied with categories from outside itself, reason cannot function at all—except perhaps in such abstract spheres as mathematics, though we need hardly discuss this point now. As Kant might have said, but did not, empirical science without principles of interpretation is void; reason without categories is blind. In empirical matters reason must derive from outside itself categories of interpretation which are not revealed or validated by its own intrinsic structure, and which may well turn out to be fruitful sources of error or distortion. This is why, though biblical science may "criticize" the literary and historical forms of the Bible, there is no human science which can pass a judgment upon the divine message of the Bible and pronounce it true or false according to the canons of human reason. In this sense, the Word of God judges us, not we the Word of God. Either we accept by faith the divine truth of the Bible, or by unfaith we reject it. We do not prove it or disprove it by reason. Revelation, like the sun, must be seen by its own light. Truth is not a human discovery but a divine gift; whatever the process of reaching it may have seemed like to us, it was in reality made known to us by the shining of the Sun of Truth. Yet the adoption of this kind of Christian theory of knowledge, if for a moment we may so speak of it, does not commit us to relativism and skepticism. The secularist thinker, when he realizes the significance of Marx and Freud, and thus begins to understand the full extent of the breakdown of rationalism as a theory of the human understanding, seems to have one of two courses open to him. He may become a skeptic, doubting the possibility of human knowledge of ultimate (or, as we should say, divine) truth, and he might then become a logical positivist and devote his talents to the task of convincing other people that philosophy is either a mistake or a disease; or, alternatively, he may bury his head in the sand, as the Marxists do, and continue to behave as if nothing had happened to upset his own categories, pretending that he alone is rational, impartial and objective in a world that is a quagmire of rationalization and relativity. Christian thought, with its realistic doctrine of human nature and of the "fallen" condition of human reason, is not impaled upon either horn of this dilemma, because it has solid grounds for believing that, though human reason cannot of itself know ultimate or divine truth, or cannot with certainty know its guesses to be true, the truth is nevertheless not inaccessible to reason. This is because the truth itself is offered to reason as a gift by means of divine revelation, and the assurance of truth is "sealed" upon the heart of the believer by the testimony of the Spirit of God. Thus, the ability to see from the divine perspective is conferred upon the human understanding through faith, which gives us the categories by which truth may be rationally apprehended and understood. The rational coherence of the whole view of life which results from the use of these Christian and biblical categories is a further reassurance that we have not been deceived by our own wishful conceits. Thus, faith comes to the aid of fallen human reason and restores, at least in anticipation, that perfection of the rational mind which was created originally in God's image and likeness. In this life, therefore, we may have, not indeed the fulness of knowledge, but light sufficient to guide us on our way; we do not attain to the open and direct vision of God, who is the truth; we still see as in a glass darkly, but nevertheless we *see*; and in this cloudy seeing we possess the earnest of the knowledge which shall be ours when at last we shall know even as we also have been known. To the pilgrims *in via* God has vouchsafed through the biblical revelation sufficient knowledge to direct our path to Him, even though not to satisfy all our intellectual curiosity, still less to meet our demand for proof, until at last we attain *in patria* the inexpressible beatitude of the *summum bonum*, the unclouded vision of God.

It is significant that the Bible itself consistently regards the divine bestowal upon the human mind of the capacity to apprehend the truth when it is revealed as no less important than the actual giving of the revelation itself. It is exactly this point which non-Christian epistemology fails to understand. We must receive not only the truth but also the capacity to receive it. The personal religion of the Old Testament, so well expressed in Psalm cxix, breathes unceasingly the fervent prayer for the opening of the eyes, without which we cannot see the truth though it be made plain before our face: "Open Thou mine eyes, that I may behold wondrous things out of Thy Law. . . . The opening of Thy words giveth light: it giveth understanding to the simple. . . . Give me understanding according to Thy Word."[1]

1 Ps. cxix. 18, 130, 169.

PCA

The prophets look forward to the coming of the Messiah as the day in which the blind eyes shall be opened; and the Gospel-writers portray Jesus as the Christ who fulfils this prophetic expectation, seeing in His healings of the physically blind the outward and visible sign of the gift of spiritual sight which the Messiah confers upon all who have faith in Him.[1] Faith itself is the gift of God, by which seeing is made possible. Jesus is known to be the Light of the world because He has brought to men the gift of sight. The Christian experience of conversion thus involves "the renewal of the mind", *metanoia*, seeing things in a new way; it provides the reason with fresh and adequate categories whereby the problems of human nature and destiny can be understood in the light of God's purpose and truth. Jesus is the Truth, and to have the mind of Christ is to be able to formulate judgments about the world and life in accordance with the will of God.[2] Faith in Christ is the means whereby our understanding is re-fashioned and equipped with those principles of interpretation by which the truth that we are capable of receiving *in via* may be apprehended. To be "otherwise minded",[3] to be conformed to (or in our twentieth-century jargon, to be conditioned by) the world is the source of false judgments of every kind, untrue philosophies and unsound behaviour. St. Augustine, who is the Christian theologian who has understood better than any other the depth of the biblical intuition that it is in God's light that we see light,[4] sums up the whole matter in a characteristic passage: "God Himself, because He is the Light, enlighteneth religious minds that they may understand the divine truths that are declared or exhibited. . . . God hath created man's mind rational and intellectual, whereby he may take in His light; . . . and He so enlighteneth it of Himself that not only those things which are displayed by the truth but even the truth itself may be perceived by the mind's eye."[5]

[1] See the present writer's *Miracle-Stories of the Gospels* (London, 1941), pp. 81–90, for an elaboration of this statement.
[2] Cf. 1 Cor. vii. 40; Phil. ii. 5.
[3] Phil. iii. 15; cf. Rom. xii. 2.
[4] Ps. xxxvi. 9.
[5] *In Ps.* CXIX, *Serm.* xviii. 4.

# CHAPTER TEN

# FAITH AND REASON

§ 1. *The Classical Christian View of the Relation between Revelation and Reason*

WE MUST now pass on to our final discussion of the relation between revelation and reason, faith and philosophy. Can it be said that there is a consensus of opinion amongst Christian thinkers down the ages upon the question of the relation between faith and reason? In a broad way this question may be answered in the affirmative. In general terms it may be said that the traditional Christian view has been that a rational understanding of the world and its purpose is attainable by men, but only through the guidance of divine revelation. Faith must take reason by the hand and lead it along the right way.[1] Reason by itself cannot discover the truth about God and human destiny, and even when it stumbles upon particular truths, it cannot with certitude know them to be true; nevertheless, when reason is guided by the insights of the Christian revelation, it can construct a philosophy that is true as far as it goes, though it is always limited by the deficiencies in our empirical knowledge. In philosophy, that is to say, reason must be justified or corrected by faith; without Christian faith philosophy might conceivably approximate to truth, but could not know that it did so. The actual course of the history of philosophy, however, shows that it is more likely to lead to positive error or to radical skepticism.

This, then, may broadly be said to be the classical Christian conception of the relation between Christian faith and man's "natural" reason. Of course, there have been individual Christian thinkers who have modified this traditional outlook in the one direction or the other, and they have occasionally given rise to schools of thought which have deviated somewhat from the central line of development. On the one hand, there have been a

[1] Aquinas, *De Veritate*, XIV, 10, Resp. Cited by E. Gilson, *The Spirit of Mediaeval Philosophy*, Eng. trans. (London, 1936), pp. 40, 429.

few who have tended to denigrate the human reason. Tertullian in some of his moods passionately rejects reason, denouncing Greek philosophy as the bridal gift of the fallen angels to the daughters of men and the Greek philosophers as the patriarchs of the heretics.[1] But Tertullian is a lawyer, eager to make the most of his brief, and on occasion he is ready to welcome the teachings of the philosophers when they support his argument, and he can speak of the human soul as naturally adapted to receive God's word (*anima naturaliter Christiana*).[2] St. Bernard of Clairvaux, provoked by the rationalism of Abelard, deprecates reliance upon reason and speculation as leading away from God. Luther, resiling from the rationalism of the Schoolmen, calls reason an "evil beast", a bitter and pestilent enemy of God, and he proposes to slay the beast and offer it up as an acceptable sacrifice to Him.[3] Some modern "Barthians" have carried their protest against rationalistic liberalism so far as to despair of reason altogether and to deny all possibility of a "natural theology".[4] But these are lonely figures, who stand aloof from the main development of Christian thought upon the subject. Most of them represent some form of reaction from an excess of rationalism in the outlook of their contemporaries and immediate predecessors.

On the other side, some Christian thinkers have inclined towards the view that reason could discover for itself the truths that revelation contains. Justin Martyr, although his own search for truth belied his theory, was willing to allow that a saving natural knowledge of God was possible through philosophy; there

[1] See, e.g., *De Praescript.* 7; *Apol.* 46; *De Anima*, 3.

[2] *De Testimonio Animae*, Chaps. 1 and 5. It is interesting that Tertullian should be the only author whom Hooker quotes in a passage in which he wishes to maintain that "the Catholic Fathers" did not deprecate the use of reason in their disputations with heretics and heathen; he cites Tertullian's *De Resur. Carnis*, iii: "We may even in matters of God be made wiser by reasons drawn from the public persuasions which are grafted in men's minds. . . . For there are some things even known by nature, as the immortality of the soul unto many, our God unto all. I will therefore myself use the sentence of some such as Plato, pronouncing every soul immortal. I myself too will use the secret acknowledgment of the commonalty, bearing record of the God of gods. . . ." (*Ecclesiastical Polity*, Bk. III, Chap. viii).

[3] *In Galat.* iii. 6.

[4] See Barth's Gifford Lectures, *The Knowledge of God and the Service of God* (London, 1938), Lect. I, for Barth's own view.

is, he thinks, practically an identity between the teachings of Christianity and the best in the philosophical schools, and he claims that Christians are the heirs of all the truth that was discovered by the Greek philosophers: "Whatever has been well said anywhere or by anyone belongs to us Christians."[1] His successors at Alexandria, such as Clement, regarded Greek philosophy along with Jewish Law and Prophecy as a *praeparatio evangelica*: Plato was Moses talking Attic Greek. Abelard in the Middle Ages revived this point of view; he did not distinguish carefully between natural and revealed theology. He held that what had been revealed to the Jews by prophecy had been given to the Greeks by philosophy and that the doctrine of the Trinity, and other Christian truths, had been taught by Heracleitus and Plato: Plato's *Anima Mundi* was none other than the Holy Spirit. By these teachings Abelard incurred St. Bernard's stricture that he had succeeded in proving that he himself was a heathen rather than that Plato was a Christian. Professor C. C. J. Webb has remarked that Abelard began a process of rationalism in theology which culminated in Kant and the attempt to confine "religion within the limits of the mere reason";[2] we may perhaps look upon him as the precursor of Lord Herbert of Cherbury and the English deists. The standpoint of the deists is clearly displayed in the titles of the works of two of the leading exponents of the school— Matthew Tindal's *Christianity as Old as the Creation; or the Gospel a Republication of the Religion of Nature* (1730) and John Toland's *Christianity not Mysterious* (1696). So prevalent were such ideas in that *saeculum rationalisticum*, the eighteenth century, that Tindal was allowed to keep his fellowship at All Souls until his death,

---

[1] *Apol.* II, 13; cf. *Apol.* I, 46. St. Augustine maintained that whatever had been rightly said by the heathen should be appropriated to Christian use; the Platonists especially have said much that is in harmony with Christian faith; cf. *De Doct. Christ.*, Bk. II, Chap. xl: "All branches of heathen learning have not only false and superstitious fancies . . . but they contain also liberal instruction which is better adapted to the use of the truth, and some most excellent precepts of morality; and some truths in regard even to the worship of the one God are found among them. Now these are, so to speak, their gold and silver, which they did not create themselves, but dug out of the mines of God's providence which are everywhere scattered abroad. . . . These therefore the Christian . . . ought to take away from them and devote to their proper use in preaching the Gospel."

[2] *Studies in the History of Natural Theology* (1915), p. 231; cf. p. 218.

and, as we have noted previously, his antagonist Bishop Butler largely shared his point of view. Toland aimed at showing that Christian doctrine contained nothing that reason could not comprehend and that faith was synonymous with knowledge. In the nineteenth and twentieth centuries this type of thought re-appears, in a milder form, in the view that the truth of Christ's revelation is directly discerned by the spiritual, rational and moral consciousness of men. But such attitudes are not representative of the main stream of Christian thought on the question of the relationship between faith and reason and must be considered an aberration from the classical Christian view.

According to the central, and on the whole consistent, development of the Christian understanding of the relationship between revelation and reason, reason becomes fruitful and capable of reaching a relatively reliable view of the universe and the purpose of man's existence in it, when it is guided by the insights of the Christian faith. This does not mean that faith supplies the *data* of empirical knowledge; the search for and examination of the empirical *data* of knowledge remains the function of the empirical sciences, including theology. It means rather that faith supplies the "clues" or categories of interpretation by which alone the empirical *data* of science and religion can be rightly understood. The *data* which each several scientific discipline presents to the philosopher for his attempt to unify them into a system do not arrange themselves into a pattern; it is the philosopher's task to construct of them an ordered and coherent whole, that is, a metaphysic. Such a task demands creative insight; it requires the employment of reason in a meaning of that word which includes artistic imagination and moral sensibility, as well as scientific induction and deduction. The philosopher himself must select his own categories of interpretation; he must seize upon a "key-feature" or find a "clue" to the making of a unity out of the many. Every philosopher who attempts to build a metaphysic is ultimately dependent upon some "faith-principle", whether he is a Christian or a non-Christian, religious or anti-religious. No metaphysic or world-view can be constructed without a "faith-principle" in this sense; and, as we have noted elsewhere, even those philosophies which claim to be based upon reason alone without any admixture of faith, always turn out upon examination to be elaborate rationalizations which conceal the initial act of faith upon which they are based. If by philosophy is meant a purely rational deduction from premises which can be known to be true, or a vast super-scientific induction that can give us practical certitude, then the verdict of most Christian thinkers down the ages has been that philosophy in this sense is impossible. Reason cannot walk by its own light, and must seek the illumination of some principle of interpretation which reason itself does not contain. The general paralysis of metaphysical speculation in an age like our own in which philosophers are reluctant to believe in anything at all or to make any kind of venture of faith is the unwitting endorsement on the part of modern skepticism itself of the truth of the Christian view that reason is blind until faith takes it by the hand. The adequacy of any particular "faith-principle" must be judged by its ability to order the whole range of *data* supplied by the empirical sciences (including theology) in a rational and coherent philosophy of life and the world.

## § 2. *The Possibility of a Christian Philosophy*

It may fairly be claimed that such a view of the relation of faith and philosophy represents a central—we would be so bold as to say, *the* central—line of development in Christian thought upon this subject since the second century. It is based not upon any *a priori* or *ex cathedra* deliverance that takes no account of the evidence, but upon the deep and searching experience of philosophers who have turned Christian and of Christians who have tried to philosophize. It was the experience of Justin Martyr, who has movingly described it;[1] he had studied in turn the teachings of the Stoics, Peripatetics, Pythagoreans and Platonists, and he had been helped most by Platonism, but the end was disappointment and incertitude. It was not until he met the venerable old man who told him about the prophets and the faith by which they should be read that his quest was triumphantly concluded. Faith came to the rescue of reason and he became fully rational: "A flame was kindled in my soul; and a love of the prophets and of those men who are Christ's friends possessed me; and whilst

[1] *Dial. Trypho*, Chaps. 1–8.

revolving his words in my mind, I found this philosophy alone to be secure and profitable. That is how and why I became a philosopher."[1] This experience of Justin's has been shared by many from his day to ours. Revelation supplies a clue which enables the distracted and compassless reason to go upon its way with confidence. To become a Christian does not mean to renounce reason; on the contrary, it enables a man to become truly rational; by becoming a Christian one may become in the true sense of the word a philosopher. By the expression "a philosopher in the true sense of the word" we mean one who is passionately and actively interested in the great metaphysical questions about God, the world and human life and destiny, but we are well aware that in our modern anaemic age there are many for whom the word "philosopher" has ceased almost entirely to bear this meaning. "There are many people to-day", writes a modern philosopher, "to whom philosophy means chiefly epistemology and logic; meaning by epistemology a discussion of how we perceive sensible objects, and in what sense they are really there to be perceived, and by logic a discussion of the general laws of thought and the methods and presuppositions of natural science."[2] Of course, these considerations are certainly not outside the sphere of philosophy, but they are not the whole of it; and it is hardly surprising that those who think of philosophy and its function primarily in these terms should be unable to see how becoming a Christian might help a man to become a philosopher. Christian faith does not have much to contribute to the discussion of how we perceive sensible objects and in what sense they are there to be perceived (despite Bishop Berkeley); but it has much to say when we come to the discussion of the proper problems of the human mind and therefore of the *philosophia perennis*, God, freedom and immortality. When a philosopher becomes a Christian, he will at least be confronted with the central problems of philosophy once again.

Many Christian thinkers, such as Lactantius, who succeeded Justin Martyr and wrestled with the problem of the relation between Christian faith and Greek philosophy—for in this form the question of the relation of revelation and reason presented

[1] *Op. cit.*, Chap. 8.

[2] H. A. Hodges, *Wilhelm Dilthey: an Introduction* (London, 1944), p. 11.

itself to them—thought that, if one accepted the Christian revelation, one would then be in a position to piece together all the elements that are true in the teachings of the different philosophical sects and so by a process of syncretism arrive at the true philosophy. It is not until we come to St. Augustine that we find the problem dealt with in a truly masterful and, one might say, definitive way. Augustine is no mere syncretist but a powerful and original thinker. At the very heart of all his thinking is the conviction that Christian faith alone enables a man to be rational, to be a philosopher. Faith is a light and guide without which reason cannot work. It is an indispensable condition of understanding. A man must believe in order that he may understand. In his Old Latin Bible St. Augustine found a text which exactly expressed his meaning: *nisi credideritis, non intelligetis*[1]—unless you believe, you will not understand. On this text (which will not be found in our English Bibles) was based the famous principle, *crede ut intellegas*, which passed into mediaeval theology as a legacy from St. Augustine. Thus, the classical Christian view of the relation between revelation and reason, faith and philosophy, may be represented in three words, "Believe to understand", and these three words sum up the whole matter. Not only St. Anselm and the Augustinians but also St. Thomas Aquinas (who would have been the first to acknowledge his master's insight) and the Thomists accept the validity of Augustine's fundamental proposition and assimilate it into their teachings.[2] Considered under this aspect, as Gilson says, Augustinianism is the very charter and enduring model of Christian philosophy: "to be Christian *qua* philosophy a philosophy must be Augustinian or nothing."[3] There are doubtless other kinds of philosophies which are compatible with Christian truth, but in so far as they consciously or unconsciously dispense with revelation as the starting-point and condition of reasoning they are not properly qualified to

[1] This is a translation of the Septuagint version of Isa. vii. 9 (b), which runs: καὶ ἐὰν μὴ πιστεύσητε, οὐδὲ μὴ συνῆτε. The Vulgate rendering (*si non credideritis, non permanebitis*), like the English versions (A.V. and R.V.: "If ye will not believe, surely ye shall not be established"), follows the Hebrew.

[2] See E. Gilson's very suggestive and helpful essay, "The Future of Augustinian Metaphysics", in *A Monument to St. Augustine*, by M. C. D'Arcy and others (London, 1945).

[3] *Ibid.*, p. 308.

be called by the name of *Christian* philosophy. The philosophy of Descartes, for example, is doubtless compatible with Christian belief, but *qua* philosophy it is not a Christian philosophy.[1] The same assertion might be made of several philosophies more recent than Descartes's; in varying degrees it may be said that, although they cannot strictly be called Christian philosophies, several philosophical systems and views of recent times are not incompatible with Christian truth, such as, for instance, those of Edward Caird, T. H. Green or Josiah Royce on the one hand, or of Pringle-Pattison, James Ward, William James or F. R. Tennant on the other. A Christian philosophy as such is one which frankly admits that reason cannot work except by the light of revelation and unashamedly follows St. Augustine in acknowledging Christian faith as the master-light of all our seeing. Unless the Christian and biblical faith is something other than it claims to be, this is necessarily what Christian philosophy must be. In the activity of the Christian philosopher we do not see reason searching for a faith to believe and live by: we see rather faith itself seeking understanding, as St. Anselm so clearly saw: *fides quaerens intellectum.*

Nothing could better illustrate the nature of Christian philosophy than the spiritual and intellectual pilgrimage of St. Augustine before and after his conversion. Before that event he is seeking through reason—but not only through reason—to find a philosophy of truth and action which should meet the need of his ardent spirit; he attaches himself to the Manichaeans; forsakes them and receives help from Cicero; then he turns to Plotinus and the Platonists; but he does not become a philosopher: he becomes a Professor of Rhetoric! After his conversion he finds illumination upon all those problems of philosophy which before he could not fathom, although this illumination came not suddenly but by degrees. Gilson sums up the effect of his conversion upon St. Augustine as a philosopher in the following luminous sentences: "Thus, the philosophy that he vainly sought by reason was offered him by faith. Those all too uncertain truths which Greek speculation reserved for an intellectual *élite*

---

[1] Cf. E. Gilson, *The Spirit of Mediaeval Philosophy*, p. 37: "I call Christian every philosophy which . . . considers the Christian revelation as an indispensable auxiliary to reason."

had already been brought together, purified, justified, completed by a revelation which put them within the reach of all the world. In this sense we might not incorrectly sum up the whole experience of St. Augustine in the title he gave to one of his own works: *De Utilitate Credendi*—On the Advantage of Believing—even for the very purpose of assuring the rationality of reason. If he so incessantly repeats the words . . . *nisi credideritis, non intelligetis*, it is because they so exactly express his personal experience."[1] In the modern phrase, Augustine's philosophy is "existential"; it is part of himself; it is not something which he thinks about with his intellect only; it is something which *happens* to him. It results from a being taken hold of, a being apprehended by the Source of Understanding itself. This is the very essence of Christian philosophy, as distinct from philosophies that are merely compatible with Christian truth. This is how and why St. Augustine became a philosopher.

The great advantage of the Augustinian conception of the relationship between faith and reason is that it conserves the central fact of Christian experience in every age, namely, that faith is not a mere guessing at indemonstrable truths, which may be dispensed with when a rational structure has been built; faith is a source of illumination which enables the building of a truly rational philosophy to begin. Faith is not a short cut; it is not a substitute for understanding but a condition of it. "Blind faith" is a contradiction in terms, as far as Christian faith is concerned, for faith is the source of light and understanding. Nor is it a believing apart from or in opposition to evidence; it is no stubborn assertion of a *credo quia absurdum*. Between faith and reason there can be no conflict, for faith is ancillary to reason; faith cannot oppose reason: it can oppose only other *faiths*, which are being used as rival conditions or pre-suppositions of reason, such as the faith-principle of Marxism or scientific humanism or anti-Christian rationalism. The fact that Christian faith is opposed to rationalism (though some notable attempts have, of course, been made to combine Christianity with rationalism in philosophy) should not lead us to suppose that faith is itself opposed to reason, for rationalism operates only through the employment of a concealed faith-principle which is nonetheless as necessary to it as is

[1] *The Spirit of Mediaeval Philosophy*, pp. 32f.

faith to Christian philosophy. It is not an objection that can be raised against Christian philosophy, in any sense that it cannot be raised against other philosophies, including naturalism and agnosticism, that it is "relativistic" or "subjective" because it admits its dependence upon a faith-principle. The naturalist who draws his categories for the interpretation of the universe from physical science has equally made an act of faith in selecting those particular categories and no others; the categories were not themselves observable like the facts of the realm of physical existence, but were applied to the total situation as a result of a judgment of significance which was not made in the laboratory of a physicist. The Christian philosopher in making his judgment of significance takes his stand upon other facts, which seem to him in the light of his whole faith and experience to be more significant. He points to other observable facts: there is such a thing as a believing and witnessing Church: there is such a thing as conversion to Christian faith. The conversion of an Augustine has altered the whole course of history and of the ways of thinking of several generations. To the believer himself, who knows the experience from within, conversion does not mean the abandoning of the effort to understand but a veritable liberation of the reason. This also is a fact of human existence, and there is nothing to be gained but everything to be lost in philosophy by the attempt to explain facts away or to pretend that they are other than they appear to be to those best qualified to judge of them. So long as there exists the Christian Church, it needs to be accounted for.

Nor is the criticism valid that Christian faith involves subjectivity, if by that word it is implied that Christian philosophy rests upon a vague mystical intuition, an "inner light" or a private and mysterious faculty for knowing truth which non-Christians do not possess. Christian theology does not claim, as we have already noted, that faith is a special department or faculty of the mind, a kind of miraculous inner eye which is superadded to the natural faculties of men. Christian faith is not *formally* different from the faith-principles which operate in other systems of thought and philosophies of life. It is a judgment of significance upon the recorded biblical facts. Again, therefore, it is not subjective in the sense that it has been excogitated from the speculations of any abstract philosophical consciousness in the manner in which (for instance) the Hegelian philosophy was. It is grounded upon historical facts, as attested and interpreted by the prophetic and apostolic witness. It is not free to invent a new history or a non-historical object of belief, because its very character of Christian faith is defined by its acceptance of an historical testimony. It is evoked by the proclamation of things which have happened altogether outside and apart from the "subjective" feelings, wishes and speculations of Christians. The facts to which it points as significant are just as truly facts as those of the physical world. It is within the historic Christian community, the Church, that the true significance of these facts is seen in a way in which it cannot be seen from outside, and there need be nothing to surprise us in this. Just as a nation's history is richer, instinct with deeper meaning, arousing stronger and tenderer emotions, for the members of that particular national-historical community than it can ever be for a foreign observer, so also is the biblical-Christian-Church history for those who stand within the historic Christian community than it can ever be for those who stand outside. Within the community the light of faith is not ineffable, incommunicable, non-verifiable; it is not in this sense "subjective".[1]

## § 3. *Faith as a Condition of Rationality*

At this point we may reflect upon the very great benefit that has been conferred upon us by the progress of modern biblical science through its demolition of the traditional theory of the inspiration of the Scriptures. As long as it was held that revelation was conveyed in propositional truths written in an infallible book, there was a very grave danger that the true nature of Christian faith would be obscured. This false theory made it fatally easy to equate Christian faith with the believing of certain propositions, the intellectual acceptance of a creed or formula.[2] St. Augustine

---

[1] Cf. H. R. Niebuhr, *The Meaning of Revelation* (New York, 1941), especially pp. 59-73, for a valuable consideration of this theme.

[2] E. Brunner in *The Divine-Human Encounter* (Eng. trans., London, 1944) has dealt effectively with this antithesis between belief in "truths" and genuinely Christian or biblical faith. Cf. pp. 73f.: "Orthodoxy thought of God as the teacher who delivered supernatural, revealed truth and proffered faith to man. In this way the Word of God was identified with doctrine, and faith was assent

himself, of course, laboured under the heavy disadvantage of the
traditional theory of biblical inspiration; allegorism helped in the
interpretation of particularly difficult biblical passages, but it
offered no assistance in the matter of understanding the nature of
faith as something quite different from the acceptance of "truths"
written down in the Bible. He had no alternative to the universally prevalent view, and so he loyally accepted it, though not with-
our misgiving. But he avoids all the grosser forms of literalism:
"the letter killeth" was a Pauline text upon which he had medi-
tated profoundly.[1] It is easy to imagine with what a great sense of
relief he would have welcomed the abandonment of the literalist
theory of inspiration, had it been possible in his day. Despite the
temptation which that theory must have presented to him to do
so, Augustine does not confuse Christian faith with the acceptance
of Scriptural propositions. He notes that the Scriptures are
unintelligible to those who do not read them with Christian eyes:
"the Spirit giveth life" to the words of Scripture. Even after his
conversion Augustine found that he had to lay aside the Book of
Isaiah, which St. Ambrose had advised him to read, because he
could not understand the first chapter; he well knew the difference
between "reading things in the letter and understanding them in
the spirit."[2] If the words of Scripture were indeed infallible
oracles it would not be necessary to read them "with new eyes".
Faith for St. Augustine is not intellectual assent to certain
scriptural propositions; it is the awakening of the mind to truth,
a new way of seeing things, a means of understanding what before
did not make sense, the acquiring of categories of interpretation
by means of which our whole experience and thought become
rational and coherent. What the believer possesses as a result of
his conversion is not a set of formulae which he can repeat like a

to this doctrine. Precisely that which is the concern of biblical faith was consequently no longer understood: that is, overcoming the Object-Subject
relation and having the real Person of God present in His Word, who as such
is also the creative Presence of the Holy Spirit. For this reason the faith of
Orthodoxy was so destitute of love. For love cannot be created by faith in a
revealed truth, but only by the presence in the heart of the Holy Spirit, who is
none other than the very love of God Himself poured out in our hearts."

[1] See, e.g., *De Spiritu et Littera*, 6.

[2] *Conf.*, Bk. IX, Chap. v and Chap. iv. 6.

parrot, nor a system of doctrines which he accepts as infallibly true, nor a book of oracles out of which he can answer every question: he possesses "new eyes". He sees the truth to which he was formerly blind. Again and again Augustine rebuts charges of credulity and subjectivism. Christian faith, he repeats, is not formally different from faith in one's doctor or in one's friend.[1] It is not wishful, since it is created by those very qualities in one's doctor or friend which have elicited it, but it is still faith and not proof. The object of faith, if it is not credulity, is what has awakened faith in us. St. Augustine realizes very clearly that it is what God has done which has created Christian faith in us, both through His great acts in the biblical history and through the revealing work of His Spirit in our minds to-day. It is God Himself who through the testimony of the Scriptures in the Church elicits the faith of believers. It is the character and deeds of Jesus, as attested by reliable witnesses, which calls forth Christian faith. It is therefore something that is objective in the sense that it is outside ourselves, something that is given in historical attestation, a divine quality exhibited in human history, which awakens faith in the hearts of Christian believers—just as it is a quality that actually exists in our doctor or our friend which leads us to put our trust and confidence in him. Therefore, though it does not cease to be a human act, faith is also and in the first place a divine act. On our part it is a response to an invitation, a gift which we are free to refuse, for God does not compel us against our will to believe. He invites, and waits for our acceptance. But it is God who has also created the very possibility of our acceptance, our capacity of response in faith, the freedom to use our reason and will rationally when the gift of faith is offered to us. God created man in His own image; and our capacity to respond to God's Word, our reason and conscience—which reflect that light which lighteth every man coming into the world—are God's "point of connection" with us; they are the vestigial remains of that original righteousness, sadly defaced, which is the divine image and likeness in man. The light of

---

[1] *De Util. Credendi*, 23. Augustine argues cogently that a man who thinks that faith is mere credulity cannot have a friend. It is reasonable to have faith in one's friend, if he is really a friend; and this should be enough to convince any rational person that faith and credulity are not the same thing.

reason and conscience, themselves always, however feeble, refractions of the divine light, must be rekindled by the brightness of the light of the biblical revelation of Christ, who is the effulgence of the Eternal Light. Reason, which is blind and helpless in questions of ultimate truth until it is illuminated again by the light from which it came, is nevertheless that capacity or part of us which through divine assistance recognizes the truth when it comes to us; will is the capacity which through divine help acts upon the truth that is thus brought to it in the operation of the divinely enlightened conscience; and the result is what Christians know by the name of faith. It is because man is capable of becoming a rational and free being that he can respond to God's gracious invitation; it is when he makes the response of faith that he becomes a truly rational and free being. It is in the response to the address of the rational word of Him who is the Supreme Reason that man learns to answer reason with reason, and thus the divine image and likeness is restored in him. Thus, it is impossible that there should be conflict between faith and reason, when faith is truly response to the source and essence of the universal reason.

Christian faith has always maintained that faith is a virtue and that lack of faith is a sin. To modern ears this seems a hard saying, because we have been brought up in an age of pseudo-democratic ideology which has conditioned us to believe that "everyone has the right to his own opinions" and that no moral stigma attaches to anyone for choosing to believe what he likes. It hardly ever occurs to us to reflect that "believing what one likes" leads inevitably to such horrors as Nazidom, since there are so many people who *like* to believe the teachings of the Nazis and other moral perverts. It ought not to be difficult to convince people, who have lived through European history since 1933, that men are responsible to society—if not to God—for what they believe, and may therefore be in the matter of their beliefs morally culpable. Beliefs, even the elaborate systems of philosophers, are so often rationalizations of personal or party or national selfishnesses, that it ought to be clear that moral responsibility attaches even to the most purely "rational" or "scientific" philosophy. No despotism or organized group-selfishness has ever lacked its philosophical apologists. But, apart from ideological motives,

even the reason of philosophers, who proudly write "prolegomena
to every future metaphysic", can be the minister of one of the
most deadly forms of human pride, the pride of intellect and the
pretension of wisdom.[1] Christian philosophers, of course, are not
immune from this temptation to sin; but the self-knowledge
which Christian faith engenders ought to be for them a prophylactic against it. Error in philosophy, or in the use of reason generally,
arises not only from the weakness and finitude of our human
intellect and the deficiencies of our empirical knowledge, but
also—and more dangerously—from the distortions occasioned by
human sinfulness and self-interest. The right use of reason is a
virtue, the product of a virtuous mind; but this is no cause for
self-satisfaction and pride, since, like every other good and
perfect gift, it comes from above. Faith is a virtue, but like every
virtue we possess, it is the gift of the divine grace. The Christian
philosopher will not boast of his truth over the non-Christian;
for he knows that his truth was not of his making and that it
is not his private possession but the treasure of the Church of the
ages, which is shared by shepherds and fishermen as well as by
kings and sages. Moreover, he will be ready to confess his sins
against the truth, which are many.

It is in the matter of self-knowledge that St. Augustine has
much to teach us. Descartes, we are told, was angry with his
friend who reminded him that his *Cogito, ergo sum* was borrowed
from St. Augustine.[2] Descartes, however, was right in claiming
that his Method was original and that he had not learned it from
Augustine, although the latter has often been unjustly blamed for
the Cartesian errors.[3] Augustine would have repudiated the
suggestion that there could be any true knowledge of the self, or
indeed of anything else, apart from God. The knowledge of the
self is bound up with the knowledge of God. Archbishop Temple
has spoken of the *Cogito, ergo sum* as the "Cartesian *faux-pas*"
which put modern philosophy on the wrong track at the outset of
its quest;[4] but the real gravamen of the charge against Descartes

[1] On this subject see R. Niebuhr, *Nature and Destiny of Man*, Vol. I (London,
1941), pp. 207–11.

[2] Augustine's form of the proposition was, "I doubt, therefore truth is"
(*De Vera Relig.* xxxix. 73). See footnote on p. 30, *supra*.

[3] Cf. E. Gilson in *A Monument to St. Augustine*, pp. 293ff.

[4] *Nature, Man and God*, Lecture III.

and the break with the Christian philosophy of the Middle Ages is more serious even than this. It is the fallacy that was deep-rooted in the thought and temper of the Renaissance, the resuscitation of the untruth that lay in the heart of classical humanism, the untruth which St. Augustine had killed.[1] This untruth is the assumption that the human reason can itself by following the rules of its own inherent nature and applying them to human experience arrive at a true philosophy of the world and life. By the fifth century A.D. the potentialities of classical philosophy had been exhausted in the effort to provide man with a basis for rational knowledge and practical action out of the resources of human reason and experience alone. Modern philosophy since Descartes has largely recapitulated the course of ancient philosophy and has ended in the same skepticism and disillusion. The time has surely come for Christian philosophy to be frankly Augustinian again and to call in Christian faith to liberate reason from the toils of rationalism and its corollary, skepticism. Rationalism loves to represent the issue between itself and Christian philosophy as one of reason *versus* "belief" or "mere opinion"; it does this by concealing its own faith-principle or by pretending that it is not a faith-principle at all but one which is either rationally demonstrable or self-evident to all thinkers. But a glance at the history of philosophy or at the condition of philosophical discussion to-day is sufficient to show that there is no key of universal understanding which is, or can

---

[1] Cf. C. N. Cochrane, *Christianity and Classical Culture* (Oxford, 1940). Cochrane traces the development of classical thought and the Christian *critique* of it, which culminated in St. Augustine. The Christians traced the error of classicism "to the acceptance of a defective logic, the logic of classical 'naturalism', to which they ascribed the characteristic *vitia* of the classical world. . . . Their revolt was not from nature; it was from the picture of nature constructed by classical *scientia*, together with its implications for practical life. And what they demanded was a radical revision of first principles as the presupposition to an adequate cosmology and anthropology. The basis for such a revision they held to lie in the *logos* of Christ, conceived as a revelation, not of 'new' truth, but of truth which was as old as the hills and as everlasting. This they accepted as an answer to the promise of illumination and power extended to mankind and, thus, the basis for a new physics, a new ethic and, above all, a new logic, the logic of human progress. In Christ, therefore, they claimed to possess a principle of understanding superior to anything existing in the classical world. By this claim they were prepared to stand or fall" (Preface, p. vi).

be made, evident to all rational beings. The history of philosophy rather proves that it is only by the creatively imaginative act of boldly grasping a faith-principle as a key of understanding that a great and noble system of philosophy can be built. All the great philosophers have done this. *Credo ut intelligam* is as true of Plato, Descartes, Spinoza, Hegel or Marx as it is of Augustine or Anselm. But the advantage enjoyed by Augustine and Anselm was that they were aware of this truth. Compared with the self-knowledge of St. Augustine and St. Anselm the others were working in the dark, with tools which they but imperfectly understood.

Faith, then, is necessarily bound up with reason, and neither reason nor faith can be understood without the other. To speak of "faithless reason" is to be ignorant of the very nature and constitution of reason; it is also to deprive faith of its most important function, that of making possible rational assent to the address of God. Our knowledge of God in this life is essentially a rational knowing made possible by faith in the biblical revelation.[1] Traditional Christian apologetics has rightly avoided all arguments from mystical experience to a direct or unmediated knowledge of God enjoyed by the human soul. The knowledge of God, as the Bible and the Church understand it, is mediated by the *word*, that is by the address of God as of one rational being to other rational beings. The final New Testament category for the understanding of God's address to the world in Jesus Christ is the

---

[1] No one understood this more clearly than St. Augustine, although he often speaks of "seeing" God—*intellectualis visio Dei*. This is, of course, a legitimate metaphor (cf. Matt. v. 8, etc.). To charge Augustine with "ontologism" in the sense in which it has been condemned by the Roman Church is to misunderstand his whole position. (Cf. Gilson in *A Monument to St. Augustine*, pp. 296–300.) Faith is always seeking understanding, not supra-rational "visions". (Cf. Cochrane, *op. cit.*, p. 503.) Aquinas taught that in this life— *in statu viatoris*—all our knowledge, including our knowledge of God, is reached by abstraction from sense-data; in the world to come—*in patria*—we shall know God's essence, that is, we shall know Him directly. Ontologism is the view that we can have a direct knowledge of God in this life through some natural or innate organ of the soul. It is to be condemned, not because it conflicts with Aquinas's somewhat doubtful theory of knowledge, but because it denies the biblical truth that revelation by the Word of God alone mediates to us our knowledge of God. (Cf. on this subject, John Baillie, *Our Knowledge of God*, pp. 166–77.) Many doctrines of an "inner light", or of "the divine spark in every man", and many theories of mysticism, are akin to ontologism and have more in common with Stoicism or Neo-Platonism than with Christianity.

conception of Christ as God's incarnate Word. The use of words is a function of rational minds and the means of communication between rational minds. Our knowledge of other minds, and particularly of their purposes or rational intentions, is mediated to us primarily by words. In this life our knowledge of God must remain rational knowledge in this sense; no wordless knowledge of God, or immediate apprehension of Him, is claimed as a result of Christian faith. Faith is not a mystical but a rational activity, and to seek "religious experiences" as an evidence for or as a consequence of Christian faith is the first false step in our religious life. Our knowledge of God is a mediated knowledge, and the One Mediator is Christ the Word.

### § 4. *Concluding Statement: St. Thomas and St. Augustine*

Thus, as we understand the central tradition of Christian thought upon the subject of the relation of faith and reason, man's "unaided" reason is not to be regarded as autonomous, capable of reaching any measure of truth without divine aid or of walking in its own light. Some of the very greatest of the Christian apologists of the past have, of course, while admitting this truth, nevertheless attempted to make reservations and to agree with the rationalists that there is a sphere of the knowledge of truth where "unaided" reason can travel quite a long way in its own strength. Bishop Butler, as we have seen, adopted much of the rationalism of the deists, and one cannot fail to admire the courage and confidence of the champion of Christian faith who is happy to fight on his opponents' ground and with his opponents' choice of weapons; but the result was that (as we should think) he failed to give a truly Christian *critique* of deism. St. Thomas Aquinas is, however, the supreme example of the apologist who loved to fight on his opponents' ground. The greatest Christian apologist of the Middle Ages, St. Thomas accepted the challenge of Mohammedans and free-thinkers to fight upon the newly re-discovered Aristotelian ground, and he undertook to show that the unaided human reason could reach a true and valuable "natural" knowledge of God and the world. But his deeply Christian mind always reserved for revelation the sole custody of our highest and saving knowledge of God. St. Thomas came to believe that the Aris-

totelian categories were the laws of reason as such, and that they
led to a permanently true natural knowledge which included even
a knowledge of God as He who is; in this sphere of natural
knowledge reason had its own laws and did not require the
illumination of Christian faith, as Aristotle had proved, if only
it were true to its own nature and followed its own inner necessity.[1] Faith supplements reason; it does not condition it, but, of
course, it may guide simple folk or busy men who have not the
ability or the time to be their own Aristotle; in the sphere of
natural knowledge it can give to children what as thoughtful men
they might later have discovered for themselves. So St. Thomas
courageously and brilliantly follows out his self-appointed task
of working out the logical conclusion of the Aristotelian categories
in every sphere of "natural knowledge", in spite of the protests
of the disapproving conservatives; and he produced that master-
piece of rational argument and classic of Christian apologetic, his
*Summa contra Gentiles*; and thus the bold innovator became the
Angelic Doctor whose modernism came to be regarded as final and
definitive by seven centuries of Roman theology.

At first St. Thomas's qualification of the Augustinian view
would seem to be almost a rejection of it and his break with his
master irreparable. But St. Thomas himself modifies his basic
theory in such a way that he does not, after all, entirely obscure
the insights of Augustinianism. In the first place (and this is
very important), he insists that even our natural knowledge "is

[1] The laws of reason were, of course, for St. Thomas the laws of God, who
also gave the supernatural revelation of the Bible; therefore there could never
be a conflict between faith and reason (cf. *Contra Gentiles*, Bk. I, Chap. vii).
St. Thomas himself provides us with many illustrations of the process which
his theory denies, namely, the "control" by faith of the conclusions which his
"autonomous" reason is supposed to discover for itself (see P. H. Wicksteed,
*Reactions between Dogma and Philosophy*, London, 1920, pp. 259f.). By handing
over to reason, operating without the aid of revelation, an important area of the
field of our total knowledge of the world and God, St. Thomas has taken the
first step in the direction later pursued by the deists, when they yielded up to
reason the whole sphere of man's possible knowledge of God and made revelation
only a "republication" of the truths of natural religion. See C. C. J. Webb,
*Studies in the History of Natural Theology*, Oxford, 1915, pp. 288f. In Chap. VI
(*supra*) we have already indicated our agreement with Dr. Webb's view that the
hard and fast delimitation of the spheres of "natural" and "revealed" theology
was St. Thomas's "cardinal mistake".

instilled into us by God, since God Himself is the author of our nature".[1] But beyond this, he admits that revelation does in fact act as a sign-post to reason and show it the way it should go. In actual practice we find that reason proves only when revelation has shown the way. Aristotle was the most wonderful illustration of what the unaided reason can achieve, but even he was not infallible, and reason sometimes led him astray—for instance, in accepting the erroneous doctrine of the eternity of the physical universe. St. Thomas remained too faithful a disciple of Augustine to believe that in practice we could trust to reason were it not for the help that reason may obtain from revelation. "Mankind would remain in the deepest darkness of ignorance", he says, "if the path of reason were the only available way to the knowledge of God".[2] There are three disadvantages, he tells us, which would result, if the truth which is theoretically attainable by reason were left solely to the investigation of reason alone. First, so many men are too stupid, or too pre-occupied with secular affairs, or too lazy, to gather the fruits of reason. Secondly, since a true philosophy requires years of study before it can be achieved, only a few elderly people would ever acquire it. Lastly, there is that *debilitas rationis*, weakness of intellect, which is common to mankind and which prevents men from ever knowing, apart from revelation, truth which they ought to have been able to discover for themselves. Here we find the most uncompromisingly rationalistic of all the great doctors of the Church accommodating his rationalism to the insights of biblical religion:

"The third disadvantage is that much falsehood is mingled with the investigations of human reason, on account of the weakness of our intellect in forming its judgments, and by reason of the admixture of phantasms. Consequently many would remain in doubt about those things even which are most truly demonstrated, through ignoring the force of the demonstration: especially when they perceive that different things are taught by the various men who are called wise.... Therefore it was necessary that definite certainty and pure truth about divine things should be offered to man by the way of faith. Accordingly the divine clemency has made this salutary

[1] *Contra Gentiles*, Bk. I, Chap. vii.    [2] *Op. cit.*, Bk. I, Chap. iv.

commandment, that even some things which reason is able to investigate must be held by faith: so that all may share in the knowledge of God easily, and without doubt or error."[1]

Thus, it will be seen that St. Thomas's view is in its practical teaching not so far distant from St. Augustine's as it might have at first sight appeared. He admits that as far as our everyday thinking and believing is concerned reason without revelation gives us little that can be called the knowledge of God and no knowledge at all of His saving purpose for the world. Nevertheless in St. Thomas's view reason without revelation is still reason, and if it is true to itself it can still think rationally. Here lies the essential difference between St. Thomas's thought and St. Augustine's. For Thomas it is still theoretically possible for a man who has no faith to think rationally, however restricted may be the area in which rational thought is possible and however small may be the likelihood of any individual thinker's becoming an Aristotle. Augustine has rejected even this degree of rationalism: reason without the light of revelation cannot function as reason, any more than a man's eye can function as an eye in a completely dark room. In St. Augustine's view faith is the lamp of reason. St. Thomas speaks of the "weakness" of the intellect: St. Augustine knows that apart from the grace of saving faith the intellect is a slave of sin, self-interest and pride—and therefore the begetter of false theories, rationalizations and of all forms of error. The "new psychology" of the twentieth century could have taught St. Augustine little that he did not know about man's ability to persuade himself that his rationalizations are reasons; the Marxian ideologists might have learnt from him the doctrine that self-interest is the source of wishful thinking. The fallacy of Thomism and of all forms of rationalism is that they obscure the classical Christian understanding of human nature as fallen: according to the insights of biblical religion the *whole* of human nature is fallen, and there is no part of it, such as the reason, which is capable without divine grace of fulfilling the purpose for which it was created. The uselessness of saying that reason has merely to follow the laws of its own nature in order to arrive at truth is that this is precisely what it cannot do; its own nature

1 *Ibid.*

has been corrupted by sin. The fall did not affect the will alone, leaving the intellect unimpaired; it is not the intellectual weakness of the reason which is the primary source of error, but its enslavement to selfishness and sin. The human reason is in just the same fallen and helpless condition as the human will. Rationalism is Pelagianism in philosophy, and Augustine will have none of it. "The truth which I would I cannot think; the error which I would not I think". The whole of us, including our reason, must be justified by faith. Reason needs more than sign-posts along the road; it·needs the light by which they can be read.

Hence the Christian philosopher needs that distinctively Christian grace of humility. Trust in one's own rationality and wisdom is the chief obstacle to becoming a Christian philosopher. It is a humbling reflection that after all one's years of toil and study one does not necessarily know the truth better than a simple shepherd or a child. The reign of God—over the things of the intellect as well as of the will—must be received as a little child. Pride of intellect is as blinding in the pursuit of truth as pride of virtue is deadly in the pursuit of righteousness. Professor Paul Tillich has well said that "no one, not even one who believes, and not even a Church, can boast of the truth, just as no one can boast of love. Orthodoxy is intellectual Pharisaism. The justification of one who doubts corresponds to the justification of one who sins. Revelation is just as paradoxical as the forgiveness of sins."[1] By "orthodoxy" Tillich here doubtless means pride in the possession of truth, as though this were a matter of self-congratulation, implying scorn of all who do not follow with us. But it would be better to define orthodoxy as thinking in and with the Church which rejoices in the light of the revelation given in Jesus Christ. Obviously orthodoxy then becomes not an occasion of pride but of humble thanksgiving, for it is of God's grace alone that the Christian believer has received the faith which enables him to have his part and lot in the company of those in all the ages upon whom the light of Christ has shone.

All truth is God's truth; it cannot be man's truth until God Himself brings the truth to men. The classical biblical and Christian tradition maintains that any recognition of truth upon man's part is due to the self-movement of God towards mankind,

[1] *The Interpretation of History* (New York, 1936), p. 34.

resulting in that self-disclosure which Christians call revelation. The general revelation whereby men "discover" truth in any sphere of human knowing, from physics to all that comes "after physics", is an outgoing of the grace of God and a testimony to God's being and goodness. The very desire for truth is a confession that God is. Knowledge is literally unthinkable apart from God; the very concept of atheism can define itself only by reference to God. If men have ever transcended the "weakness of intellect" or the ideological promptings of self-interest, they have done so only through the grace of God. If Plato and Spinoza and Marx taught anything that was true, they did so only because the truth itself had come to them, and Christians are therefore the legitimate inheritors of their truth. "Whatever has been well said belongs to us Christians." But Christians can know what has been *well* said only by virtue of the special self-movement of God towards mankind in the biblical history, culminating in the special revelation through Jesus Christ. Special revelation lights up the meaning of all general revelation and enables the Christian philosopher to discern, at least in outline or by analogy, the meaning of the whole. Above all, special revelation makes clear the character of all knowledge of truth, namely, that it comes from God and is the result of His loving-kindness towards man. Apart from the biblical revelation we should have been very ignorant of the source and nature of knowledge and truth. We should perhaps have had some degree of wisdom, but the Source of Wisdom, making us wise, we could not have known, save dimly and afar off. The Gospel of Jesus Christ, which the whole Bible attests and which the universal Church proclaims, tells us of a God who not only satisfies our desire for truth but Himself is the source of that desire, who is not only the answer to our questions but the author of them within us, the end of our quest for goodness and also its origin: "He whom we desire to receive Himself causes us to ask; He whom we wish to find Himself causes us to seek; He unto whom we strive to come causes us to knock. . . . And when He is received, He works to make men desire to receive Him more fully by further asking, seeking and knocking. For if men are seeking either the good life or to live well, as many as are led by the Spirit of God, these are the sons of God."[1]

[1] *In Ps.* CXIX, *Serm.* xiv. 2.

# INDEX